THE ART OF WAR
AND OTHER CHINESE MILITARY CLASSICS

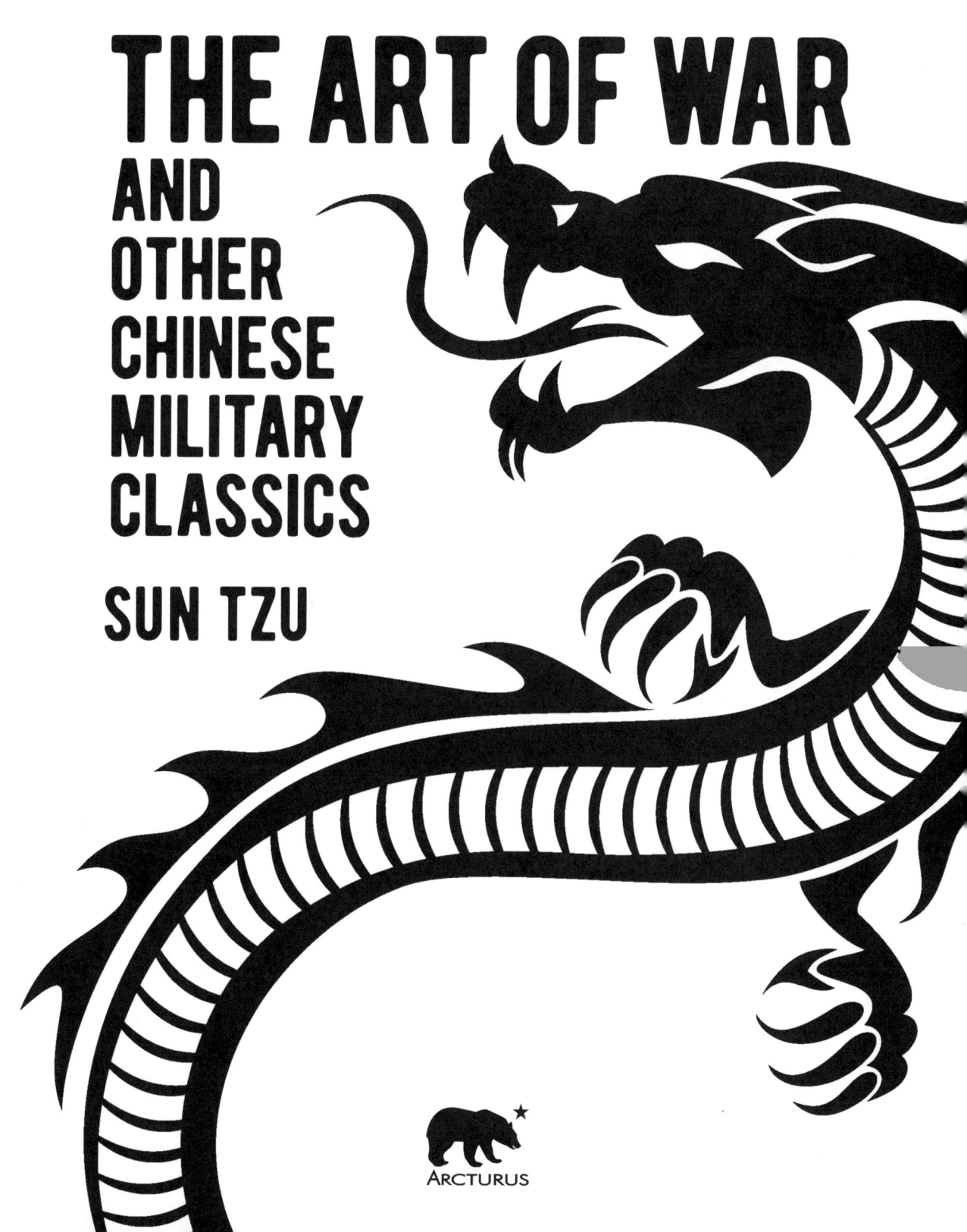

THE ART OF WAR
AND OTHER CHINESE MILITARY CLASSICS

SUN TZU

ARCTURUS

ARCTURUS

This edition published in 2023 by Arcturus Publishing Limited
26/27 Bickels Yard, 151–153 Bermondsey Street,
London SE1 3HA

Copyright © Arcturus Holdings Limited

All rights reserved. No part of this publication may be reproduced, stored in a retrieval system, or transmitted, in any form or by any means, electronic, mechanical, photocopying, recording or otherwise, without prior written permission in accordance with the provisions of the Copyright Act 1956 (as amended). Any person or persons who do any unauthorised act in relation to this publication may be liable to criminal prosecution and civil claims for damages.

ISBN: 978-1-83940-159-6
AD005634UK

Printed in China

CONTENTS

INTRODUCTION 7

六韜
TAIGONG'S SIX SECRET TEACHINGS 17

司馬法
METHODS OF THE SIMA 105

孫子兵法
THE ART OF WAR 135

吳子
WUZI 199

尉繚子
WEI LIAOZI 231

三略
THREE STRATEGIES OF HUANG SHIGONG 297

唐太宗李衛公問對
QUESTIONS AND REPLIES BETWEEN EMPEROR TAIZONG OF TANG AND GENERAL LI JING 331

介紹
INTRODUCTION

Combat and warfare have been features of civilization since mankind first evolved. It is no surprise that in every civilization, one finds debates, discussions, and discourses surrounding battle and warfare. Nowhere is this truer than in China, where scholars and rulers of successive empires facing the realities of combat and warfare, debated and discussed these matters for centuries.

Warfare was a fact of life for all premodern Chinese empires. Chinese history is the story of these empires, states, and dynasties that arose in periods of strife and conflict. They succeeded each other in warfare and relied on military might to consolidate their rule. The system of dynastic empires that marked Imperial China began with the establishment of the short-lived Qin Empire (221–206 BCE), the first imperial dynasty, and its longer-lived successor the Han (206 BCE–220 CE) that established many of the basic principles and traditions of imperial rule. The Qin state existed for centuries before it established the first empire, existing uncomfortably alongside other polities that eventually fell prey to their ambition.

The Warring States

This period is today referred to as the Warring States (c. 475–221 BCE), and it is from this period that many of

介紹 INTRODUCTION

the texts in this volume emerge. This period witnessed rapid technological change and social innovation. Warfare transformed from staged contests between individual opponents to large campaigns involving mobilized and specialized troops. The Trans-Eurasian trade brought metallurgical technology and horses from Central Asia, leading to advances in weaponry, particularly the crossbow, and the development and use of cavalry and charioteers.

The relatively flat lands of the North China plain, where most of these states were located, led to the development of complex defenses to make up for the lack of natural hills and waterways. These evolved into complex walls and fortifications, several of which served as precursors to the Great Wall built centuries later. These heavy fortifications also meant that not only were tactics and strategies necessary for campaigns against large armies, but also that siege warfare was a necessary and vital aspect of contemporary warfare.

The era also saw an expansion in literacy and scholarship. The development of bamboo as a cheap writing medium coupled with the increased need for educated bureaucrats and advisors led to the production of texts and the growth of communities of scholars. These communities were diverse and scattered among the many different states of the time, and the texts they produced discussed a wide variety of topics. Given that war and combat were facts of life, rulers naturally sought out advice and offered patronage to those who could help develop strategies and ensure success in these matters.

Imperial China

Both the Qin and the Han, and the empires that followed them, continued this trend of involving the burgeoning scholarly class in statecraft, recruiting them into their governments and patronizing academic endeavors through promoting writing, establishing schools and academies, and even supporting academic projects. Alongside these developments were military campaigns that saw the deployment of large-scale armies made up of infantry, cavalry, and archery troops alongside extensive wall and fortification building campaigns, just as had occurred in the Warring States that preceded them.

These empires set the standard of including scholarly and ideological matters alongside their military and empire building projects, a pattern that would remain throughout all successive Chinese empires. By the time of the Song Dynasty (960–1279 CE), scholars in China were not mere imperial advisors or individuals hiding in ivory towers, but instead were the dominant social class of an empire entirely staffed and run by those trained in a standardized scholarly tradition. As the concerns and culture of these scholars increasingly shaped the vagaries of life, so too did they begin to shape and influence military tradition. Scholarly concerns of textuality, ideology, and philosophy became just as important as battlefield tactics, troop deployments, and military training with regard to combat and warfare. The discussion of the nature of texts, their provenance, and origin became an active part of providing advice and justifying the choice of tactics to the Emperor. It was in this rich interplay of perspectives that the Chinese military tradition was formed through the canonization of what became known as the *Seven Military Classics*.

The Seven Military Classics

Canonized in 1080 CE under the reign of Emperor Shenzong of the Song (r. 1067–1085 CE), this collection of texts is as much a representation of scholarly activity in forming a military tradition as it is a matter of practical concern. Military matters played a dramatic role in the Song alongside its burgeoning intellectual community. The Song existed in a near constant state of conflict with their rivals the Liao (907–1125 CE) and Jin (1115–1234 CE) empires, battling for control of China. But this canonization was done with texts that predated the Song and reflect the standardized intellectual traditions they developed, such as canonizing and anthologizing earlier texts, and considering those earlier texts as the primary font of knowledge. The seven chosen texts range from as early as the Warring States to the end of the Tang Dynasty (618–907 CE). They are complex texts made up of different components, as can be seen in *Taigong's Six Secret Teachings* (also known as the *Liu Tao*), and have multiple versions and iterations, as in the case of *The Art of War*. Reading these texts yields much more than simply a list of military techniques. It provides an insight into the development of both text and thought on the subject.

The seven texts—*Taigong's Six Secret Teachings*, *The Methods of the Sima*, *The Art of War*, *Wuzi*, *Wei Liaozi*, *Three Strategies of Huang Shigong*, and *Questions and Replies Between Emperor Taizong of Tang and General Li Jing*—have been preserved as a body of knowledge on warfare and combat and their study forms the cornerstone of Chinese military tradition. They became required reading for those who sought military careers and martial success and are still read by world leaders today. The knowledge they contain is diverse and the manner in which they speak about military matters is at times complex. The seven texts come from many different time periods and scholarly communities, and they are informed by conventions and standards that would have been common at the time of their composition, though perhaps alien to later readers.

Taigong's Six Secret Teachings, though most likely composed in the Warring States, is purported to be the work of a general of antiquity, Jiang Ziya (11th century BCE), who aided in the overthrowing of the last tyrannical King of the Shang, Zhou (r. 1075–1046 BCE). Placed as the "first" chronologically amongst the seven, it is divided into six sections that blend ideological concerns with tactical necessities, a cornerstone of the seven. It is written from the perspective of the overthrow of a kingdom, that of the Shang (c. 1600–1046 BCE), in keeping with its historical narrative.

The Methods of the Sima is attributed directly to the Warring States, though with much debate over its provenance, particularly many parts associated with the Han. It speaks much about the issue of ritual and propriety, directly relating those issues to military matters. It shows a strong concern with the organization of forces and the situations of battle over explicit tactics.

The Art of War is also attributed to the Warring States and specifically to a scholar-character known as Sunzi (554–496 BCE). One of the more complex texts in the collection, it exists in multiple versions and is one of the most researched by scholars both modern and premodern. The text contains detailed discussions of not only military organisation and tactics, but also reconnaissance, geography, and espionage.

Both the *Wuzi* and the *Wei Liaozi* are of unclear origin, though both are usually attributed to the Warring States. They are both concerned with the organization of the military and the state during times of war. The *Wuzi* emphasizes how best to run and discipline an army and particularly emphasizes maintaining a strong cavalry, reflecting the importance of horses in warfare in the Warring States and early imperial China. The *Wei Liaozi* explains how to maintain civilian support for military campaigns and secure supplies and material in times of war.

The Three Strategies of Huang Shigong is attributed to the Han, notably the Han general Zhang Liang (c. 3rd century–186 BCE), and like the *Wuzi* and *Wei Liaozi* discusses much in the way of administrative matters with a strong ideological focus. It directly compares these to combat and emphasizes how they lead to success. The text also directly comments on and discusses matters presented in the *The Art of War*, the first text in the collection directly to reference another text.

The final text of the seven, *Questions and Replies Between Emperor Taizong of Tang and General Li Jing*, is attributed to the late Tang (618–907 CE). The text, as the title suggests, is framed as a series of questions and answers between the famed Tang general Li Jing (571–649 CE); who aided the establishment of the Tang Dynasty in their overthrow of the Sui, the Tang's expansion into Central Asia; and the second Tang Emperor Taizong (r. 626–649 CE). It discusses many of the lessons from the earlier texts of the seven, illustrating how to adapt them for the changing military realities of the Tang, in which newer military technologies were being introduced and a greater number of empires vied for control of Asia.

As one reads through these texts, one quickly sees that matters pertaining to philosophy, politics, and ritual are given high prominence and at times seem more of a concern than purely military tactics. Discussions of personal self-cultivation are not uncommon and reference to metaphysical phenomena and other ideas common to scholars of different times are also brought up alongside discussions of battlefield strategies. The ease with which these topics are melded together speaks both to the lack of discrete disciplines in these times and the permeation of battle and military matters into other realms of life. Likewise, the reader will note a number of references to other texts and individuals, a common method of debate in Chinese texts. This also serves to further the construction of a tradition based on texts and commentary to other texts.

These texts have many voices and perspectives. These voices and perspectives are added to through the act of translation. Translation is not easy; translators must deal with ideas and concepts unfamiliar to themselves and their community, yet try to make them comprehensible. They must try to understand tone and register that may seem awkward in a different language. They must also try to make sense of technical terms and esoteric references, and understand that these texts were not developed in isolation, but are the result of many hands and interactions over an extended period of time, leading to many nuances and idiosyncrasies. Additionally, translators face linguistic features such as punning, rhymes and visual and graphic aspects of the orthography are naturally not easily replicated in the source language.

Though these may seem like daunting challenges, the careful consideration of these matters in this volume bring out the complex interactions and developments that these texts convey. The translators who contributed to this edition have done a masterful job in addressing these concerns and putting forward not only effective and understandable translations, but translations that engage the reader and welcome them into the multiple voices and perspectives of the texts. These translations take account of the complex philological, philosophical, and ideological developments represented alongside the military and strategic.

Through their fine efforts, the reader will join these multiple voices and observe the complex world of both the Chinese military tradition, and the methods by which this tradition was constructed. The reader will discover many different worlds from the dawn of Chinese civilization to its late Imperial period and become familiar with the concerns and issues that the people who wrote these texts faced and how they propose to solve them. The wealth of military tactics and strategy in these texts has always been noted, as they are still read by generals in East Asia today, but these texts offer much more. Combat and warfare may be common, but the methods of dealing with them are as diverse and complex as the worlds of these texts.

Dr Justin Winslett, University of Cambridge

A NOTE ON THE TEXT

Two systems have generally been used for romanizing Chinese characters. Traditionally, the Wade-Giles system was the most common, and it is this older system that is employed in the translation of *The Art of War* in this volume. Since the 1980s, the newer system of Pinyin has become the standard method of writing Chinese in Latin characters. The two systems can appear surprisingly different. For example, in Wade-Giles, the author of *The Art of War* is written as "Sun Tzu." In Pinyin, this same name is represented as "Sunzi." For the introduction and the other six texts included here, the Pinyin system has been used to avoid confusion. Where traditional Chinese measurements appear, modern equivalents have been inserted in brackets.

六韜
TAIGONG'S SIX SECRET TEACHINGS

*Translated by
Anjie Cai Anderson
and Mengchen Wang*

文韜
CIVIL SECRET TEACHING

文師
KING WEN'S TEACHER

King Wen of Zhou planned a hunting trip. After practicing divination, the Scribe Bian advised: "You will catch something special from your trip to the north bank of the Wei River. What you will catch is not a dragon, nor the son of a dragon, or a tiger or a bear, instead it will be a master strategist. He is a teacher sent from Heaven, and he will assist with your running of the country, and benefit your offspring for generation after generation."

King Wen asked: "Is the sign given by the divination truly auspicious?"

Scribe Bian replied: "My forefather Scribe Chou used to practice divination for Emperor Yu. The divination from that time is very similar to today's. That is how Emperor Yu met his strategist Gao Yao."

After fasting for three days, King Wen rode his hunting chariot along the north bank of the Wei River. He found Taigong sitting on an overgrown river bank with a fishing rod in his hand.

King Wen acquainted himself with Taigong. "Sir, do you enjoy fishing?" he inquired.

Taigong answered: "I heard a wise man achieves his ambitions, while an ordinary man concentrates on his own affairs. Fishing is very similar to this."

"What are the differences?" asked King Wen.

Taigong answered: "Fishing resembles the management of the people. There are three lures you can use to attract talents: generous compensation, rewards, and high positions. The purpose of fishing is to catch the fish [you want]. From this, you gain a glimpse into the true philosophy of life."

King Wen said: "I am keen to listen to your thoughts."

Taigong explained: "The deeper the source, the swifter the water, the more numerous the fish: this is the Way [Tao] of nature. The deeper the roots, the lusher the leaves, the more bountiful the fruits. The more two gentlemen can relate to each other, the closer the bond, the more successful the business. Sometimes words are used to conceal true feelings. Sharing thoughts truthfully is the foundation of mutual understanding. If I say things without reservation, will my straightforwardness offend you?"

King Wen said: "Only people with virtue can accept harsh advice without holding grudges. How could I be offended?"

Taigong elaborated: "When the fishing line is thin and the bait catches the eye, small fish will take it. When the line is moderate and the bait is appetizing, medium-sized fish will take it. When the line is long and thick and the bait is generous, big fish will take it. Those who are keen on fragrant bait will be hooked by the line. Those who take the emperor's salary will follow the emperor's orders. If you catch fish with fragrant bait, the fish can be cooked. If you attract talents with compensation, they can be used according to their strengths. If you use family to acquire a state, the state can be conquered. If you use the state as the basis to acquire the world, the world can be conquered.

"Alas, the wealth gathered by a magnificent country will eventually be scattered to the winds. If the country prepares silently, its glory will extend far. Such a subtle endeavor! The virtues of a wise ruler lie in the ingenious and subtle ways of seeking talents. What preoccupies a wise ruler is how to help each individual accomplish [their goals] and gather the people's support."

King Wen asked: "How do I gain the people's support?"

Taigong replied: "The world does not belong to one person; instead it is shared by everyone. Those who share in the benefits of the world can gain the world; those who try to monopolize them, lose them. Heaven has its four seasons; Earth has its wealth. Those who share such wealth are benevolent. All people will follow a benevolent ruler. Sparing the people from death, removing their suffering, eliminating their misfortune, and rescuing them from emergency: this is grace. Where grace goes, people follow. Sharing your happiness and sorrows, your likes and dislikes with the people, is righteousness. People follow where righteousness leads. People prefer life to death. They appreciate grace and pursue profit. Seeking profits on people's behalf is the Kingly Way [Tao]. People follow the Kingly Way [Tao]."

King Wen bowed again and showed his gratitude: "Teacher, what you said is insightful. Do I dare ignore the message from Heaven?" He invited Taigong to join him in the hunting chariot and returned to the capital. He performed a ceremony to honor Taigong as his teacher.

盈虛
FULLNESS AND EMPTINESS

King Wen asked Taigong: "The world is in a confusing state of prosperity and weakness, peace and chaos. What is the cause? Is it due to the wisdom and incompetence of rulers? Or is it the result of destiny and nature?"

Taigong replied: "If the ruler is not wise, the country will suffer from crisis and uprisings. If the ruler is a Sage, the country will be peaceful and its citizens obedient. Therefore, the fortunes and misfortunes of the Zhou Dynasty lie in the wisdom and foolishness of its ruler. It is not the result of the twist of fate."

King Wen asked: "Could you tell me the story of wise rulers in ancient times?"

Taigong said: "Emperor Yao was referred to as a Sage in his day."

King Wen asked: "How did he administer his country?"

Taigong explained: "When Emperor Yao was the sovereign, he did not use gold, silver, pearl, or jade as accessories. He did not wear over-embellished clothes. He did not appreciate rare and precious things. He did not collect antiques nor listen to sensual music. He did not decorate his palace walls, nor add intricate beams and pillars. He did not trim the grass in his garden. He wore deerskin and sackcloth in winter to cover his body. He ate simple food and drank wild vegetable soup. He did not impose labor service on the people to protect their agricultural and weaving activities. He restrained his own desires and greed. He ran his country peacefully and without intervening unnecessarily. He promoted officials who were just and loyal and increased the salary of officials who were incorruptible and loving. He respected those who were filial toward their seniors and affectionate toward their juniors. He encouraged the people to focus on agricultural activities. He could tell virtue from evil. He rewarded compassionate families and promoted fairness and morality. He made laws to punish evil-doers. He rewarded the people he disliked based on their accomplishments. He punished the people he liked who had committed crimes. He looked after orphans, widows, and those left on their own. He assisted those who suffered from misfortune and loss. Emperor Yao himself lived a humble life and imposed only a meager tax upon his people. All under Heaven lived a prosperous and contented life, without any trace of hunger or poverty. People loved him just as they worshiped the sun and the moon. They viewed him like they did their own parents."

King Wen said: "What a great and virtuous ruler!"

國務
STATE AFFAIRS

King Wen spoke to Taigong: "I would like to know the principles of running a country. I would like the ruler to be respected and the people to live harmoniously. What should I do to achieve this?"

Taigong answered: "Just love your people."

King Wen inquired: "How do I love the people?"

Taigong answered: "Help the people rather than harm them. Empower the people to achieve success rather than sabotaging them. Protect the people from being killed. Give rather than take. Bring the people safety and joy rather than suffering. Fill the people with delight rather than anger."

King Wen asked: "Could you clarify the reasons?"

Taigong said: "People benefit from keeping their jobs. People must keep to the agricultural seasons. Reducing [criminal] sentences protects the livelihood of the people. Lowering taxes favors the people. Limiting the building of palaces and leisure gardens benefits the people. Honest and undemanding officials bring the people joy. On the contrary, depriving people of their jobs hurts them. Distracting farmers from agricultural seasons is damaging. Executing innocent people is murder. Imposing heavy taxes is exploitation. Building extravagant palaces and gardens wears out people and causes pain. Corruption and harassment from officials irritate the people.

"Therefore, a wise ruler should treat people like parents treat their children, or like elder brothers care for their younger brothers and sisters. A ruler should worry about the people's hunger and grieve for their toil. Rewards and punishment should be imposed as if upon himself. Imposing taxes should be treated as stealing from yourself. These are the principles of loving your people."

大禮
PROPRIETIES

King Wen asked Taigong: "What are the proprieties between a ruler and his subordinates?"

Taigong answered: "A ruler should be compassionate toward his subordinates. Subordinates should be submissive to their chief. A ruler should not be distant from his ministers, while ministers should be submissive without concealing anything. A ruler should extend his grace to everyone. Ministers should commit themselves to their positions. His grace should be as wide as the sky that covers all creatures. His devotion should be as steady and reliable as the Earth. A ruler should follow the example of Heaven, while ministers should follow the example of Earth. Heaven and Earth complete each other."

King Wen asked: "How should the sovereign act?"

Taigong explained: "The sovereign should be calm, peaceful, gentle, restrained, and confident. He is gracious rather than exploitative. He is humble, selfless, and fair."

King Wen asked: "How should a ruler listen to people's opinions?"

Taigong answered: "Do not accept them hastily, nor reject them harshly. Haste causes the loss of his independence. Harsh rejection discourages good advice. A wise ruler should be like a magnificent mountain which arouses admiration. He should be like an abyss which is deep and mysterious. A virtuous and sagely ruler pushes tranquility and righteousness to their extremes."

King Wen asked: "How can a ruler be insightful?"

Taigong replied: "Eyes are for observing things with clarity, and ears are for receiving opinions from many sources. If you rely on the eyes of all people under Heaven, you can see everything. If you listen through the ears of all people under Heaven, you can hear everything. If you think with the brains of all people under Heaven, you will know everything. If all information is channeled into the ruler, he can understand everything without being blinded."

明傳
CLEAR INSTRUCTIONS

King Wen was sick in bed with Prince Fa by his side. King Wen summoned Taigong and said: "Alas! Heaven is about to end my life. I will entrust the future of the Kingdom of Zhou to you. Now I would like to hear your wisdom in order to pass on the essence to my offspring."

Taigong asked: "What would you like to know?"

King Wen said: "Drawing on the practices of wise rulers of ancient times, what should be encouraged and what should be abandoned?"

Taigong answered: "Being too lazy to do good deeds, being indecisive when facing good opportunities, to know of mistakes and bear with them—these three things should be abandoned. Being gentle and tranquil, modest and discreet, strong yet humble, restrained yet strong—these are four things that should be encouraged. In this way a country prospers when justice overcomes greed, and a country suffers when greed overcomes justice. A country is blessed when respect overwhelms slackness. A country will be destroyed if slackness overtakes respect."

六守
SIX RULES

King Wen asked Taigong: "What are the reasons a ruler loses his country and the support of his people?"

Taigong said: "This is due to using the wrong people. The sovereign should follow the Six Rules and pay special attention to the Three Treasures."

King Wen asked: "What are the Six Rules?"

Taigong answered: "They are benevolence, righteousness, loyalty, trustworthiness, bravery, and resourcefulness. These are the Six Rules."

King Wen asked: "How do I select talents who follow the Six Rules?"

Taigong explained: "Make them rich in order to see if they [continue to] observe the law. Make them distinguished to see if they become arrogant. Allocate them important roles to see if they can accomplish their duties with determination. Command them to deal with problems to see if they conceal anything or deceive you. Trap them in crisis to see if they can face danger fearlessly. Let them tackle emergencies to see if they can handle them smoothly. Those who are rich and law-abiding are benevolent. Those who are distinguished and humble are righteous. Those who can undertake important jobs with determination are loyal. Those who deal with problems without deception are trustworthy. Those who are fearless in the face of danger are brave. Those who handle emergencies smoothly are resourceful. A ruler should not hand the Three Treasures to others. Otherwise, a ruler will lose his authority."

King Wen asked: "Where are the Three Treasures you are referring to?"

Taigong replied: "Agriculture, craft, and trade are the Three Treasures. If farmers are gathered together in certain areas to work, grain will be plentiful. If artisans are gathered together to make things, tools will be sufficient. If merchants are gathered together to trade, goods will be ample. If these Three Treasures are settled in the right places, the people will not start uprisings. Districts should not be disturbed, and families should not be separated. Subordinates should not be richer than the ruler. Other cities should not be larger than the capital. If people who follow the Six Rules are appointed, a ruler's career will be prosperous. If the Three Treasures are valued, a country will be stable and secure."

守土
GUARDING THE TERRITORY

King Wen asked Taigong: "How do I guard the country's territory?"

Taigong replied: "Do not estrange your clans. Do not neglect your people. Pacify the neighboring states and control the Four Corners under Heaven. Do not hand the administration of the country to others. Otherwise, a ruler will lose his authority. Do not dig valleys in order to build hills. Do not focus on the branches and ignore the roots. Dry things when it is midday. If you are holding a knife, cut immediately. If you are holding an ax, fight at the right time. If you do not dry things when the sun is the strongest, you will miss the chance. If you hold a knife without cutting, the opportunity will pass you by.

If you hold an ax without attacking enemies, they will swoop in. If small streams are not blocked, they will become big rivers. If faint sparks are not smothered, they will become a great fire. If tender leaves are not trimmed, you will have to use an ax to chop them. In this way, a ruler should strive to make his country flourish. If the country is not wealthy, it cannot be benevolent. If a country is not benevolent, it cannot unite its clans. Estranging the clans will be harmful. Losing the support of the people will result in defeat. Do not allocate the power of running your country to others. It will lead to a disastrous ending."

King Wen asked: "What is benevolence?"

Taigong answered: "Respect your own people and unite the clans. Respect contributes to harmony. Unity brings joy to the clans. This is the principle of benevolence. Do not let others usurp your power. Rely on your observation and insight to deal with affairs. Reward and appoint people who are submissive. Eradicate people who oppose you. If you follow these principles without hesitation, the world will be harmonious and obedient."

GUARDING THE COUNTRY

King Wen asked Taigong: "How does one guard his country?"

Taigong replied: "Once you have fasted, I will tell you the principles of Heaven and Earth, the reason of creatures growing in four seasons, the truth of the Sages, and the nature of people's hearts."

King Wen fasted for seven days. He bowed toward Taigong in the same manner as a student treats his teacher.

Taigong said: "There are four seasons. The Earth produces millions of creatures. The

Sage rules for all the people under Heaven. The Way [Tao] of spring is birth. Everything flourishes. The Way [Tao] of summer is growth. Everything prospers. The Way [Tao] of autumn is harvest. Everything matures and ripens. The Way [Tao] of winter is storage. Everything hibernates. Once things are ripe, they should be stored away. Afterward, they will be reborn and thrive. This everlasting cycle has no end or beginning. The Sage follows the rule of nature and uses it as a principle for administering the world. When the world is peaceful and prosperous, the Sage lives like a hermit. When the world is chaotic, the Sage makes things right and builds a prosperous country. This is inevitable. The Sage resides between Heaven and Earth and holds significant positions. He rules the country and orders the people according to the rule of nature. Unsettled hearts breed riots and a struggle for power will ensue. The Sage secretly develops his power and fights for justice when the time is right. First, he will eradicate violence and quieten the people. Then the world will follow his lead. When the riot is pacified and order restored, he does not need recognition of his benevolence. If you can guard your country in this manner, you will share the glory of Heaven and Earth, and the splendor of the sun and moon."

上賢
HONORING THE WISE

King Wen asked Taigong: "As a ruler, who shall I respect? Who shall I control? Who shall I appoint? Who shall I eradicate? What shall I ban? What shall I discourage?"

Taigong answered: "A ruler should respect talents with virtues and control people without talent or virtue. He should appoint loyal and trustworthy people, and eradicate deceiving and insincere people. He should ban violence and riots, and discourage extravagance. Therefore, a ruler should be aware of the Six Thieves and the Seven Harms."

King Wen said: "I would like to hear more."

Taigong explained: "These are the Six Thieves:

"First, if ministers build extravagant palaces and terraces for pleasure, a ruler's virtues will be compromised.

"Second, if people do not commit to agricultural activities, but instead remain idle, become wandering bandits, commit crimes, do not follow officials' regulations, a society's values will be harmed.

"Third, if ministers band together for selfish reasons, push aside the wise and worthy, and obscure the sovereign's insights, a ruler's power will be impaired.

"Fourth, if ministers are arrogant, aloof, and presumptuous, associate with lords of other states, and show no respect for their own rulers, a ruler's dignity will be crippled.

"Fifth, if ministers scorn titles and superiors are unwilling to take risks for the sovereign, the drive and motivation of loyal ministers will be injured.

"Sixth, if strong clans fight each other, and exploit the weak and poor, the livelihood of the people will be damaged.

"These are the Seven Harms:

"First, those who have no wit or strategy go to battle for the sake of reward and titles. They are reckless and opportunistic. They should never be appointed generals.

"Second, they have an undeserved reputation.

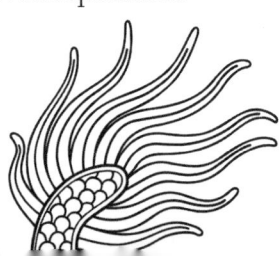

Their deceiving words are matched by their deeds. They conceal others' kindness and expose others' shortcomings. They are exploitative. A ruler should never work with them.

"Third, people appear modest and wear humble clothes. They claim to be inactive and unambitious in order to seek fame and profit. A ruler should never make acquaintance with hypocrites.

"Fourth, they wear strange accessories and splendid clothes. They appear to be knowledgeable and talk about lofty ideas in order to impress others. They live in distant and poor places and spend all their time criticizing the current state of affairs. A ruler should not favor these crafty people.

"Fifth, they slander and flatter unscrupulously to seek titles and positions. They pursue remuneration recklessly. They neglect the big picture and seek only personal gain. They talk with eloquence to please the sovereign. A ruler should not appoint them.

"Sixth, they desire luxurious crafts. They desire intricate carvings, inlays, and embroideries, which prevents the people from focusing on agricultural activities. A ruler should ban them.

"Seventh, they perform witchcraft and deception. They fool and confuse the public. A ruler should forbid them.

"In this way, people who do not commit to agricultural activities are not good. Officers who are not loyal and trustworthy are not decent. Ministers who dare not challenge authority are not honorable. Officials who are not righteous or compassionate are not noble. Chancellors who cannot enhance prosperity and military power, are unable to deal with conflicts and affairs, who stabilize neither the sovereign's position nor the people's work and life, are not helpful. A ruler is like the head of a dragon. He stands high and sees far. He is insightful and visionary. He listens to people's opinions with discretion. He appears solemn while revealing his emotions. He is as high and limitless as the sky. He is as deep and immeasurable as the abyss. If a ruler does not show his justified anger, evil ministers will take advantage. If a ruler does not prosecute, riots will ensue. If a ruler does not send his troops to neighboring states, other states will thrive."

King Wen: "How wise!"

舉賢
APPOINTING THE WISE

King Wen asked Taigong: "A ruler seeks the wise, but the results are not satisfactory. Society becomes more and more unsettled, causing a crisis. Why is that?"

Taigong answered: "If one seeks the wise without appointing them [to a position], it is superficial. It lacks the substance of employing the wise."

King Wen inquired: "What are the causes of the mistake?"

Taigong said: "If a ruler appoints people because they are valued by the people, he cannot obtain truly wise talents."

King Wen asked: "Why do you say that?"

Taigong said: "If a ruler values those who are complimented by worldly voices, and disdains those who are judged poorly by worldly opinions, those with strong and supportive cliques will be appointed. Those with smaller cliques will be rejected. Evildoers will unite to dismiss the wise, and loyal and innocent ministers will be executed. Treacherous court officials gain titles and positions. In this way the country becomes turbulent. It is inevitable that such a state will fall apart."

King Wen asked: "How should one appoint the wise?"

Taigong replied: "The tasks of generals and chancellors should be divided. Officials of various ranks should be advanced on merit. Performance should be assessed according to officials' roles. Talents of all kinds should be selected. Titles and positions should be matched by candidates' ability and virtue. This is the essence of appointing the wise."

賞罰
REWARD AND PUNISHMENT

King Wen asked Taigong: "Rewards are used to motivate people, and punishments are used to warn people. I would like to motivate a hundred people by rewarding one man, and warn the masses by punishing one man. How can that be achieved?"

Taigong answered: "To use rewards effectively, value credibility, and to use punishments effectively, value certainty. The credibility and certainty from reward and punishment can be seen and heard by the people, and even when they do not see or hear, its subtle influence will still reach them. As [the ruler's] trustworthiness is appreciated by both Heaven and Earth, it extends to the deity as well as men."

兵道
PRINCIPLES OF MILITARY MANEUVER

King Wu (the heir of King Wen) asked Taigong: "What are the principles of military maneuver?"

Taigong answered: "In military maneuver, nothing can be more important than unity and consistency. Unified troops can fight independently without enemies. The legendary Yellow Emperor said: 'Unified command is marvelous and unpredictable.' Unity is about timing. It lies in the utilization of situations. Its success lies with the sovereign. In this way, the ancient Sage Kings described wars as 'evil instruments,' which should only be used when they were inevitable. Today, the Shang King realizes the existence of other countries only when his own country is facing crisis. He has only known indulgence, not disaster. The long-term survival of a country is not just about the present, it is about contemplating potential danger. A [wise] ruler's true pleasure comes not from immediate indulgence but in foreseeing future crisis. Now you ponder the question of survival. Why do you worry about other details?"

King Wu asked: "Two armies encounter each other. The enemy cannot attack, but our side cannot advance either. Knowing the opposing side has strong defense, neither side dares to go forward. I would like to attack the enemy, but lack advantageous conditions. What shall I do?"

Taigong answered: "Give the appearance of chaos while in truth you remain disciplined. Pretend to lack supplies while having sufficient. Pretend to be weak while strong. Divide or assemble the army, making it appear disordered to confuse the enemy. Conceal your own tactics and intentions, and build high barriers. Allocate your elite troops to ambush. Be concealed, invisible, and quiet. The enemy cannot fathom your strategy. If you want to attack from the west, pretend to advance from the east."

King Wu asked: "If the enemy already knows our situation and tactics, what shall I do?"

Taigong replied: "The secret of success lies in observing the enemy's movements and seizing favorable opportunities. Attack them swiftly and unexpectedly."

武韜
MARTIAL SECRET TEACHING

發啟
OPENING INSTRUCTIONS

King Wen summoned Taigong to the Capital of Feng. King Wen said: "Alas! King Shang is cruel and bloodthirsty. He kills innocent people on a whim. Tell me how to save All under Heaven. What shall I do?"

Taigong answered: "A ruler should cultivate his virtue and character. He should be benevolent toward people and observe the signs of Heaven. If ill signs are not visible, you cannot begin a revolt. If you cannot see natural disasters and misfortunes, you can make plans to attack King Shang. By comparing his public utterances and behavior to his secret activities, you can understand his real thoughts. By weighing his external behaviors against his internal activities, you can work out his real intentions. By knowing who he neglects and who he advances, you can understand his true feelings. Your political goal can be achieved by punishing evil-doers. The ideal of unifying the world can be achieved by adopting the right strategy. Appropriate discipline guarantees success. Establishing an advantage allows you to conquer strong enemies. Gaining victory without battle or injury is the realm of God. How subtle!

"If you suffer the same misfortunes and illness as other people, you can save each other; if you share the same emotions, you can look out for each other; if you have the same hatreds and dislikes, you can aid each other; if you have the same likings and pursue the same goal—you can gain victory without an army, you can attack without chariots and bows, you can defend without moats and ditches. Real wisdom, tactics, bravery, and profit are hidden beneath the surface. People across the world welcome those who help, people are against those who harm. The world does not belong to one man. It belongs to everyone under Heaven. Gaining the world is like chasing wild animals. Everyone has the desire to share the meat from beasts. It is the same as crossing a river in a single boat—all will benefit from the successful crossing. However, all will suffer from an unsuccessful attempt. If a ruler brings them together in this way, people across the world will welcome him and no one will object to him. A ruler profits by not exploiting his people or the world. People will support him and allow him to thrive. If a country does not take advantage of other countries, it will benefit. The Way [Tao] cannot be seen or heard, and the victory cannot be known. How subtle!

"When an eagle is ready to attack, it first draws back its wings and descends; when a beast is about to attack, it presses back its ears and crouches down low; when a Sage is about to take action, he exhibits his foolishness and slowness.

Take the example of the Shang, shaken by rumors and riots, while the king remains vicious beyond measure. This is the omen of destruction. I have observed their fields where weeds overwhelm their crops. I have observed their officials who are brutal and immoral. Their court is still not aware of their doom. It is the time for them to perish. When the sun rises, all creatures bask in sunshine. When justice appears, everything benefits. When the righteous army arrives, everyone follows. How great! The virtues and insights of the Sage are the greatest joy!"

文啟
CIVIL INSTRUCTIONS

King Wen asked Taigong: "What principles should a Sage follow?"

Taigong answered: "There is no need to worry or limit yourself. All creation will flourish and thrive. People should be transformed by policies without realizing, just like the passing of time. If the Sage follows this principle, all creation will be influenced. The cycle repeats itself endlessly. A ruler should pursue the art of governing without interfering. If he seeks the Way [Tao], he must keep it in his heart; if he keeps it in his heart, he must implement it; if he implements it, he must not declare it. Heaven and Earth do not reveal themselves and so allow all creation to thrive. The Sage does not parade himself so he is able to achieve great things.

"The Sages of ancient times assembled people into families, assembled families into countries, and assembled countries into the world. They appointed the wise as feudal lords and gave them the task of administration. They promoted civilization and complied with local customs. They transformed crime into righteousness. Despite the differences of different countries, people felt settled and respected their rulers. This is called the establishment of a state. Alas! The Sage is committed to inaction and tranquility, while a worthy ruler is committed to rectifying body and soul. With skewed mind and body, an ignorant ruler opposes the people. Excessive laws lead to enormous and demanding punishments, which create a disturbed people. A disturbed people will try to leave. If the people are not settled and agricultural activities are interrupted, society will be unsteady: this is called the great political loss. People's hearts are like the flow of water. If you block the water, it stops; if you free it, it runs clear. Alas! How marvelous! Only the Sage can see the germination and predict its flowering."

King Wen asked: "How do you make the world peaceful?"

Taigong said: "Heaven changes according to certain patterns. People have their livelihood. If a ruler and his people can come to terms, the world will be peaceful. Therefore, the best policy is the one which follows the people's heart. The second-best policy is the one which moves and transforms them. When people are transformed, they will follow instructions. All creation thrives without Heaven's actions. People thrive without charity. This is the Sage's virtuous administration."

King Wen said: "Your words resonate with me. I will reflect on them day and night and use them as the principle to rule the world."

文伐
CIVIL ATTACK

King Wen asked Taigong: "How do you attack without military methods?"

Taigong said: "There are 12 ways:

"First, appeal to your enemy's preferences and follow his wishes. He will become increasingly proud and arrogant and do erroneous things. If you guide him in this way, you will be able to eradicate him.

"Second, acquaint yourself with those who are close to your enemy in order to divide his power. If the ministers have second thoughts, their loyalty will be compromised. A country without loyal ministers faces doom.

"Third, bribe your enemy's ministers and build a relationship with them. As long as they reside in their own country, their hearts will lean toward your side. Their country will be in danger.

"Fourth, foster your enemy's indulgence and extravagance, encourage his lust and desire, bribe him with rare jewels, and gift him beautiful women. Speak humbly, listen attentively, follow his orders obediently, and accommodate his wishes. Therefore, he will forget the conflict with you and develop his evil behaviors without restraint.

"Fifth, respect your enemy's loyal ministers and send them small presents. Delay communication with his ambassadors and ignore their questions. Urge him to send new ambassadors and treat them with sincerity in order to gain his trust. Your enemy will feel close to you again. Treat your enemy's ministers differently to create division between a ruler and his officials. Then you can plot against them.

"Sixth, bribe your enemy's favored ministers and keep the less favored at a distance. Those talented ministers will reach out to foreign countries and this will result in internal conflict. Then the country you oppose cannot survive.

"Seventh, if you want the enemy ruler to trust you blindly, you should offer him enormous gifts. Secretly bribe his favored minister and it will cause him to neglect agricultural production and result in a shortage of grain and wealth.

"Eighth, bribe your enemy with treasure and persuade him to attack other countries. Once he benefits, he will trust you. The closer you get to him, the more you can take advantage of him. When a state is exploited by an opposing country, it will end in disaster.

"Ninth, honor him with a glorious title and protect him from danger. Make him feel important and powerful and obey his wishes to gain his trust. Praise his accomplishments in order to raise him to a paramount position. Tell him he is as virtuous as a Sage. This will make him so arrogant that he abandons his government duties.

"Tenth, pretend to be humble and obedient toward your enemy. Gain his trust and see how he is positioned. Accommodate his thoughts and wishes and treat him like a brother.

After gaining his trust, you can manipulate him subtly. Once the timing is right, you can destroy him as if you had help from Heaven itself.

"Eleventh, block his access to information. All his officers and people adore wealth and position, while abhorring death and misfortune. You should promise distinguished positions and significant treasure to bribe your enemy's talents. Pretend to be weak and poor while your country is self-sufficient and wealthy. Make alliances with your enemy's strategic talents and make plans with them. Make acquaintance with your enemy's military talents in order to boost your capabilities. Satisfy those people's desire for wealth and foster their greed. Your enemy's talents will be enlisted on your side. This is the Way [Tao] to block his access to information. Although he still rules the country, he cannot run it without information.

"Twelfth, support your enemy's disloyal ministers to confuse his heart and mind. Offer him beautiful women and erotic music to weaken his willpower. Give him good dogs and horses to exhaust him. Report to him only good situations to blind him. Then wait for your opportunity to usurp his country.

"After applying these 12 tactics, you can take military actions. When the omens from Heaven and Earth are right and all the auspicious signs are evident, you can attack him."

順啟
INSTRUCTIONS ON FOLLOWING THE HEARTS OF THE PEOPLE

King Wen asked Taigong: "How do you administer All under Heaven?"

Taigong replied: "When your tolerance covers the world, you can encompass the world. When your trustworthiness covers the world, you can discipline the world. When your benevolence covers the world, you can conciliate the world. When your favor covers the world, you can preserve the world. When your power covers the world, you can own the world. Be decisive and bold. Then the running of the stars and the changing of the four seasons cannot shift you from your path. When all these requirements are met, you can administer the world. If a ruler benefits All under Heaven, the people will welcome him. If a ruler harms All Under Heaven, the people will oppose him. If a ruler kills All under Heaven, the people will be hostile to his cruelty. If a ruler follows the will of All under Heaven, the people will follow him. If a ruler imposes poverty on All under Heaven, the people will hate him. If a ruler settles All under Heaven, the people will rely on him. If a ruler brings calamity, the people will regard him as a disaster. The world does not belong to one man. Only a man with great virtue can be the ruler of the world."

三疑
THREE DOUBTS

King Wu asked Taigong: "I want to achieve great things. However, I have three doubts. I'm afraid I do not have enough strength to attack my enemy, to alienate his close subordinates, or to scatter his population. What shall I do?"

Taigong answered: "First, guide your enemy according to his circumstances. Second, employ tactics cautiously. Third, use your resources wisely. When you attack a strong enemy, you should indulge him so that he becomes arrogant and reckless. An audacious and arrogant enemy will surely be defeated. Before attacking a strong enemy, you should nurture his capacity for violence. If you want to drive a wedge between him and his close supporters, you should bribe his closest subordinates first. If you intend to scatter his population, you should win over the people's hearts.

"Thoroughness is the key to developing strategies. If you bribe your enemy, it will definitely cause internal conflicts. If you intend to alienate his supporters, you should promise them favors and generous benefits. They will be pleased by the gifts and they will not have any doubts as to your intentions.

"The Way [Tao] to defeat a strong enemy is to blind the ruler. Then you can attack his army, destroy his enormous country, and rescue his suffering people. There are many ways to blind him. You can corrupt him with beautiful women, tempt him with generous gifts, indulge him with exquisite food, and seduce him with erotic music.

"Since you have alienated his supporters, you should also estrange him from his people. Do not let him uncover your plot. Entice him into your trap without him realizing. Your plan will be successful.

"If you want to benefit the people, do not begrudge them wealth. People are like cows and horses. The more you feed them, the more obedient they become. The mind produces wisdom; wisdom produces wealth, wealth nurtures the people. Talents come from among the people. A ruler can be assisted by wise talents to rule the world."

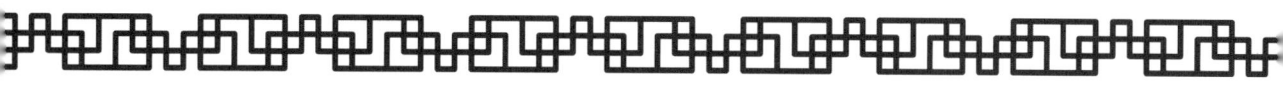

龍韜
DRAGON SECRET TEACHING

王翼
THE KING'S WINGS

King Wu asked Taigong: "When the sovereign leads his army, he should be assisted by competent people to create extraordinary power. How should it be done?"

Taigong replied: "A general grasps the destiny of an army. As a general, the most important thing is to know every situation and circumstance. Never rely on one specialization. In this way, you should allocate positions according to talent and make the most of the people's strength. Be flexible and use your principles to make criteria. A general needs 72 people to assist in order to follow the Way [Tao] of Heaven and cope with attendant circumstances. If you set up in this manner, you will master the principles of being a general. When people's talents are employed fully, all tasks can be accomplished successfully."

King Wu asked: "Can you explain the details?"

Taigong said: "One trusted chief is in charge of advising and planning. He can deal with emergencies, observe the stars, eliminate calamities, supervise general strategies, and protect people's lives.

"Five advisors are in charge of security and planning for danger, observing how the situation changes, judging officers' virtue and talent, maintaining military discipline, assigning titles and positions, answering difficult questions, and judging what measures to take.

"Three astrologers are responsible for investigating the stars and measuring the wind and weather. They can predict if the timing is auspicious or ominous, check for omens, abnormalities and potential disaster, and they can observe Heaven's attitude.

"Three topographers are responsible for choosing the terrain for the army to billet on or march across. They can analyze the advantages and disadvantages of the terrain, observe near and far, easy and difficult, river and mountain, to ensure the army enjoys an advantage.

"Nine strategists are responsible for discussing the similarities and differences of situations, analyzing the reasons for success and failure, inspecting the weapons, and uncovering those who disobey orders.

"Four supply officers are in charge of managing supplies and storage. They ensure the flow of rations and the collection of military supplies, and make sure there are no shortages.

"Four frontline officers are in charge of selecting brave soldiers, allocating superior weapons, and organizing shock troops for rapid attacks.

"Three signals officers are responsible for the flags and drums of the army. They ensure signals are correct and create fake signals to confuse the enemy.

"Four peripheral officers are responsible for important and difficult tasks. They dig ditches and build moats to defend against the enemy.

"Two staff officers make up for implementing the general's shortcomings and rectify the general's mistakes. They receive guests, answer questions, eliminate disasters, and resolve conflicts.

"Three Officers of Authority are responsible for carrying out the strategy of deception. They set up unusual traps and snares without being recognized by the enemy. Their tactics are endless.

"Seven information officers are responsible for interacting with the outside world. They observe the movements, situations, and circumstances of the enemy and the direction of the wind.

"Five Claw and Tooth officers are responsible for raising the prestige of your army and motivating your soldiers. In this way, soldiers can take risks, face challenges, and attack the enemy's elite troops without doubt or fear.

"Four Feather and Wing officers are responsible for promoting the reputation of your general in order to frighten your neighboring countries and weaken their morale.

"Eight roaming officers are responsible for instigating disloyalty among the enemy's officers, spying on conflicts, manipulating their people's thoughts, observing their intentions, and carrying out espionage activities.

"Two wizards are responsible for spreading rumors and confusing the enemy with witchcraft.

"Two medical officers are in charge of managing medical supplies and curing the injured and the sick.

"Two accounting officers are responsible for working out the balance of food supplies, income, and expenses."

論將
THE EVALUATION OF GENERALS

King Wu asked Taigong: "What are the principles for assessing generals?"

Taigong answered: "Generals should have Five Virtues and avoid Ten Defects."

King Wu asked: "Can you clarify the details?"

Taigong said: "The Five Virtues are: bravery, wisdom, benevolence, integrity, and loyalty. Those who are brave will not be discouraged; those who are wise will not be dismayed; those who are benevolent will love their soldiers; those who have integrity will not deceive; and those who are loyal will not be half-hearted.

"The Ten Defects are: being reckless and taking death lightly; being hasty and rushing to success; being greedy; being kind but complacent; being clever but cowardly; being trustworthy but gullible; being honest but mean toward subordinates; being resourceful but indecisive; being determined but arrogant; being weak and dependent. Those who are reckless and take death lightly can be enraged easily; those who are hasty and are overeager for success can be destroyed by persistence; those who are greedy can be bribed; those who are kind but complacent can be worn down; those who are clever but cowardly can be threatened; those who are trustworthy but gullible can be deceived; those who are honest but mean can be insulted; those who are resourceful but indecisive will be unprepared for surprise attacks; those who are determined but arrogant can be schemed against; those who are weak and dependent can be fooled.

"Warfare is vital to the survival of a country. The destiny of a country is in the hands of generals. Generals support a country. They are valued by generations of sovereigns. In this way, the appointments of generals should not be done in haste. Both sides cannot win the battle. Once an army leaves its borders, within ten days either one country perishes or the general of the other country is killed."

King Wu said: "That is well said!"

選將
THE SELECTION OF GENERALS

King Wu asked Taigong: "When a ruler plans to raise an army, how should he select a wise and brave general with virtues?"

Taigong said: "There are 15 cases when a general's actions do not match his outward appearances. He appears to be wise but is unworthy. He appears to be kind but is a thief. He appears to be respectful but is arrogant. He appears to be polite and cautious but is insincere. He appears to be competent but is ignorant. He appears to be reliable but is dishonest. He appears to be resourceful but is indecisive. He appears to be decisive but is incompetent. He appears to be trustworthy but is faithless. He appears to be wavering but is loyal. He appears to be unfocused but is efficient. He appears to be brave but is cowardly. He appears to be serious and distant but is friendly. He appears to be harsh but is warm. He appears to be weak and vacuous but is capable of all tasks. Those who are looked down on are valued by the Sage. Ordinary people do not have insightful understanding of human nature and cannot clarify the mystery. These are the cases when a man's appearance and actions do not match."

King Wu asked: "How can we truly understand this?"

Taigong said: "There are eight ways to understand this. First, ask him [the general] questions and see if he can explain clearly. Second, interrogate him to test his adaptability. Third, spy on him to make sure of his loyalty. Fourth, ask him questions you already know [the answer to] to see if he is hiding something. Fifth, appoint him to manage your possessions to test his honesty. Sixth, test him with beautiful women to observe his integrity. Seventh, confront him with urgent and difficult situations to test his bravery. Eighth, get him drunk to see how he carries himself. After these eight tests, you can tell if he is worthy or not."

立將
THE APPOINTMENT OF GENERALS

King Wu asked Taigong: "What is the procedure for appointing a general?"

Taigong answered: "When a country is in crisis, a ruler will vacate the main hall and summon his commanding general to the side hall, saying: 'The security of our country lies in your hands. Now a certain country is revolting against us. Please lead our army to pacify them.'

"After the commanding general accepts the order, the ruler will order the Scribe to practice divination. He will fast for three days, go to the imperial shrine, burn tortoiseshell, select an auspicious day, and grant the commanding general a ceremonial ax. On the special day, the ruler will enter the shrine and stand facing west. The commanding general follows and stands facing north. The ruler holds the upper part of the ax and gives the handle to the general, declaring: 'From now, all the army's affairs will be in your hands.' Then he will say: 'When the enemy is weak, you should advance. When the enemy is strong, you should halt. Do not underestimate them when we are strong. Do not risk your life just because you have been given heavy responsibilities. Do not despise your subordinates when you are in control. Do not be headstrong when other people think differently. Do not be arrogant because you are articulate. Do not sit when your soldiers are not seated. Do not eat when your soldiers are hungry. Share the heat and cold with them. Then your soldiers will commit their lives to the battle.'

"After the general receives his mandate, the general will bow and say: 'I heard a country's affairs should not be interfered with by other countries. A ruler should not give orders to his army when he is still in the court. If I have second thoughts, I cannot serve the sovereign faithfully. If the general and his officers are controlled by the ruler, they cannot attack the enemy wholeheartedly. I have received the order from your majesty. I shall only return alive if we win. Please allow me to take control of the army. If not, I dare not undertake the responsibility.'

"After receiving permission from the ruler, the commanding general will bid farewell and lead the army. From then on, everything in the army will come under the control of the general rather than the ruler. When the general can focus on battle, he will not be constrained by Heaven, Earth, the enemy, or the ruler. The wise will be willing to plan, and the brave will be willing to do battle. Morale will be high and action will be rapid. The enemy will submit even before battle commences. In this way, the war will be won beyond the borders, accomplishments will be established in the court, the general will be promoted, soldiers will be rewarded, the people will celebrate, and there will be no casualties among the senior officers. The wind and rain will be smooth, grain will be sufficient, and the country will be peaceful."

King Wu said: "That is very well said!"

將威
THE AUTHORITY OF THE GENERAL

King Wu asked Taigong: "How do you establish the authority of the general? How does he show his wisdom? How does he command and forbid effectively?"

Taigong replied: "The general will build his authority by prosecuting people in high positions, and show his wisdom by rewarding people of humble background. He can command and forbid effectively by strict reward and punishments. If the execution of one man can terrify the entire army, he should be killed. If the reward of one man can please the entire army, he should be rewarded. If you prosecute the privileged, your punishments will reach the elite. If you reward cowherds, stablemen, and feeders, you reward the lowest. Your authority will be established if you punish the elites and reward the lowest."

勵軍
MOTIVATING THE ARMY

King Wu asked Taigong: "I want the officers and soldiers of the army to contend to conquer the city, to compete to attack in the battlefield, to be angry when hearing the command to retreat and to be pleased to hear the signal to advance. How can I achieve that?"

Taigong said: "There are three key factors you must consider if you wish to conquer the enemy."

King Wu said: "Can you explain them?"

Taigong said: "A general does not wear a leather coat in winter, does not use a fan in summer, and does not use a canopy when it rains. Then he can be called a general with proper manners. If a general does not set himself up as an example, he will not experience the same cold and warm as his soldiers. When negotiating narrow tunnels and passing muddy lanes, a general should leave his chariot and walk. Then he can be called a general of strength. If he does not take the first step, he will not understand the hardships of his soldiers. A general only enters his tent when all the other tents have been set up. He only begins his meal after his soldiers' food has been served. If the army has no fire, the general cannot have any either. Then he can be called a general of restraint. If a general cannot restrain himself, he cannot understand the hunger of his soldiers. If a general can share the cold, heat, hardships, and hunger with his people, all the officers and soldiers will rejoice at the sound to advance and be angry at the signal to retreat. When they attack high walls and deep moats and face the danger of stones and arrows, they will contend to conquer the city. On the battlefield, once the fighting starts, the soldiers will advance with bravery and without hesitation. This is not because soldiers are born to love death and rejoice in injury, but because the general shares their heat, cold, hunger, and hardships, so that they are willing to fully commit themselves."

陰符
SECRET COMMANDER'S SEAL

King Wu asked Taigong: "When the general leads the army into the enemy territory, there is an emergency. The situation might be beneficial or harmful. I would like to inform the general [of the situation] from afar. What shall I do?"

Taigong said: "There are eight types of secret commanding seals for the ruler to inform the general with. The one which signifies great victory is one foot long. The one which signifies defeating the enemy and capturing their general is nine inches long. The one which signifies the surrender of the enemy's army and the occupation of their cities is eight inches long. The one which signifies repelling the enemy and reporting the situation is seven inches long. The one which motivates the soldiers and people to enhance the defenses is six inches long. The one which requests supplies and additional support is five inches long. The one which reports defeat and the death of the general is four inches long. The one which reports defeat and the loss of soldiers is three inches long. For those who are in charge of delivering commanding seals, any delay or leak of information will mean a death sentence. These eight secret commanding seals are used by the ruler and general to pass information in secret without revealing any details. Even though the enemy is wise, the seals cannot be decoded."

King Wu said: "That is brilliant!"

陰書
SECRET LETTERS

King Wu asked Taigong: "When the general leads the army into enemy territory, the ruler and the general want to gather the army and develop new strategies. But the secret commanding seals cannot explain the numerous details while the army is separated by vast distances and is unable to communicate. What shall we do?"

Taigong answered: "All secret plans require secret letters rather than secret commanding seals. The ruler uses secret letters to inform the general, and the general sends them to the ruler to ask questions. Each letter is divided into three parts and sent by three couriers. Each courier carries one part of the letter. Even the couriers do not know the contents of the letter. This is called a secret letter. No matter how clever the enemy is, our secrets will not be revealed."

King Wu said: "That is brilliant!"

軍勢
THE ARMY'S STRATEGY

King Wu asked Taigong: "What are the principles behind attacking?"

Taigong answered: "Attacking strategy should be determined by the enemy's dynamics. Changes emerge from the confrontation between both sides. Unconventional tactics come from the infinite wisdom and thoughts of the general. The most important military secrets cannot be revealed. The deployment of the troops cannot be spoken of. The most important secrets can only be hidden in the heart. The key affairs of the army cannot be exposed to the enemy. The deployment of troops is unpredictable. If the enemy knows your plan or discovers your movements, they will plot against you. If the enemy works out your pattern, you will be in danger. The true experts win before the armies are deployed. Those who are good at eliminating disaster will eradicate danger before it occurs. Those who excel at battles can win before the enemy has appeared. The ultimate victory is achieved without military forces. Those who achieve victory with blades and struggles to the death are not great generals. Those who set up defenses after they have been defeated are not wise. Those who have the same wisdom as ordinary people cannot be regarded as teachers of the nation. Those who have the same skills as ordinary people cannot be considered as artisans of the nation. Deployment is the key to victory. Secrets are the key to battle. Unpredictability is the key to movement and tactics. If you want to attain victory before the battle, you should show your weakness first and then attack. It will yield twice the result with half the effort.

"The Sage observes the changes of Heaven and Earth. He studies the law of the sun and moon, the changes of the seasons, and the length of day and night to deduce the general pattern of the creation. Life and death come from the changes of Heaven and Earth. If a general goes into battle without first ascertaining the situation, even with an enormous army, he is destined to be defeated.

"The general who is good in command will not be confused by false appearances. He will advance when the timing is right and retreat when there is no possibility of victory. Do not fear. Do not hesitate. In military deployment, he who hesitates is lost. The greatest failure in military affairs is doubt. An experienced general does not let go of any advantageous situation or hesitate when presented with an opportunity. Otherwise, disaster occurs. A wise general will strike like lightning, rapidly and powerfully. Those who obstruct him will be defeated. Those who get too near will be destroyed. Who can defend against this type of army?

"A general who has great confidence without revealing his secrets is spirit-like. He who grasps the situation instantly is wise. If he masters the law of the spirit and wisdom, no opponents can fight him on equal terms. No country will dare to challenge him."

King Wu said: "This is brilliant!"

奇兵
THE UNCONVENTIONAL ARMY

King Wu asked Taigong: "What are the principles for employing the troops?"

Taigong answered: "The great generals of ancient times did not attack from Heaven or from below Earth. Their success lay in unpredictable military strategy. Those who achieved it thrived, those who did not failed. When two armies opposed each other, they unloaded armor and weapons, released troops, and created chaos to deceive the enemy. They occupied lush terrain to conceal their retreats. They used dangerous valleys to attack with a limited number of soldiers. Downs and marsh lands were used to stop the enemy's chariots and cavalry. Narrow passes and mountain forests were used for concealing troop movements. Open and wide terrain was used for attacking directly with courage and strength.

"If you are as swift as an arrow and as strong as a crossbow, you can disrupt the enemy's tactics. Setting up traps, employing unconventional troops, and performing acts of deception are used to attack the enemy and capture their general. Attack from four directions to break the enemy's circular and square formations. Attack while the enemy are in panic and fear and one can overcome ten. Attack the enemy while they are fatigued and encamped and 10 can overcome 100. Build bridges and boats with exceptional skills to cross deep waters and large rivers. Use crossbows and long-reaching weapons for battle on water. Set borders and send scouts to occupy the enemy's territory. Make noises by drumming to disturb and confuse the enemy. Take action on stormy nights to strike the front and the rear. Pretend to be enemy emissaries to cut off their supply channels. Use the enemy's commands and wear their uniforms to prepare for their retreat. Motivate the troops with talks of righteousness to boost morale. Grant titles and rewards to encourage the troops to commit. Strict punishments force the weary troops to persevere. Use joy and anger, reward and punishment, courtesy and dignity, slowness and swiftness, to coordinate the army's actions. Occupy high and open terrain to guard and defend. Protect narrow passes to stabilize the defenses. Occupy deep forests to conceal the troops' actions. Dig deep moats, build high walls, and store sufficient supplies for long-term battle.

"In this way, if a general does not understand strategies, he cannot lead the army into war. If he does not know how to divide and employ troops, he does not know how to gain an unconventional victory. If he does not grasp the meaning of order and chaos, he does not know how to adjust according to changing circumstances. If the general is not benevolent, his troops will not support him. If the general is not brave, his troops cannot fight with vigor. If the general is not intelligent, his troops will have fears and doubts. If the general is not shrewd, his troops will be defeated. If the general is not thorough, he will miss great opportunities. If the general is not alert, his troops will neglect defense. If the general is not strong, his troops will be derelict in their duties. The general dominates the army. The army is ordered with him, and they are chaotic without him. A wise and capable general will ensure a thriving army. Without a general, the army and the state will perish."

King Wu said: "Well said!"

五音
THE FIVE NOTES

King Wu asked Taigong: "From the music of the pitch pipe, can we tell the dynamics of the army and predict the result of battle?"

Taigong answered: "This is a very profound topic! There are twelve scales and the five major ones are: *Gong, Shang, Jiao, Zhi,* and *Yu.* These are basic and unchanging sounds. Five elements reinforce and counteract each other, which are the laws of Heaven and Earth. You can use them to foretell the changes of your opponent. Metal, wood, water, fire, and earth complement and neutralize each other. They can be applied to attacking the enemy.

"In the ancient time of three Sage Kings, the principle of inaction was used to restrain the strong and the cruel. Without words and writings, everything was operated according to the Law of Five Elements. The Law of Five Elements is the law of the changes in Heaven and Earth. The six divisions of time are very subtle. Here are the methods of using five notes and five elements:

"When the day is clear and dry, send light cavalry to attack the enemy's camps in the middle of the night. Standing 900 steps from the camp, you should hold the pitch pipe to your ear and shout at the enemy to disturb them. You will hear their response from the pitch pipe. The noise is very weak. If the *Jiao* sound is reflected in the pipe, you should attack from White Tiger, signifying the west. If the *Zhi* sound is reflected in the pipe, you should attack from Tortoise, signifying the north. If the *Shang* sound is reflected in the pipe, you should attack from Rosefinch, signifying the south. If the *Yu* sound is reflected, you should attack from Unicorn, signifying the center. If there is no sound, which is the *Gong* sound, you should attack from Green Dragon, signifying the east. The application of five elements is the key to victory."

King Wu said: "This is marvelous!"

Taigong said: "Subtle sounds have great effects."

King Wu asked: "How can we know?"

Taigong replied: "When the enemy are disturbed, listen to them. The sound of the drum is the response of the *Jiao* sound. The response to seeing the light of their fire should be the *Zhi* note. The response to the sound of the clash of armor should be the *Shang* note. The response to the shouting of the enemy should be the *Yu* note. The response to silence should be the *Gong* note. These five notes match external movements."

兵徵
THE SIGNS OF MILITARY MANEUVER

King Wu asked Taigong: "I would like to know the enemy's strengths and weaknesses in order to foresee the result of the battle. What shall I do?"

Taigong said: "A shrewd general can observe the signs of victory and defeat can be seen in the enemy's spirit. He can use these signs to defeat them. Investigate the enemy's comings and goings thoroughly. Observe their movements, the auspicious signs and ominous tones of their conversations. If the soldiers are joyful, if they fear the law and respect orders from the general, if they rejoice in defeating the enemy and take pride in bravery and power: these are the signs of a strong army. If the army is constantly disturbed, if troops are chaotic, if they fear the power of their enemy, if they talk of defeat, if they spread rumors, if they deceive each other, if they do not fear the law or respect their general: these are the signs of a weak army. If the army is ordered, the battle array is solid, the moats are deep and the walls are high, the flags point to the front, gongs and drums are loud and clear, and they enjoy advantageous weather like wind and rain: these are the signs when the army receives help from spirits and will gain a great victory. If the formation is not solid, the flags are disoriented, the army is against the wind and rain, soldiers are scared, morale is low, horses are frightened and prone to panic, chariots have broken shafts, gongs and drums sound soft and depressing, these are the signs of defeat. When attacking a city, if the color of their qi [vitality] above the city is like dead ashes, the city can be destroyed. If the qi flows north, the city can be conquered. If the qi flows west, the city might surrender. If the qi flows south, it cannot be crushed. If the qi flows east, the city cannot be attacked. If the qi covers your troops, you will experience misfortune. If the qi continues rising, the battle will be long. When surrounding the city, if there is no lightning or rain after ten days, you have to retreat, because there is a Sage assisting it. Thus, you can understand when you can attack and when you should halt."

King Wu said: "Brilliant!"

農器
AGRICULTURAL INSTRUMENTS

King Wu asked Taigong: "When the world is peaceful and harmonious and there is no warfare among countries, can we dispense with the production of weapons of war? Can we stop making defensive equipment?"

Taigong answered: "The tools of offense and defense are all found in agricultural instruments. Plows can be used to clear obstructions such as barriers and barbs. Horse and ox carts can be used to build camps. Hoes can be used as spears. Rain capes, umbrellas, and bamboo hats can be used as armors and shields. Spades, axes, mortars, and pestles can be used to attack walls. Horses and oxen can be used to transport supplies. Chickens and dogs can be used for time-keeping and lookouts. The fabric women weave can be used to make flags. The methods for leveling the fields can be used to attack walls. The technique of weeding in spring is the same as fighting the enemy's chariots and cavalry. The technique of plowing in summer is the same as fighting the enemy's infantry. The harvest in autumn can be used as supplies for battle. In winter, the full warehouse is a prerequisite for long-term warfare. People from the same village work together, which is the foundation for enlistment. Village chiefs and officers can serve as army officials during wartime. The walls between villages can serve as divisions of platoons. The transportation of grain and the harvest of feed serve as army logistics. The skills for repairing walls and unblocking tunnels are the same as those for digging ditches and building fortifications. In this way, the equipment for warfare can be found in agricultural activities. A wise ruler will emphasize agricultural affairs. People should rear animals, cultivate fields, and settle in their own places. Men should farm their own acres of land, and women should weave lengths of fabric. These are the ways of strengthening a country and its military power."

King Wu said: "This is brilliant!"

虎韜
TIGER SECRET TEACHING

軍用
MILITARY EQUIPMENT

King Wu asked Taigong: "When the ruler leads his army to war, are there any rules for the type and quantity of military equipment?"

Taigong answered: "This is an important question! The type and quantity of offensive and defensive instruments varies, which affects the strength of the army."

King Wu said: "I would like to hear more details."

Taigong said: "There is a basic standard for employing the troops. For 10,000 soldiers, the weapons and equipment needed are: 36 *Wuchong* large chariots with skillful and brave warriors guarding both sides. The warriors hold crossbows, spears, and halberds. Each chariot needs 24 people to push it. The height of the wheel is 8 feet. There are flags and drums on the chariots. In military strategy, these chariots are called Shock and Fear. They can be used to attack solid formations and to defeat strong enemies.

"Seventy-two *Wuyi* chariots with large shields and halberds are guarded by warriors holding crossbows, spears, and halberds on both sides. The height of the wheel is 5 feet. The crossbows fire continuous arrows. They are used to attack solid formations and defeat strong enemies.

"One hundred and forty *Tiyi* chariots with small shields are equipped with winch-powered crossbows to fire continuous arrows. These chariots have a single wheel. They are used to attack solid formations and defeat strong enemies.

"Thirty-six Large Yellow Chariots equipped with strong crossbows will be guarded by skillful and brave warriors with crossbows, spears, and halberds on both sides. Two types of flags named Flying Bird and Lightning Shadow are planted on the chariots. Flying Bird has a red pole, a white feather, and a bronze top. Lightning Shadow has a green pole, a red feather, and an iron top. The flags used in the daytime are made of red silk, which are 6 inches long and 6 inches wide. They are called Light Glory. The flags used at nighttime are made of white silk, which are 6 inches long and 6 inches wide. They are called Meteors. This type of chariot can be used to attack solid formations and defeat strong enemies.

"Thirty-six Great Attack chariots will carry Praying Mantis warriors. They are used to attack strong enemies in both vertical and horizontal formations.

"Canopy chariots are also called Lightning Chariots. In military strategy, they are used for lightning attacks. They can be used to attack the enemy's infantry and cavalry to penetrate solid formations.

"If the enemy attack in the darkness, use 160 Spear and Halberd Light Chariots. Each chariot carries three Praying Mantis warriors. This is referred to as a Lightning Attack. They are used to penetrate solid formations and defeat the enemy's infantry.

"Square-headed iron sticks weigh 12 catties with shafts more than 5 feet long. There are 1,200 of them. They are called Heaven's Truncheon. Long-shaft axes called Big Stems have 8-inch blades and 5-foot-long shafts and weigh 8 catties. There are 1,200 of them. They are also called Heaven's Yue. Square-headed hammers weigh 8 catties with shafts of over 5 feet. There are 1,200 of them. They are also called Heaven's Hammer. These can be used to defeat the enemy's infantry.

"Flying Hooks are 8 inches long with 4-inch-long curved hooks and over 6-foot-long shafts. There are 1,200 of them. They can be thrown toward enemies.

"When in defensive positions, use the 20-foot wide wooden chariots equipped with Praying Mantis warriors and sword blades. There are 120 of them. They are also called Flying Horses. When used on flat and open terrain, infantry can use them to block the movement of cavalry.

"Wooden caltrops should be set up at 2 feet, 5 inches above the ground. There are 120 of them. These can be used to delay the movement of the enemy's infantry and cavalry, stop desperate invaders, and intercept fleeing soldiers.

"There are 120 short-axle quick-turning Spear and Halberd Light Chariots. They were used by the Yellow Emperor to defeat Chiyou. They can be used to defeat the enemy's infantry and cavalry, stop desperate invaders, and intercept fleeing soldiers.

"On narrow routes, set iron caltrops. They are 8 inches wide and 6 inches long with 4-inch-long thorns. There are 1,200 of them. They can be employed to stop the enemy's infantry and cavalry.

"If the enemy press the attack in darkness and naked blades clash, set out ground snares, 2 arrowhead caltrops, and the Weaving Girl barrier. The sharp blades should be 2 inches apart. There are 12,000 of them. When fighting in wilderness with deep grass, set out 1,200 arrow-shaped spear barriers. They should be 1 foot, 5 inches above the ground. These can be used to defeat the enemy's infantry and cavalry, stop desperate invaders, and intercept fleeing soldiers.

"On narrow roads, small by-paths, and low-lying marshland, set out Iron Chain barriers. There are 120 of them. They can be employed to defeat the enemy's infantry and cavalry, stop desperate invaders, and intercept fleeing soldiers.

"When guarding camp gates, use 12 sets of spears, axes, and small shields, and winch-activated crossbows. When in defensive position, set Heaven's Snares and Tiger Chain barriers, which are 15 feet wide and 8 feet tall. One hundred and twenty of them. Launch chariots with Tiger Chains and sword blades attached, which measure 15 feet wide and 8 feet tall. There are 520 of them.

"When crossing trenches, set up eight Flying Bridges, which are 15 feet wide and over 20 feet long with swivel winches. Chains and long ropes are needed for this. When crossing rivers, use eight Flying Bridges, which are 15 feet wide and over 20 feet long. They are connected by chains and ropes. The Heavenly Float has iron Praying Mantis anchors. They are circular inside, 4 feet in diameter, and connected by iron loops and ropes. There are 32 of them. They can be used to cross wide rivers. They are called 'Heaven's Huang' or 'Heaven's Boat.'

"When making camp in forests and wilderness, use wood to build ramparts and connect the Tiger Chains to make a fence. Use iron loops, long ropes, and chains. Each one is over 20 feet long. There are 1,200 of them. There are 600 large ropes with iron loops. Loops are 4 inches long. The ropes are over 40 feet long. There are 300 medium-sized ropes with 2-inch loops and 40-foot ropes. There are 12,000 small ropes with over 20-foot ropes.

"When it rains, cover the heavy chariots with wooden boards. These are equipped with serrated seams to match the chariots. Each board is 4 feet wide and over 40 feet long. Each chariot is fixed with iron nails.

"There are 300 large axes for cutting trees. They weigh 8 catties and have shafts that are over 3 foot long. There are 300 large hoes which have 6-inch-wide blades and shafts over 5 feet long. There are 300 Eagle Claws, square-shaft iron rakes with shafts over 7 feet long. There are 300 square-shafted iron pitchforks with shafts over 7 feet long.

"There are 300 large sickles to cut grass with shafts over seven feet long. There are 300 big oar blades which weigh 8 catties and have shafts 6 feet long. There are 300 iron stakes with rings, which are over 3 feet long. There are 120 large hammers for pounding posts which weigh 5 catties and have shafts over 2 feet long.

"Ten thousand soldiers need 6,000 strong crossbows, 2,000 sets of axes and large shields, 2,000 sets of spears and shields, and 300 artisans to repair and make weapons and equipment. These are the approximate numbers of weapons and equipment required for 10,000 soldiers."

King Wu said: "Indeed!"

三陳
THREE DEPLOYMENTS

King Wu asked Taigong: "During the battle, what are Heavenly Deployment, Earthly Deployment, and Human Deployment?"

Taigong said: "When you follow the sun, the moon, the stars, and the Big Dipper, it is Heavenly Deployment. When you follow the terrain such as hills and lakes, it is Earthly Deployment. When you follow the chariots, cavalry, or civil and military instructions, it is Human Deployment."

King Wu said: "Brilliant!"

疾戰
RAPID BATTLE

King Wu asked Taigong: "If the enemy surrounds us from all four directions, cuts off our communications from outside support, and severs our supply routes, what should we do?"

Taigong said: "This is the most difficult situation. Under these circumstances, if you break out from the siege quickly, you can succeed. Any hesitation will cause failure. Here is the Way [Tao] to break out: deploy the troops into formations in all four directions, use the powerful chariots and brave cavalry to attack and confuse the enemy. Then assault them rapidly. You will advance without any obstacles."

King Wu asked: "After the successful break-out, if we want to attack the enemy, what should we do?"

Taigong replied: "Command the left wing of your troops to attack the left wing of the enemy, and the right wing of your troops to attack the right wing of the enemy. Do not fight the enemy on the roads since it will disperse your forces. At the same time, command the central troops to attack the front and back of the enemy in turn. You can defeat them despite the odds."

必出
SURE ESCAPE

King Wu asked Taigong: "Our troops are deep in enemy territory, the enemy surrounds our army from four sides, cuts off our retreat and blocks our supply channels. The enemy is numerous and plentifully supplied. The enemy occupies advantageous terrain and establishes solid formations. How can we break out?"

Taigong said: "When attempting to break out, weapons and equipment are vital, while bravery is of utmost importance. Investigate the weaknesses of the enemy's troops and unguarded areas. You can escape by attacking their weaknesses. The formation for the break-out is as follows: Officers hold black flags and weapons in their hands and carry gags in their mouths. They act in the darkness of the night. The officers at the front are the brave, the strong, the flexible, and those willing to take risks. They attack the enemy camps and create a path for your troops. The skillful and courageous warriors will use crossbows and act as an ambushing force to cover the movement of troops. The old and weak soldiers, chariots, and cavalry will be in the middle. After deployment, be calm and cautious. Do not panic. Use Attack Chariots to protect the front and back, and use Covered Chariots to protect left and right. If the enemy notices your moves, your brave and strong pioneer troops should advance and attack immediately, followed by the weak soldiers, the chariots, and the cavalry. Warriors equipped with crossbows will hide in secret. When the enemy chases you, your ambushing force can attack their rear and use lights and drums to disturb them, in order to make them feel that we rise from below Earth and descend from above Heaven. If the entire army fights courageously, the enemy cannot stop us."

King Wu asked: "There are wide rivers, broad moats, and deep burrows ahead of us. We must cross over but we have no boats. The enemy has numerous soldiers, moats, and high walls. They try to block our advance and cut off our road of retreat. The patrols are watchful and strategic terrains are occupied. Chariots and cavalry block us in the front, and warriors attack us in the rear. What should we do?"

Taigong said: "Normally, the enemy does not guard wide rivers, broad moats, and deep burrows. Even if they are guarded, the soldiers will not be numerous. We can use tools such as Flying Rivers, Twisting Passes, and Heaven's Huang to help us cross. Send brave warriors to attack and fight to the death. Burn your heavy equipment and supplies. Inform your officers and soldiers that persistent fighting leads to life and cowards face death. When escaping from danger, the front troops should send out firework signals to troops far away to occupy forests, graveyards, and strategic terrains. Enemy chariots and cavalry will not dare to chase us. Firework signals are to gather the front troops to assemble and consolidate into a four-direction formation. When all your officers and soldiers are brave and fierce, you are unstoppable."

King Wu said: "Brilliant!"

軍略
MILITARY STRATEGY

King Wu asked Taigong: "I am leading my troops into enemy territory. We face deep valleys and wide rivers. Before we can cross, rain falls from Heaven, resulting in a flood. Our troops in the rear are cut off without any boats, bridges, or equipment to stop the water. If we want the entire army to cross without delay, what should we do?"

Taigong said: "When leading troops to battle, if plans are not formed beforehand, weapons and equipment are not prepared, drills and practice are not perfected, skills are not honed, an army cannot be called the king's troops. Before major military campaigns, soldiers should be trained to use weapons skillfully. If the army needs to surround and attack walls and ramparts, chariots such as Assault Chariots, Tower Chariots, and Charging Chariots should be used. When observing the enemy's activities inside the walls, Flying

Ladders and Flying Towers should be used. When advancing the troops and building tents, large Wuchong chariots and Wing Chariots should cover the troops. To block the roads, brave and skillful soldiers should use crossbows to guard both sides. When setting up camps, equipment such as Heaven's Snare, Martial Drop, Running Horse, and caltrops should be set around the camp. In daytime, officers should climb the Cloud Ladder to look into the distance and use five colored flags to signal with. In the evening, set off fireworks, beat Thunder Drums and War Drums, strike big bells, blow whistles as signals. When crossing valleys, use Flying Bridges, Twisting Passes, and Wheels and Cogs. When crossing wide rivers, use boats such as Heaven Huang and Flying River. When crossing against the current, use equipment such as Floating Sea [rafts] and [the rope-pulled] River Severance. When all equipment is prepared, the general has nothing to worry about."

臨境
REACHING THE BORDER

King Wu asked Taigong: "Our army confronts the enemy at the border. The enemy can attack us, while we can attack them. Both sides have strong formations. Neither dares take action first. I would like to attack them but worry about being attacked. What should I do?"

Taigong answered: "Under such circumstances, divide your troops into three sections: front, middle, and rear. The front troops dig deep moats and build high ramparts without initiating battle. They set up flags and beat drums. They prepare for defense. They accumulate food supplies without being noticed by enemy spies. Then, secretly send your strong middle troop to attack the enemy's center. Attack without being noticed.

Attack when they are not prepared. When the enemy is unaware of your maneuver, they will not dare to attack you."

King Wu asked: "If the enemy knows our situation and perceives our attempts, they know our intentions. They will send their strong troops to ambush us in the deep grass, attempt to cut off our troops on narrow roads, and attack our weak points. What should we do?"

Taigong said: "Command your frontline troops to provoke the enemy every day to wear them out. Command your old and weak soldiers to drag tree branches to raise dust, beat the drums, create a clamor, and run back and forth, to make your army appear more impressive. Your troops then show up to the left or the right of the enemy, less than 100 paces from them. After your persistent harassment, the enemy's general will be fatigued and his soldiers will be frightened. In this way, they will not dare to attack you. You pester them ceaselessly and attack them internally and externally. When you engage in battle rapidly, the enemy will be defeated."

動靜
MOVEMENT AND INACTIVITY

King Wu asked Taigong: "We lead the troops deep inside enemy territory. Both sides are equal in strength and numbers and confront each other. Both sides dare not initiate the battle. Under such circumstances, I would like the enemy general to be fearful, his troops low in morale, his formations fragmented, his soldiers in the rear on the verge of flight, and his frontline formation unstable. When we beat the drums and shout, our attack will force the enemy to escape. What shall we do?"

Taigong said: "Send troops 10 miles behind the enemy. Ambush them from both sides of the road. Send chariots and cavalry about 100 miles away. Behind the enemy's troops, command your soldiers to prepare numerous flags, drums, and gongs. When battle commences, beat the drums and shout. At the same time, have all the troops attack the enemy. The enemy's general is sure to be scared, and his soldiers will panic. Their troops cannot rescue each other. Officers and soldiers will not watch out for each other. They will definitely be defeated."

King Wu asked: "The terrain which the enemy occupies is not convenient for an ambush. Our chariots and cavalry cannot reach the rear of the enemy. At the same time, they notice our attempts and make preparations. Our officers and soldiers are pessimistic and dismayed. Our general is fearful and cannot gain victory. What should we do?"

Taigong replied: "How subtle! In this situation, patrols should be sent five days before the battle. Your spies and officers should observe enemy movements, investigate the signs of enemy advances, and set up traps ahead of them. You should fight on the terrain which puts the enemy at a disadvantage. Space out your flags and troops. Assault the enemy with equal strength and numbers. Retreat once the battle begins. Beat the gongs and pretend to halt. Withdraw three miles, then fight back. The ambushing force will begin the battle on both sides of the enemy, or attack the front and rear. If your entire army fights fiercely, the enemy will definitely be defeated."

King Wu said: "Well said!"

金鼓
GONGS AND DRUMS

King Wu asked Taigong: "I am leading troops in enemy territory. Both sides are equal in strength and numbers. The weather is extremely hot or cold, or it rains heavily for ten days non-stop, resulting in damage to the ditches and ramparts. Narrow passes and barricades are not guarded. Patrols are slack and negligent. If the enemy attacks at night, our Three Armies are not prepared and our officers and soldiers are all confused. What should we do?"

Taigong said: "If the army is alert, it will come together, while slackness leads to failure. Command your soldiers on the ramparts to challenge everyone. Sentinels should hold flags and communicate orders internally and externally. Gongs and drums should not stop. Officers and soldiers should face the enemy and be ready for imminent battle. Soldiers should be grouped into units of 3,000. Instruct and discipline them. Ask them to be on alert. If the enemy comes, they will see your discipline and readiness and turn around in fear. Then, you can send strong troops to chase and attack them when they are weary."

King Wu asked: "The enemy knows we are going to chase. So they hide their strong soldiers in advance and pretend to retreat. When we enter their trap, they turn around to collaborate with their ambushing force. They attack the front, the rear, and the ramparts. Our army is in panic and disturbed. The formation is disrupted. Soldiers leave their positions. What shall we do?"

Taigong said: "You should divide your troops into three sections. The front unit chases the enemy. Take care not to enter the ambushed area. The first three units should attack the front and both flanks of the enemy. Give clear and strict orders. Command soldiers to advance rapidly. The enemy will definitely be defeated."

絕道
SEVERED ROADS

King Wu asked Taigong: "After leading our troops deep into enemy territory, we are confronted by enemy troops. They have cut off our supply routes and attacked us in the front and rear. I would like to fight, but we might not win. I would like to defend, but we cannot last long. What should I do?"

Taigong replied: "When you fight deep in the enemy's territory, you must investigate the terrain and enemy positions. Occupy advantageous terrain. Strengthen the formations by using forests, mountains, springs, and rivers. Guard passes and bridges carefully. You should also occupy advantageous areas such as cities, towns, hills, and graveyards. In this way, your defense will be solid. The enemy cannot cut off your supply routes or attack you from the front and rear."

King Wu asked: "We cross large forests, wide marshes, and flat terrain and our troops are delayed. The enemy suddenly attacks. If we advance, we cannot win. If we defend, we cannot be secure. The enemy surrounds us on both flanks and follows us in the rear. Our troops are fearful. What should we do?"

Taigong said: "When you engage in battle, you should send patrols to faraway places. When you are 200 li[1] from the enemy, you should understand their position in detail. If the terrain is disadvantageous, you should use the Attack Chariots as your ramparts and advance. Send two rear guard troops in the rear. The distance between the rear troops and the main troops should be between 50 and 100 li[1]. Troops can rescue each other when an emergency occurs. If your army can maintain such complete and solid formations, you will not suffer from loss and failure."

King Wu said: "Brilliant!"

---

1. One li is approximately one-third of a mile.

略地
OCCUPYING TERRITORIES

King Wu asked Taigong: "Our troops have penetrated deep into enemy territory and occupied their land. However, we still have not managed to conquer their great cities. A unit from the enemy confronts us on disadvantageous terrain. I would like to attack their cities, but I am worried that troops inside the cities will cooperate with troops outside the cities to attack our flanks, causing chaos and fear in our ranks. What should we do?"

Taigong said: "When besieging cities, you should allocate chariots and cavalry to places far away. The guarding and patrolling forces should cut off the enemy's internal and external communications. Then, when the city dwellers lack food, supplies cannot be brought in. Inhabitants and soldiers inside the city will panic. The general in charge will surrender."

King Wu asked: "When supplies in the city are cut off, food cannot be transported in. The enemy secretly communicates inside and outside the city, planning to break out. They fight to their death at night. Their strong cavalry attacks us from within and without. Our officers and soldiers are frightened. The army is chaotic and defeated. What should we do?"

Taigong said: "Under such circumstances, you should divide your troops into three sections and position them according to the terrain. Investigate the position of the enemy troops outside the city as well as their fortifications. Leave a route for fleeing troops and encourage them to escape. Guard them with alertness. Do not let them escape. Under siege, they will escape into the woods or to a different city. One section of your troops should attack the enemy outside the city. The elite cavalry stops the enemy from escaping. In this situation, troops inside the city will think the first group has escaped successfully and has found an escape route. Their elite soldiers will follow the route from the city, leaving the old and weak behind. Your third unit of chariots and cavalry should attack the rear of the enemy. Those remaining in the city will not dare to break out. Your troops should be very cautious. Do not engage in battle in a rush. Sever the supply routes and besiege them. After some time, the enemy will definitely surrender. After conquering the city, do not burn the food in storage, do not destroy inhabitants' houses, do not cut down the trees in graveyards and shrines, do not kill surrendering soldiers, and do not abuse captives. Take this opportunity to show mercy and benevolence. Explain to their people that their ruler is the only guilty man. The whole world will obey your orders."

King Wu said: "Excellent!"

火戰
FIRE IN WARFARE

King Wu asked Taigong: "After leading our troops deep into enemy territory, we are surrounded by thick grass and bushes. After marching for several hundred li, the soldiers and horses are exhausted and need rest. The enemy takes advantage of dry weather and a strong wind and lights a fire upwind. Their elite cavalry also ambush us in the rear, causing our Three Armies to panic and scatter. What should we do?"

Taigong said: "Under these circumstances, you should set up Cloud Ladders and Flying Towers to observe the situation from the front, back, left, and right. If the enemy sets a fire, you should light a fire in the spacious area in front of your troops and spread it. At the same time, light a fire to the rear of your troops to create a burnt and blackened area. If the enemy advances, the troops should defend this blackened space. When the enemy sees the fire, they will retreat. You establish your formation on the blackened ground, use strong soldiers and crossbows to protect both flanks, and continue igniting grassland to the front and rear. The enemy will not be able to do any damage to you."

King Wu asked: "If the enemy lights a fire to our left, right, front, and back, the smoke will cover our troops. At the same time, the enemy attacks the blackened ground. What should we do?"

Taigong answered: "In this situation, allocate Attack Chariots to four sides and cover both flanks with strong crossbows. This formation will not lead to victory but will prevent defeat."

壘虛
EMPTY FORTIFICATIONS

King Wu asked Taigong: "How can we know whether the enemy's fortifications are empty or occupied? How can we discern the movement of the enemy's troops?"

Taigong said: "A general should know Heaven's trends, Earth's advantages and disadvantages, and the affairs of the people. From the high ground you can observe the changes in the enemy's situation. By observing fortifications from afar, you can tell whether they are empty or occupied. By observing the movement of soldiers, you can see the maneuvers of the enemy."

King Wu asked: "How can you know such things?"

Taigong answered: "If you cannot hear drums or bells, if the birds are undisturbed, if dust is not raised, you can tell the fortification is empty. The enemy is using dummies to deceive you. If the enemy retreats in a rush, but not very far, and returns too hastily, the maneuver will be chaotic and disordered. Without order, their formation will be chaotic. In this situation, you can attack them rapidly. Even if your number is small, you will gain victory."

豹韜
LEOPARD SECRET TEACHING

林戰
FOREST WARFARE

King Wu asked Taigong: "When leading our troops deep into enemy territory, we confront the enemy in a large forest. If I want the defense to be solid and the attack to be victorious, what should I do?"

Taigong said: "Deploy your troops into the Assault Formation and station them in an advantageous place. Crossbows should be on the outside, and shields and axes inside. Chop down trees and long grass and widen the road to improve your movement. Set up the flags and discipline the army. Do not let the enemy know your intentions. This is forest warfare. Here are the methods: form soldiers with weapons such as spears and halberds into a combat squad. If the trees are not dense, cavalry will assist the assault. Station chariots at the front and engage in battle when the situation is advantageous. If the terrain is difficult in the forest, deploy an Assault Formation to prevent the enemy attacking your front and rear. If you attack rapidly and fiercely, the enemy will be defeated despite their large number. Your troops should take turns to fight and rest within their sections. This is the general principle of forest warfare."

突戰
RAPID WARFARE

King Wu asked Taigong: "Suppose the enemy's troops have penetrated into our territory, occupied our land, and plundered our cattle and horses. They swarm toward us and besiege our cities. Our officers and soldiers are fearful. Our people are held captive. If I want our defense to be solid and our forces to be victorious, what should I do?"

Taigong said: "This is referred to as rapid assault. The enemy's cattle and horses will lack feed and the soldiers will lack rations. Therefore, they will attack you fiercely. In this case, command your troops stationed in distant areas to select elite soldiers and attack the rear of the enemy without delay. Calculate and confirm the exact time of attack. Make sure they meet you in the darkness of the night. Your entire army will fight the enemy rapidly and fiercely. Though the enemy is numerous, their general will be captured."

King Wu asked: "The enemy divides into three or four sections: one section attacks us to occupy our land and one section plunders our cattle, horses, and other properties. Their main troops have not arrived yet, but they send one section to besiege our city to frighten us. What should we do?"

Taigong answered: "Observe the situation carefully. Prepare cautiously and await them before they arrive. Build camps and ramparts four li from the city. Beat gongs and drums, and set up all the flags. Send a unit as an ambushing force. Equip troops on the ramparts with crossbows. Set up a secret gate for troops to attack from every 100 steps. Place barricades in front of the gates. Chariots and cavalry are stationed next to the ramparts. Brave elite soldiers hide nearby. When the enemy arrives, send your light-armored soldiers to engage in battle and feign a retreat. Command your guards to set up flags on the walls and beat the drums to prepare for defense. If the enemy thinks your main force is guarding the city, they will advance to the city walls. Send your ambushing force to penetrate the enemy ranks and attack their formations. At the same time, command your entire army to assault the enemy's front and rear rapidly and bravely. Their brave soldiers will not be able to fight, and their swift soldiers will not be able to escape. This is called rapid warfare. Even though they are numerous, their general will definitely be defeated and flee."

King Wu said: "Brilliant!"

敵強
STRONG ENEMIES

King Wu asked Taigong: "When leading our troops deep into enemy territory, we are confronted by the enemy. They are numerous while we are few. They use darkness as cover to assault our left or right flank, causing us to be fearful. If I want our attack to be victorious and our defense to be solid, what should I do?"

Taigong answered: "They are called Shaking Invaders. It is better for you to attack than defend. Select strong soldiers armed with crossbows, use chariots and cavalry on your flanks, attack their front fiercely, and attack their rear rapidly. Attack from the outside and inside. Their soldiers will definitely be chaotic. Their general will be frightened and defeated."

King Wu asked: "The enemy obstructs our front, attacks our rear rapidly, cuts off our elite troops, and severs our supply lines. Our front and rear lose communication, causing the army to be disturbed and chaotic. The soldiers have no will to fight. Officers are not motivated to defend. What should we do?"

Taigong said: "It is wise of you to raise this question. In this case, be clear about your orders. Deploy your strong and elite soldiers. Each one holds a torch. Two men beat one drum. Discover the exact location of the enemy. Then attack externally and internally. Troops should carry secret codes to identify each other. When the troops have communicated the secret codes to each other, put out the torches and cease drumming. Act according to the pre-agreed plan. The entire army will attack rapidly and fight courageously. The enemy will definitely be defeated."

King Wu said: "Brilliant!"

敵武
MARTIAL ENEMIES

King Wu asked Taigong: "When leading troops deep into enemy territory, we are confronted by the enemy. They are numerous, courageous, and ferocious. They use Attack Chariots and cavalry to surround our flanks. Our army is shaken. Soldiers and officers desert in droves. What should we do?"

Taigong said: "This is called a defeated army. Those who excel in maneuvering can win. Those who do not will be defeated."

King Wu asked: "In this case, what should we do?"

Taigong said: "Deploy strong soldiers and crossbowmen in ambushing positions about three li from your main troops. Station powerful chariots and gallant cavalry on two flanks. If the enemy chases you, dispatch your chariots and cavalry to attack both their flanks. They will be chaotic. Your fleeing soldiers will hold their ground."

King Wu asked: "Our chariots and cavalry confront the enemy. They are numerous while we are weak. Their formation is ordered and disciplined. Their soldiers are skillful. Our formation is not strong enough to defend. What should we do?"

Taigong said: "In this case, choose your strongest soldiers and crossbowmen to ambush from both sides. Deploy your chariots and cavalry into a strong formation to defend. When the enemy passes your concealed troops, soldiers armed with crossbows should shoot at both flanks intensively. Your chariots, cavalry, and gallant soldiers should attack the enemy's front or rear fiercely. In this way, even if they are numerous, they will definitely be defeated."

King Wu said: "Brilliant!"

鳥雲山兵
BIRD AND CLOUD FORMATION IN THE MOUNTAINS

King Wu asked Taigong: "When leading our troops deep into enemy territory, we encounter high mountains, giant rocks, and tall peaks. There are no trees or grass. We are surrounded on four sides. Our army is fearful. Our soldiers are confused and fearful. I would like the defense to be solid and the assault to be victorious. What should I do?"

Taigong said: "If the army is deployed on a mountaintop, it is easily besieged by the enemy. When the troops are stationed at the foot of a mountain, they are prone to capture. If you are fighting in mountains, you should apply the Bird and Cloud Formation, which means guarding the south and north of the mountains. If the army sets up camp at the south of the mountain, they should guard the north, and vice versa. If the army sets up camp on the west side of the mountain, they should guard the east side, and vice versa.

Guard every pass the enemy can climb. Use chariots to cut off main routes and valleys. Set up flags for communication. Discipline the Three Armies and await the enemy. Do not let them know your situation. This is how you turn a mountain into a walled city. Plan the troop's formation, line up the soldiers, give the orders, confirm the tactics, deploy into Assault Formation, and station your army in the high places. Then deploy your chariots and cavalry into the Bird and Cloud Formation. When the enemy approaches, your troops will fight fiercely. Though they are numerous, they will be defeated. Their general will be captured."

鳥雲澤兵
BIRD AND CLOUD FORMATION IN MARSHES

King Wu asked Taigong: "After leading the troops deep into enemy territory, we are confronted by the enemy across the river. Their supplies are plentiful and they are numerous. We lack supplies and have few soldiers. I would like to cross the river to attack but I lack the power. I would like to wait but lack food. We are positioned in barren and salty ground without cities or vegetation nearby. Our troops cannot plunder supplies. The cattle and horses have nothing to feed on. What should I do?"

Taigong said: "When your troops have no supplies, cattle and horses have no feed, and your soldiers have no food, you should seek opportunities to deceive the enemy and retreat. Set up ambushes in the rear to stop them from chasing you."

King Wu asked: "Suppose they are not deceived. Our officers and soldiers are confused and fearful. Our army is defeated and fleeing. What shall we do?"

Taigong said: "In this case, use treasure such as gold and silver to entice the enemy. At the same time, bribe the enemy's emissaries. The job should be done discreetly. Do not let the enemy notice."

King Wu asked: "The enemy knows that we have ambushes. Their main force is not willing to cross the river. Instead, they send a smaller force to attack. Our army is shaken. What should we do?"

Taigong said: "In this case, deploy your troops into Assault Formation in an advantageous position. After they have crossed, strike at their rear with your ambushing force and use crossbows to shoot their flanks. Deploy your chariots and cavalry into the Bird and Cloud Formation, guard the front and back, and fight fiercely. Realizing that their small force is engaged in battle with you, the enemy's main force will cross the river to support them. Command your ambushing soldiers to savage the enemy's rear. Send your chariots and cavalry to attack both flanks of the enemy. Though they are numerous, they will be defeated. Their general will flee. When it comes to the basic principle of military maneuver, deploy troops into the Assault Formation, station them in an advantageous position, and divide the chariots and cavalry into the Bird and Cloud Formation. The term Bird and Cloud comes from the soldiers dispersing like birds and unifying like clouds, which is flexible and endless."

King Wu said: "Brilliant!"

少眾
THE FEW AND THE MANY

King Wu asked Taigong: "I would like to defeat a large number with a few, and attack the strong with the weak. What should I do?"

Taigong said: "If you want to defeat a large number with a few, you should take advantage of the sunset. Deploy an ambushing force in tall grass and cut off the enemy at narrow passes. If you want to attack the strong with the weak, you should get the support from big states and neighboring countries."

King Wu asked: "Suppose we do not have terrain with tall grass for ambushes or narrow routes to guard. The enemy troops do not arrive at sunset. We do not have any support of large states or neighboring countries. What should we do?"

Taigong answered: "Use tactics of seduction and deception to confuse the enemy. Lure them into the tall grass. Encourage them to take the long route so they are delayed and engage in battle at sunset. When the enemy's advance troops have not finished crossing the river, and the troops behind have not yet set up camp, launch your ambushing forces to attack both their flanks. Command your chariots and cavalry to harass the front and back of the enemy. Though they are numerous, they will be defeated. Treat the rulers of the large states with respect, honor neighboring countries' talents with money and generous presents, and speak to them with reverence. That is how you can obtain the support of large states and neighboring countries."

King Wu said: "Brilliant!"

分險
DIVIDED STRATEGIC POSITIONS

King Wu asked: "When leading troops deep into enemy territory, we encounter the enemy in narrow passes. We have mountains on the left and water on the right. The enemy have mountains on the right and water on the left. In this case, both sides would like the defense to be solid and the attack to succeed. What should we do?"

Taigong said: "If you occupy the left side of the mountain, you should prepare to guard the right side immediately, and vice versa. If you have no boats to cross large rivers, you should use floating equipment such as Heaven's Huang. The advance force which has already crossed the river should clear the route and occupy advantageous terrain, allowing the main troop to follow. Use Assault Chariots to cover the front and rear of your army. Deploy strong crossbowmen to make your lines and formation solid. Block important passes and valleys with Assault Chariots and set up flags, forming a Chariot City. In strategic places, deploy Assault Chariots at the front, use large shields as a protective force, and deploy strong crossbowmen to protect both flanks. Group 3,000 men into one unit and deploy them in an Attack Formation. Position them on advantageous terrain. During battle, the left army should advance on the left, the right army should advance on the right, and the central army should advance up the middle. All should attack and advance in concert. Troops which have already fought should return to camp to rest. Those which are yet to engage in battle should fight until victory is achieved."

King Wu said: "Marvelous!"

犬韜
DOG SECRET TEACHING

分兵
DIVISION AND ASSEMBLY

King Wu asked Taigong: "The ruler leads his troops and divides his forces into Three Armies encamped in different locations. The general assembles soldiers at specific times to battle with the enemy. He commands all the officers and soldiers and clarifies rules for reward and punishment. How can that be achieved?"

Taigong said: "Since the soldiers of the Three Armies are so numerous, they must divide and reassemble often. The general should first confirm the location and date of the battle. Then he should pass the battle documents to officers, confirm the city to be attacked and besieged, the location for assembling, the date of the battle, and the arrival time for each unit. The general should arrive at the assembly point in advance to set up camp, to establish the formation, and to erect poles to observe their shadows and calculate the time. He will move on passers-by and wait for the officers to arrive. When the officers have arrived, he should check the schedule to see who was late and who was not. Reward those who arrive early and behead those who arrive late. Whether they come from far or near, officers must arrive at the assembly point on time. After the arrival of the Three Armies, you can unite their strength to fight the enemy."

武鋒
MARTIAL ADVANTAGE

King Wu asked Taigong: "One of the important principles of military maneuver is to have strong chariots and cavalry, assault troops to charge and shatter the enemy, and soldiers to exploit any opportunities to attack. What are the ideal opportunities for attacking?"

Taigong answered: "If you want to strike at the enemy, you should observe and investigate 14 cases which put them at a disadvantage. Once any of them arise, you can launch the assault. They will definitely be defeated."

King Wu asked: "Can you explain the 14 cases?"

Taigong said: "You can attack when the enemy has just assembled without any chance to consolidate. You can attack when the enemy's horses are starving. You can attack when the weather is disadvantageous to them. You can attack when the terrain is disadvantageous to them. You can attack when they are in a hurry. You can attack when they are off guard. You can attack when they are weary. You can attack when the soldiers are without a general. You can attack when they are marching on a long journey. You can attack when they are crossing the river. You can attack when they are chaotic. You can attack when they are negotiating narrow passes. You can attack when their formation is disordered. You can attack when they are panicking."

練士
SELECTING SOLDIERS

King Wu asked Taigong: "How should I select soldiers?"

Taigong said: "Assemble those with exceptional courage and who do not fear death or injury into a unit called Blade Warriors. Assemble the sharp, young, strong, brave, and aggressive into a unit called Penetrating Formation Warriors. Assemble those with unique physiques, steady steps and coordinated movements, and who are skilled in swordsmanship, into a unit called Brave and Sharp Warriors. Assemble those who have extremely strong arms and can destroy the enemy's gongs, drums, and flags into a unit called Courageous and Strong Warriors. Assemble those who can climb over high mountains, walk long distances, and run fast into a unit called Invading Army Warriors. Assemble those who used to be royalty and ministers and aspire to regain their reputation into a unit called Death Fight Warriors. Assemble those who are the sons or brothers of dead soldiers and keen to exact revenge into a unit called Dare Death Warriors. Assemble those who live in their in-laws' family and used to be captives of the enemy and want to bury their shame into a unit called Inspirational Warriors. Assemble those who are dissatisfied with poverty and want to be rich and successful into a unit called Death Committed Warriors. Assemble those criminals who are spared and want to hide their humiliation into a unit called Grateful to be Used Warriors. Assemble those with exceptional skills and talents and are able to undertake great responsibility to a unit called Awaiting Orders Warriors. These are the ways of selecting soldiers. Close examination should never be neglected."

教戰
TEACHING COMBAT

King Wu asked Taigong: "When we assemble our army, how can we train them to be skillful in combat?"

Taigong said: "When leading the Three Armies, use gongs and drums to synchronize their movements. The general should teach the details of drill and train them to use weapons and familiarize them with military maneuvers according to the changes of flag signals. When training the army, instruct one man. Then extend the practice to ten men. When studying military tactics, instruct ten men to start with. Then extend the practice to 100, to a 1,000, 10,000 and finally the entire army. The powerful army will be indestructible in the world."

King Wu said: "Brilliant!"

均兵
EQUIVALENT FORCES

King Wu asked Taigong: "When chariots and infantry engage in battle, one chariot is equivalent to how many infantry soldiers? How many infantry soldiers are equivalent to one chariot? When cavalry and infantry enter battle, one cavalry soldier is equivalent to how many infantry soldiers? How many infantry soldiers are equivalent to one cavalry soldier? When chariots and cavalry soldiers engage in battle, one chariot is equivalent to how many cavalry soldiers? How many cavalry soldiers are equivalent to one chariot?"

Taigong said: "Chariots are the feathers and wings of an army and are powerful in combat. They are for penetrating formations, pressuring strong enemies, and cutting off retreat routes. Cavalry are the eyes of an army. They are for investigating and guarding, chasing fleeing enemies, severing supply routes, and pursuing scattered enemies. In this way, if not used properly, one cavalry soldier is less powerful than one infantry soldier. If chariots, infantry, and cavalry coordinate well, when fighting on flat terrain, one chariot is equivalent to 80 cavalry soldiers. Eighty infantry soldiers are equivalent to one chariot. One cavalry soldier is equivalent to eight infantry soldiers. Eight infantry soldiers are equivalent to one cavalry soldier. One chariot is equivalent to ten cavalry soldiers. Ten cavalry soldiers are equivalent to one chariot. The rules of fighting on dangerous and difficult terrain are: one chariot is equivalent to 40 infantry soldiers. Forty infantry soldiers are equivalent to one chariot. One cavalry soldier is equivalent to four infantry soldiers. Four infantry soldiers are equivalent to one cavalry soldier. One chariot is equivalent to six cavalry soldiers. Six cavalry soldiers are equivalent to one chariot. Chariots and cavalry are the most powerful forces in an army. Ten chariots can defeat 1,000 men. A hundred chariots can defeat 10,000 men. Ten cavalry soldiers can defeat 100 men. A hundred cavalry soldiers can defeat 1,000 men. These are the approximate numbers."

King Wu asked: "What is the proportion of chariots to cavalry soldiers? What are the methods of fighting?"

Taigong said: "For the chariots: 1 leader for every 5 chariots, 1 official for every 10 chariots, 1 commander for every 50 chariots, and 1 general for every 100 chariots. When fighting on flat terrain: 5 chariots make 1 line, with lines 40 steps apart from front to rear, spaced

10 steps apart from right to left and detachments 60 steps apart. When fighting on dangerous and difficult terrains, chariots should follow the roads. Ten chariots form 1 company. Twenty chariots form 1 detachment. The lines of chariots should be spaced 20 steps apart from front to rear, spaced 6 steps apart from left to right and detachments should be 36 steps apart. There is 1 leader for every 5 chariots. Their range is 2 li. After the battle, chariots should return the way they came. For the cavalry: there should be 1 leader for every 5 soldiers, 1 official for every 10 soldiers, 1 commander for every 100 soldiers and 1 general for every 200 soldiers. When fighting on flat terrain 5 cavalry soldiers form 1 line. The lines of cavalry should be spaced 20 steps apart from front to rear, spaced 4 steps apart from left to right and detachments should be 50 steps apart. When fighting on dangerous and difficult terrain the lines of cavalry should be spaced 10 steps apart from front to rear, spaced 2 steps apart from left to right, and detachments should be 25 steps apart. Thirty cavalry soldiers form 1 detachment, and 60 cavalry soldiers form 1 regiment. There should be 1 official for every 10 chariot soldiers. They must not range more than 100 steps. After the battle, they should return to their original positions."

King Wu said: "Marvelous!"

武車士
MARTIAL CHARIOT WARRIORS

King Wu asked Taigong: "How do I select chariot warriors?"

Taigong answered: "Here are the standards: select those who are under 40 years old and taller than six foot. They can keep up with a galloping horse and jump on a charging chariot. They can ride forward and back, left and right, up and down on the chariot. They can hold flags, draw an eight-*picul* crossbow and shoot to the left, right, front, or rear skillfully. These men are called Martial Chariot Warriors. They should be given generous rewards."

武騎士
MARTIAL CAVALRY WARRIORS

King Wu asked Taigong: "How do I select cavalry warriors?"

Taigong said: "Here are the standards: select men who are under 40 years old and taller than 6 foot. They are exceptionally strong and nimble. They can ride a galloping horse and shoot a crossbow on the horse. They can ride a horse forward, back, left, and right. They can jump over ditches and hills, charge toward dangerous and difficult roads, cross wide rivers, and chase strong and numerous enemies. They are called Martial Cavalry Warriors. They should be given generous rewards."

戰車
CHARIOT WARFARE

King Wu asked Taigong: "How do I deploy chariots?"

Taigong said: "The essence of infantry warfare lies in the understanding of changing situations. The essence of chariot warfare lies in the understanding of terrains. The essence of cavalry warfare lies in the understanding of unusual routes and shortcuts. These Three Armies share a name, but the method of their deployment varies. There are ten fatal terrains and eight advantageous situations."

King Wu asked: "What are the ten fatal terrains?"

Taigong said: "When there is only a path to advance and no turning back, this is the fatal land for chariots. When crossing narrow passes and obstacles to chase the enemy, this is the land of exhaustion for chariots. When the land ahead is flat and smooth, but the rear is tricky and dangerous, this is the land that traps chariots. When trapped in dangerous terrain that is difficult to escape from, this is the land of desperation. When the land is a collapsing and muddy marsh, this is the land of hardship. When the land on the left is difficult and the right is flat, and the chariots need to climb over a hill, this is the land of adversity. When the land is covered with grass, and chariots need to cross deep water, this is the land of obstacles. When chariots are few in number, the terrain is flat, and cavalry do not coordinate well, this is the land of failure. When there are ditches to the rear, deep waters to the left and high hills to the right, this is the chariots' land of destruction. When it rains heavily for days, roads are destroyed, and chariots can neither advance nor retreat, this is the land of sinking. These are the ten fatal terrains for chariots. An ignorant general will be defeated and captured if he does not understand their dangers. A wise one can avoid them and gain victory."

King Wu asked: "What are eight advantageous situations?"

Taigong replied: "When the enemy's front and rear formations are not settled, assault them with chariots. When the enemy's flags are chaotic and the soldiers and horses are constantly moving, strike them with chariots. When some of the enemy's soldiers move forward, some go back, some move to the left, and some move to the right, penetrate them with chariots. When the enemy's lines are not solid, and soldiers glance fearfully at each other, strike at them. When the enemy are hesitant to advance and fearful to go back, penetrate with chariots. When the enemy's entire army becomes terrified and chaotic, penetrate them with chariots. When the enemy engage in battle with you on flat terrain, and the battle is yet to be finished by sunset, strike at them. When the enemy march a long distance, set up camp in the dark, and their Three Armies are terrified and uneasy, strike them with chariots. These eight situations are all advantageous in chariot warfare. When a general knows the ten fatal terrains and eight advantageous situations, even if the enemy surround you from four directions, attack you with 1,000 chariots and 10,000 cavalry, and assaults your flanks, you can win each battle."

King Wu said: "Brilliant!"

戰騎
CAVALRY WARFARE

King Wu asked Taigong: "How do I fight with cavalry?"

Taigong said: "There are Ten Victories and Nine Defeats in cavalry battle."

King Wu asked: "What are the ten situations which produce victory?"

Taigong replied: "When the enemy has just arrived, has yet to settle or coordinate their formations, use cavalry to attack their forward cavalry and two flanks. They will definitely flee. When they have built solid fortifications and their spirits are high, assault them ceaselessly. Some should race toward them and some race away, as fast as the wind, as strong as the thunder. From daytime to dusk, change your flags and uniforms constantly in order to scare and confuse them. When the enemy's formation is not solid and soldiers are unwilling to fight, your cavalry should besiege their front and rear and attack their flanks; they will definitely be terrified. When the enemy's troops return to their camps at sunset and their soldiers are fearful, send your cavalry to assault their flanks, rapidly attack their rear, push toward the entrance to their ramparts, and stop them from entering their camp. They will definitely be defeated. When the enemy has no strategic terrain to rely on, your cavalry should penetrate and cut off their supply tunnels. They will be starved. When their troops occupy flat terrain, which can be attacked from four sides, your cavalry should coordinate with your chariots to attack them. They will definitely be chaotic. When the enemy is defeated and their soldiers scatter, send your cavalry to assault their flanks, front and rear. Then their general can be captured. When the enemy return to their camp at sunset, their troops will be disordered. Assemble ten cavalry soldiers into a unit, 100 soldiers into a regiment. Group five chariots into a unit and ten chariots into a squad. Set up flags and protect them with strong crossbowmen to shoot at the enemy flanks, front and rear. The enemy's general will be captured. These are the ten opportunities of gaining victory."

King Wu asked: "What are the nine situations leading to defeat?"

Taigong said: "When your cavalry fails to penetrate the enemy's formation and they feign to flee in order to assemble their chariots and cavalry to attack your rear, your cavalry will be defeated. When chasing the fleeing enemy over dangerous and difficult terrain, penetrating deep into enemy territory without stopping, and the enemy ambush you on both sides and cut off your retreat route, this is an encircled situation. When you are unable to retreat after advancing, unable to get out after entering, this is called being trapped in the courtyard or the earth cave. This is the death terrain. When the road ahead is narrow and the road back is long and winding, the enemy can beat the strong with the weak and strike at the many with the few. This is the place of elimination. When there are deep valleys and lush forests, and it is difficult for troops to maneuver, this is the place of exhaustion. When there are waters on both sides, big mountains at the front, high peaks in the rear, you are fighting between waters. The enemy can rely on strategic mountains and rivers. This is the difficult place for cavalry. When the enemy severs your supply routes, you can only go forward without a route to go back. This is the trapped place for cavalry. When the terrain is low and muddy with marsh land everywhere, it is difficult to advance or retreat. This is the land of worry. When there are deep valleys on the left, gullies on the right, and the ground looks even but in fact rises and falls, you will be attacked whether you advance or retreat. This is the land of pitfalls. These are the nine fatal terrains. A wise general should avoid them. A fatuous general will be defeated by them."

戰步
INFANTRY WARFARE

King Wu asked Taigong: "What is it like for the infantry to engage in battle with chariots and cavalry?"

Taigong said: "When engaging in battle with chariots and cavalry, the infantry should assemble its formation in hills and strategic terrain. They should station long weapons and strong crossbows at the front, and short weapons and weak crossbows at the back. They should take turns to fight and rest. When the enemy's numerous chariots and infantry arrive, guard your formation, fight persistently, and use warriors with crossbows to guard the rear."

King Wu asked: "Suppose we do not have hills or strategic terrain to rely on, the enemy's army is strong and numerous, chariots and cavalry attack our flanks, front, and rear, causing our troops to be fearful and fleeing. What should I do?"

Taigong said: "Command your soldiers to make barrier weapons such as Running Horses and caltrops, assemble cattle and horses, and form up the infantry into the Assault Formation. After seeing the enemy's chariots and cavalry coming, set up caltrops and dig ditches which are five feet deep and wide. They are called Death Traps. The infantry move with Running Horses. Connect chariots into a moving rampart. Push it back and forth. When it stops, it serves as a military camp. Set brave warriors with strong crossbows to guard the left and right, then command your entire army to fight fiercely without delinquency."

King Wu said: "Brilliant!"

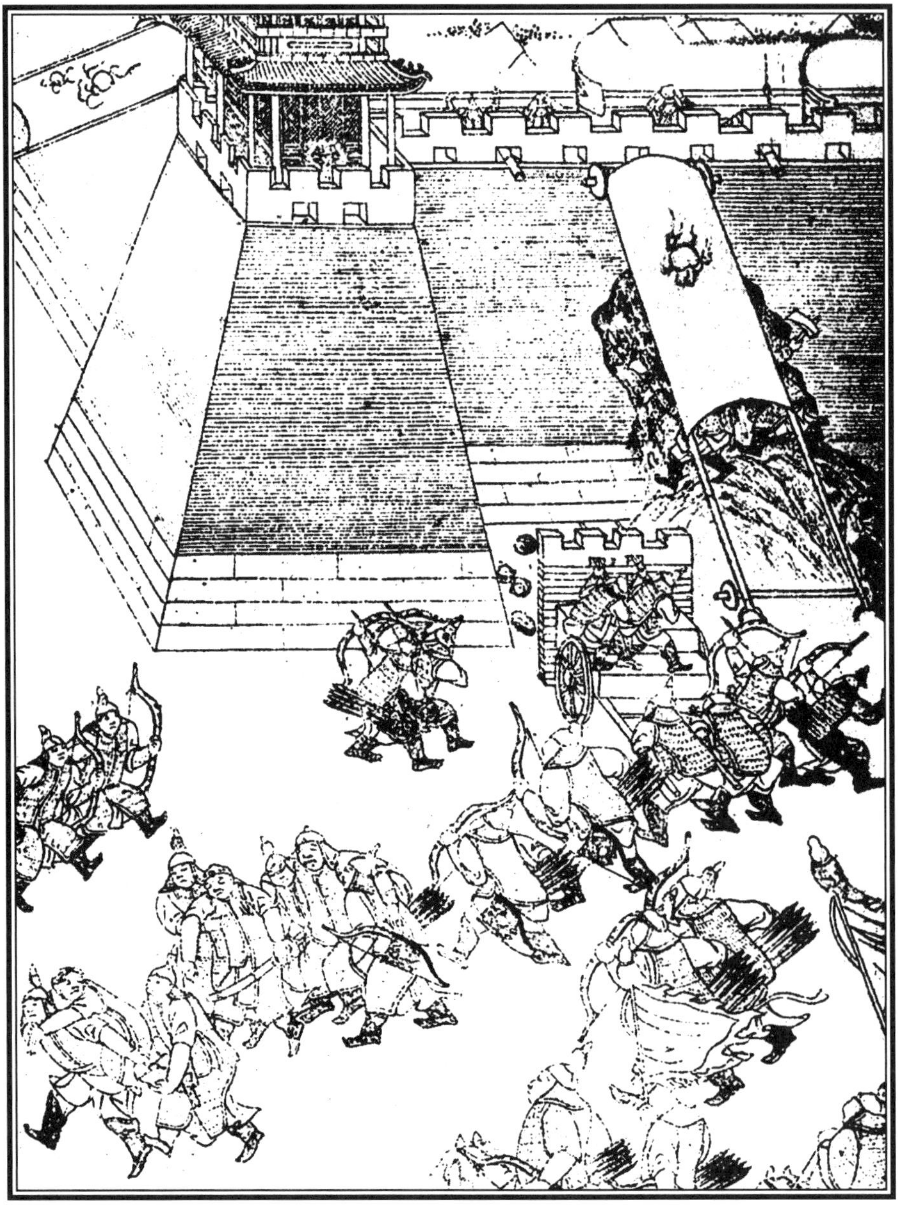

司馬法
METHODS OF THE SIMA

Translated by Stefan Harvey in association
with First Edition Translations Ltd.

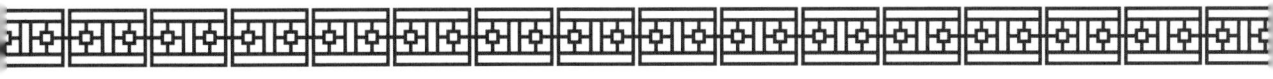

仁本
THE ORIGINS OF BENEVOLENCE

1   In ancient times, benevolence was considered essential and the use of righteousness to govern was considered just. If justice did not take root in the minds of the people, then one had to resort to authority. [To obtain authority] those with power went out to war; they did not remain at court. To kill men to save others makes the killing permissible. When one attacks a state out of love for its people, it makes the invasion permissible. To stop war with war, then it is permitted. For this reason, benevolence is cherished, righteousness is appreciated, knowledge is relied upon, courage is seen as proper, and trust is understood as honorable. These principles gain the love of those at home, so [the government] uses them to defend the people. Those abroad feel threatened by these values, so we use them to attack them.

2   As for the Way [Tao] of war: do not deviate from the seasons, do not allow the people's ills to continue unabated. This is what is done to love our people. Do not increase suffering; do not give cause for malfeasance. This is what is done to love even [the enemy's] people. Dispatch troops neither in winter nor summer. This is what is done to love both your own people and theirs. This is why although the state may be large, taking pleasure in war is bound to end in loss. Although the world is tranquil, disregarding [preparations for] war is bound to bring peril.

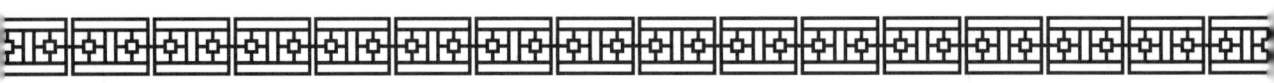

3 When the world was fully at peace, the emperor felt great joy and held [social] gatherings. In the spring and autumn, he hunted. All the dukes mustered their troops in the spring and drilled them in the autumn. This is what was done so that war was not forgotten.

4 In ancient times, when chasing those who fled, one never exceeded 100 paces. When following a retreating enemy, one never exceeded three days of movement. Thus they demonstrated their adherence to the rites [li].[2] They did not exhaust the weakest among them and they showed compassion to the wounded and sick. This showed their adherence to benevolence. They waited until all were in formation before they beat the drum to signal the attack. This highlighted their trustworthiness. They fought for righteousness and not for profit. This highlighted their adherence to righteousness. They were expert in determining whom to abandon and whom to pardon, according to their courage. They knew when to end and when to begin, highlighting their wisdom. These Six Virtues[3] were taught in a timely manner and became the Way [Tao] of the people's ascent. This has been the nature of government since antiquity.

5 As for the First Kings' governance: they followed the Way [Tao] of Heaven; established the suitability of the land; managed the virtue of the people;

---

2. The li were the forms and rituals of proper behavior that were gradually codified into a system similar to the code of chivalry of medieval Europe. The word originally meant a religious sacrifice but came to encompass all forms of human interaction and social behavior.
3. The Six Virtues were wisdom, benevolence, sagacity, righteousness, loyalty, and harmony.

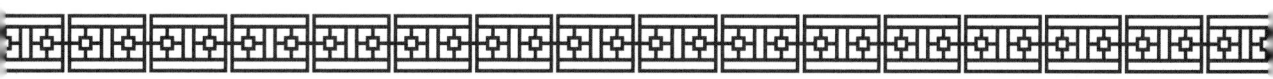

rectified names, and governed all things. They established the matters of the state, dividing salaries among the nobility. All of the dukes had hearts filled with joy. Some came from overseas to serve [the state]. The prisons were calm, while the troops rested. This was the governance of sagacity and virtue.

6 Then there were the Sage Kings. They controlled the rites [li], music, regulations, and measures, implemented the five imperial punishments,[4] and mobilized armored troops to suppress injustice. They carried out tours of inspection across every province, meeting all the dukes, examining their differences. When the dukes lost command and disorder became common, when they turned their back on virtue and went against the seasons of Heaven, they endangered good rulers. The Sage Kings would inform their dukes all over the country of their negligence. The kings informed the Lord of High Heaven, the Sun, the Moon, and the Stars of the transgressions. They prayed to Earth and all the deities of the world. They would give offerings at the tombs of the First Kings. Only then would the Chief Minister summon the troops before all the dukes and say:

"A certain state has deviated from the Way [Tao] and we are to attack it. A date will be set for the troops to arrive and meet with the emperor in order to punish and rectify that state."

---

4. The five chief forms of punishment in feudal China up to Han times: tattooing characters on the forehead (墨 mo); cutting off the nose (劓 yi); amputation of one or both feet (刖 yue); castration (宮 gong); and execution (大辟 da pi).

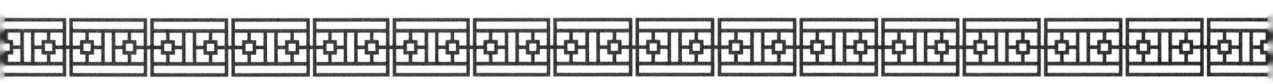

7 The Chief Minister and all the other officials would issue orders to the army, saying:

"When entering the land of the maleficent, do not terrorize their gods, do not go to their fields to hunt, do not destroy their engineering projects, do not set fire to their walls and houses, do not chop the trees in their woods, do not seize their livestock, grain, or tools. Observe their elderly and their young and return them out of harm's way. Although you will meet those in the prime of their lives, do not confront them, or view them as enemies. If you come across an injured enemy, treat them and return them."

8 When the king had executed the criminals, along with all the dukes, he reformed their state to restore justice. They elevated the virtuous and reinstated the intelligent, so that just rule could be returned.

9 These are the six principles by which the king and the senior officials governed all the dukes:

    By apportioning the local terrain to organize the dukes.
    By using government commands to keep the dukes at peace.
    By using ritual and trust to keep the dukes on good terms.
    By using skill and strength to keep the dukes content.
    By using the strategies of advisers to keep the dukes cohesive.
    By using the armed forces to keep the dukes subservient.

They allowed the lords to suffer and benefit as one, so as to unify them. They had states collaborate, making smaller powers serve larger ones, to keep the dukes in harmony.

10 They assembled the dukes to announce the nine prohibitions:

If they prevail over the weak and attack the solitary, then they will be weakened.

If they mistreat the virtuous and harm the people, then they will be attacked.

If they cause terror within their borders and run rampant outside, then they will be made to pay.

If their fields are barren and their people are idle, then [their activities] will be curtailed.

If they rely on their natural circumstances for defense and do not follow orders, then they will be invaded.

If they attack and kill their kin, then they will be brought to justice.

If they oust and murder a superior, then they will be destroyed.

If they violate orders and breach the terms of government, then they will be cut off.

If they are disorderly inside and outside their borders, conducting themselves like birds and beasts, then they will be exterminated.

天子之義
THE RIGHTEOUSNESS OF THE EMPEROR

1 For the righteousness of the emperor to be untainted, he must grasp the ways of the world and observe the First Sages. For the nobility and commoners, righteousness must involve revering one's parents and acting justly toward one's sovereign. This is why, if the nobility are not first educated, enlightened rulers are of no use.

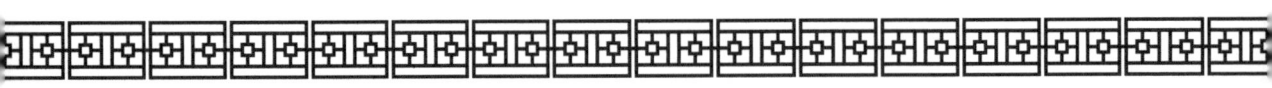

2. In antiquity, when educating the people, the ancients had to establish standard relations between the noble and the lowly. They made sure the classes did not encroach upon each other; that virtue and righteousness did not become separated; that talent and skill did not obstruct each other; that courage and strength did not come into conflict. In this way their strength was unified and all outlooks were in harmony.

3. In ancient times, state affairs would not interfere with the military and military affairs would not interfere with those of the state. In this way virtue and righteousness did not become separated. Those high up valued modest scholars, since modest scholars are the most useful to superiors. If one is modest, then one makes no demands. If one makes no demands, then there is no conflict. When attending to interior affairs, one had to grasp the state's true circumstances. When attending to the army, one had to grasp what it was suited to. In this way talent and skill did not obstruct each other. Scholars who followed orders were held in utmost esteem, while scholars who violated orders were treated with utmost contempt. In this way courage and strength did not disrupt one another.

4. Once the people have been properly educated, then one can carefully select and employ them. If affairs are regulated to the highest standard, then officials are well provided for. If education is scrutinized to the highest standard, then

天子之義 THE RIGHTEOUSNESS OF THE EMPEROR

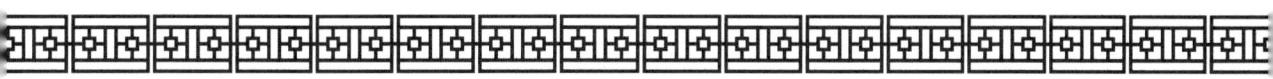

the people will flourish. If these practices become the habit, then the people will embody the customs. This is the epitome of enlightenment.

5 In ancient times, they did not chase those who fled very far, or follow those who retreated very closely. If they did not pursue [the enemy very] far, it was difficult for the enemy to lure them. If they did not stay close [to the enemy], it was difficult for the enemy to trap them. They used the rites [li] to become robust. They used their benevolence to become victorious. After victory their teachings could be reproduced. This shows why they are valued by the nobleman.

6 The nobility of the Yu dynasty[5] swore their oaths in the state capital as they wanted the people to carry out their commands. The rulers of the Xia dynasty made their pledges among the troops as they first wanted the people to articulate their concerns. The Yin[6] made their pledges outside the military camp, as they first wanted the people to attend to military affairs. Following the clash of arms, the Zhou made a pledge to comply with the will of the people. The rulers of the Xia rectified their virtue and did not use their swords, so the [different types of] weapons were not brought together. The Yin were righteous and began by using their swords. The Zhou were strong and used their swords throughout. The Xia gave rewards in court to show that they valued the good. The Yin staged executions in the

---

5. Supposedly established by the Sage-King Shun 舜.
6. Alternative name for the Shang 商 dynasty after its capital was moved to Yin.

marketplace to threaten the bad. The Zhou both gave rewards in court and staged executions in the market place to exhort the noblemen and frighten the lowly. And so the three kings expressed their virtue as one.

7 If the [five] weapons are not brought together, there will be no gain. Long weapons are used for long-range defense, while short weapons are used for protection at close quarters. If a weapon is too long, then it is difficult to attack. If it is too short, then it will not reach [the enemy]. If it is too light, then it will be nimble but feeble and will lead to chaos. If it is too heavy, then it will be clumsy and of no use.

8 As for chariots, the Xia called them "hook chariots," since they prioritized uprightness. The Yin called them "tiger chariots," since they prioritized speed. The Zhou called them "premier chariots," since they prioritized quality.

9 As for flags, the Xia had a black one at the head representing command of the men. The Yin had a white one, for the righteousness of Heaven. The Zhou had a yellow one, for the Way [Tao] of the Earth.

10 As for insignia, the Xia used the sun and moon to emphasize brightness. The Yin used a tiger to emphasize domination. The Zhou used a dragon to emphasize refinement.

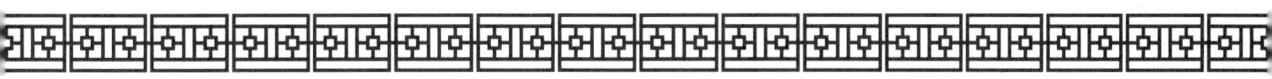

11 If the army focuses excessively on domination, then the state will be submissive, but if the army is lacking in domination, the state will not be victorious. If superiors prevent the people from achieving righteousness, then the common people will be disorganized; they will not benefit from their skills and practices; the cows and horses will not carry out their tasks. When officials encroach upon the people, this is called excessive domination. Excessive domination causes the people to be submissive. When superiors do not respect virtue but permit cheating and wickedness; when they do not respect the Way [Tao] but permit bravery and strength; when they do not value those who obey commands but instead those who violate them; when they do not value good conduct but destructive conduct; when officials are humiliated, this is what is called a lack of domination. If there is a lack of domination, the people will not be victorious. If an army prioritizes a measured pace, if the people are at ease, then they will have adequate strength. Even in a state of war when swords clash, the infantry will not rush and the chariot horses will not gallop. When pursuing a fleeing enemy, they will not forsake their formation, and so they will avoid chaos. The robustness of the army lies in regulation and discipline, so that nobody falls out of rank and no man or horse is cut off. Whether the troops move slowly or fast, they will not ignore commands and orders.

12 In ancient times, the state did not interfere with military affairs, and the military did not interfere with state affairs. If the military interfered with the state, then the people's virtue would be wasted. If the state interfered with the military, then the people's virtue would be weak. In this way, in state affairs, language was cultured and warm in tone. In court, one was humble out of respect and cultivated oneself to serve others. One did not come unless summoned, nor speak unless questioned. It was difficult to move forward but easy to withdraw. In the military sphere, one was unyielding and stood one's ground. When in formation, one was compliant and got results. In time of crisis they need not be submissive. Those in armor need not pay respect, chariots need not follow the rites [li], and those on the city walls need not scurry. In this way societal norms and military methods are like outside and inside. The arts and the military are like left and right.

13 In ancient times, the Sage Kings were clear about the people's virtue and maximized the people's goodness. In this way no virtue was wasted and the people were not diminished. Neither were rewards given nor punishments handed down. The Yu neither rewarded nor punished so the people could still be used effectively. This was the epitome of virtue. The Xia gave out rewards but not punishments. This was the epitome of education. The Yin gave out punishments but not rewards. This was the epitome of domination. The Zhou used both rewards and punishments, so virtue suffered. If one wants the people quickly to see the benefits of behaving well, rewards must not last any longer than appropriate. If one wants the people quickly to see the harm in behaving badly, punishments must not lower people's rank. Great victories are not to be rewarded, since neither superiors nor subordinates should boast of their excellence. If superiors do not boast, then they avoid being seen as arrogant. If subordinates do not boast, then one can do away with ranks [as all appear equal]. If superiors and subordinates do not boast of their excellence in this way, this is the epitome of deference. Great losses are not to be punished, so that superiors and subordinates will all perceive the lack of excellence to lie within themselves. If superiors feel this way, they are bound to regret their mistakes. If subordinates feel this way, they are bound to avoid their [previous] errors. If superiors and subordinates share the shame in such a manner, this is the epitome of deference.

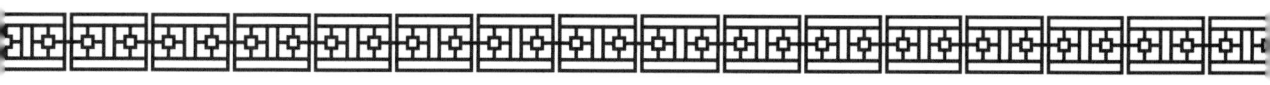

14 In ancient times those who served on garrison duty were excused from labor duty for three years.[7] If superiors and subordinates all reported to each other, this was the pinnacle of harmony. When the state achieved its aims they sang joyful songs to express their happiness. The rulers laid their arms to rest and erected the Spirit Terrace[8] and acknowledged the people's labors to show that it was time to rest.

---

7. In ancient China kingdoms were often very small so rulers could personally observe their subjects on garrison duty.
8. The Spirit Terrace was a platform for welcoming back troops from their labors but also an altar on which coffins were placed. Terraces were often unpopular with the common people, as they became the symbols of the enslavement of their labor by local rulers.

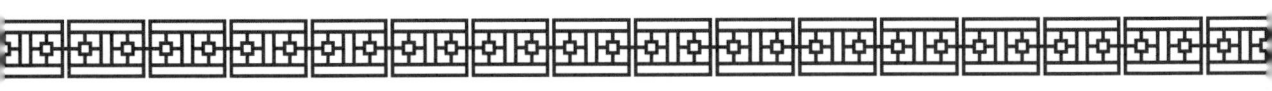

定爵
ESTABLISHING TITLES

1 In every case of war: Establish the positions of nobility; distinguish between success and failure; admit traveling experts[9]; clearly state one's teachings and instructions; inquire after your people; request [the aid of] those who are skilled: only then should you consider killing. Overcome the people's aversions and rid them of doubt; cultivate strength and seek out adeptness; act according to the people's hearts.

2 In every case of war: Make the masses robust; assess the potential benefits of the terrain; control chaos; manage advancing and coming to a halt; cater to justice; develop a sense of shame among them; agree on methods; and scrutinize punishments. If petty crimes result in death, then so should grave crimes.

3 Be harmonious with Heaven; make resources abundant; please the masses; profit from the terrain; prioritize arms. These are called the Five Considerations. To be harmonious with Heaven, conform to the seasons. [To obtain] abundant resources, seize [them] with hostility. Make every effort to please the masses. Profit from the terrain's constrictions and impasses. Prioritizing arms, use bows and arrows for resisting attacks, [maces and]

---

9. The Warring States period created a class of "stateless wanderers" made up of nobles who had defected from their state. They were people of varying talents—martial, technical, and administrative—who could offer their services to any state.

定爵 ESTABLISHING TITLES

spears for defense and halberds [and spear-tipped halberds] for assistance. In general, these five weapons each have their own use. That which is long protects the short. That which is short rescues the long. If used one after the other in war, the battle will endure. If used all at once, an army will be strong. When one views [the enemy's] situation and considers one's own alike, this is called a measured judgment.

4 Prioritize robustness and stand fast. Spot the enemy and only then advance. Ensure the general's and the masses' mind are as one. Livestock, chariots, weapons, rest, and a good diet will give the army strength. Orders are determined by preparation, while wars are determined by limitations. The general is the body, the troops are the limbs, and squadrons of five are the thumb and fingers.

5 In every instance, war is a case of authority, battle is a case of bravery, and establishing military formations is a case of skill. Employ what the troops want and go with their abilities. Do away with what they do not want, or are incapable of, and turn it against the enemy.

6 In every case of war, one should have Heaven, resources, and excellence on one's side. When the day [of battle] has been set and does not change; when the turtle shell divines victory and officials move about mysteriously,[10] this is called having Heaven. When the masses are well supplied and what

---

10. Heating turtle shells and interpreting the cracks was a form of divination in ancient China.

they produce is of fine quality, this is called having resources. When men are accustomed to advantageous formations and fully capitalize on things when making preparations, this is called having excellence. When men do their utmost to meet their responsibilities, this is called having enthusiastic men. Expanding the army for robustness; increasing its strength to cause trouble; being competent with simple management; remaining observant and responding with haste: this is called carrying out preparations. Light chariots, swift infantry, bows and arrows, and solid defense, this is called a great army. Keeping ranks tight and calm, with much internal strength, this is called a solid formation. Knowing on which grounds to advance and retreat, this is called increasing strength. When resting superiors must give the men instructions, this is called training the formation. When everyone has their appropriate post, this is called being competent. Knowing on which grounds to discuss things, this is called simple management.

7 When considering [the extent of] your masses, give thought to terrain, give thought to the enemy, and then order your formations. When attacking, doing battle, defending, advancing, retreating, and halting, everyone is ordered from front to back. The chariots and infantry rely on each other. These are called the ranks of war. When there is no obedience, no trust, no harmony; negligence, suspicion, disgust, fear; when people are contradictory, submissive, troubled, unrestrained, corrupted or sluggish: these are called the ills of war. When there is arrogance, intimidation, groaning and neglect, anxiety and fear, dealing with regret: these are called the ruin and loss of war. To be great or small, solid or soft, work in threes or fives, work en masse or as few, always to be a match for the enemy: these are called the balance of power in war.

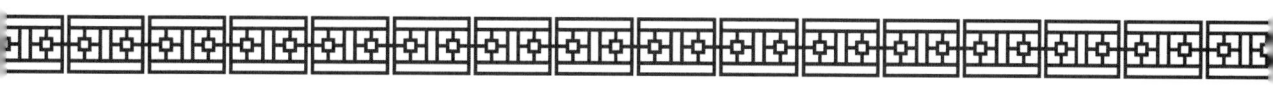

8 In every case of war, spy on those far away and observe those nearby. Stay in harmony with the seasons and work with your resources, value those with conviction and despise those with doubts. Arouse the soldiers with the feeling of righteousness. Command the men with consideration and complete your actions at the appropriate time. When you see the enemy, remain calm; when you see chaos, remain relaxed; when you see crisis and difficulty, do not fail to think of your masses. When living in the state, be faithful out of kindness; in the army, be valiant out of broad-mindedness. When blades clash, react with nimbleness. Living in the state should be harmonious; life in the army should be measured; when blades clash, investigate the situation. Living in the state should be enjoyable; life in the army should be regulated; when blades clash, the people must be trusted.

9 In all formations: When marching, men should be well dispersed; when battling, men should be close-knit; and men must have an array of armaments. Instructions for men should be detailed; once they are calm, then they can be managed; domination benefits from well-ordered men. If everyone defends each other's righteousness, then the men will exert themselves. When many [good] ideas blossom, then the men will be compliant. If men are compliant at the appropriate time, then order will follow. When things are well ordered, one's eyes see clearly. When ideas are consolidated, one's heart is strong. When advancing or retreating, men have no doubts—they see the enemy and make their plans. When listening to [legal] affairs or handing out punishments, do not arbitrarily change people's title or alter their flag.

10 In all affairs: If they are carried out well, they will endure. If they follow the ancients, then they can be successful. When the vows are well set out, then the men will be strong, eliminating menacing and propitious omens. The ways of eliminating omens are as follows. One is called righteousness, blanketing the people with trust, ruling over them with strength. Establish the foundation [of good government] and unify the [strategic] form of All under Heaven. Where nobody is unhappy, this is called employing your people in multiple ways. Another is called [using] the balance of power, making something of the enemy's excesses, seizing what they love. In this way, even from the outside we can affect the enemy's interior.

11 The first is called men; the second is called justice; the third is called expression; the fourth is called skill; the fifth is called fire; the sixth is called water; the seventh is called armaments. These are called the Seven Matters of Government. Honor, profit, shame, and death, these are called the four things to preserve. To appear accommodating, while accumulating domination, is to stop transgressions and alter ideas. In any case, these are the ways [of eliminating omens]. If you only cherish benevolence but not trustworthiness, you will fail and defeat only yourself. Treat men as men, be just toward the just, use appropriate expressions, and employ fire only when necessary.

定爵 ESTABLISHING TITLES

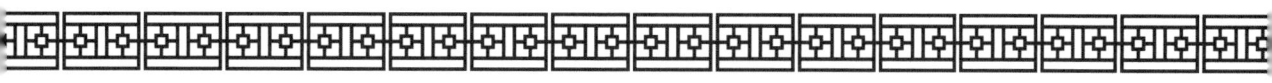

12 In every case of war: Once you have aroused the people's energy and applied it to the issue of your policies, appear to be lenient and show them the Way [Tao] through your countenance. Direct them in accordance with their fears, manage them in accordance with their desires. When you have destroyed the enemy and control their land, give order by assigning men to [administrative] posts. These are called the methods of war.

13 Seek all types of men among the masses. Measure them by how they conduct their role, for they must be good at what they do. If they do not conduct their role [well], you must take charge yourself. If they do conduct their role [well], then they must comply with commands and forget nothing. If they fulfill their role three times, then you can hold them up as a good example. That which benefits human life is called the people's method.

14 Those who wish to bring order out of chaos: first turn to benevolence; second to trust; third to straightforwardness; fourth to unity; fifth to righteousness; sixth to change; and seventh to monopoly. Establish laws: first through acceptance; second through proper methods; third through the establishment [of the talented and the upright]; fourth through haste; fifth through managing men's insignia; sixth through arranging categories; seventh through ensuring that all the officials do not go about their orders in wanton ways. In every army: controlling methods without consulting others is called monopoly. To use fearful methods with subordinates is called the law. When the army does not heed even the smallest orders, it will not gain even the smallest advantages in battle. If, on the day, everything comes together subtly, this is called the Way [Tao].

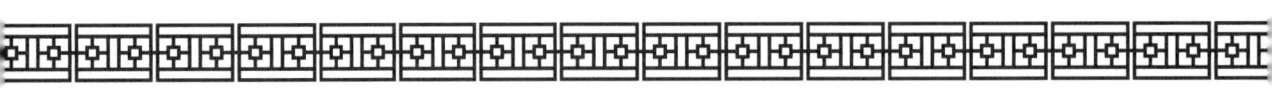

15 In every case of war, if justice does not work, then [control of] affairs must be monopolized. If people are not compliant, then the laws must be applied. If people do not trust one another, then they must be unified. If people are idle, then incite them into activity. If people are suspicious, then change their views. If the men do not trust their superiors, then do not repeat previous [bad] conduct. This has been the nature of government since antiquity.

嚴位
DISCIPLINED FORMATIONS

1 In every case of war: Ranks must be strictly established; government must rule with fear; soldiers should be given time for leisure; the people should be free of care; and all minds must be as one.

2 In every case of war: Consider the Way [Tao] and righteousness; in establishing your squadrons and platoons[11] clearly define the formations, arrange your alliances, and examine your reputation and achievements. Soldiers [who stand] in formation must advance and lie down. Soldiers

---

11. The characters 卒 zu and 伍 wu refer to groups of 100 and 5 soldiers respectively.

who sit [to fire] must kneel. If the soldiers are fearful, then they must stay close-knit; if they are in danger, then they must stay entrenched. If the enemy are seen from afar, then your troops will have no fear. If the enemy are near but unable to see [your troops], then they will not disperse. Below those officers and below the ministers sit the common soldiers, who vow to proceed with dignity. Both the officers and the foot soldiers wear armor. Decide where to position your principal and supporting forces. The thunder of cavalry may cause turmoil among the foot soldiers. If they are fearful, keep them close-knit. If they are kneeling, they should sit: if sitting, they must lie down. Have them crawl forward on their knees, swear the oath, and perform the rites [li]. Raise a clamor of drums and enter the field. Then ring the bell to signal the troops to stop. Defend against nighttime ambushes and keep to eating dried foods. Have the troops withdraw on their knees from the advance of the enemy. Make a display of corpses to prevent your soldiers from having second thoughts. Create a commotion to lead on the enemy. If the fear is overwhelming, then do not threaten them with death. Show your true colors, and let them know that you value life itself. Scrutinize them as they go about their duties.

3 In general, all members of every rank fast for half the day. Encourage men to rest and they should not share their food. If they doubt whether they really are soldiers, alleviate their doubts and then they will respect their leaders.

4 In every case of war: Use strength to sustain the battle; use [the spirit of] vitality for victory. Use robustness for longevity, but achieve victory through

danger. Use the robust mind as the foundation; use [the spirit of] vitality for victory. Armor is the means of robustness; weapons are the means of victory.

5 In general, chariots stay strong through remaining close-knit; foot soldiers stay strong through holding their ground; armor stays strong through being dense; weapons are victorious through their lightness and ease of use. Those with victorious minds only see the enemy. Those with fearful minds only see fear. These two minds are better than one alone as each benefits from the other. To achieve their combined action is the [general's] goal. Only those with authority can see this.

6 In every case of war: If you advance with a light force into the enemy's periphery, this is dangerous; if you advance with great force deep into the enemy's territory, you will achieve nothing; if you advance with a light force deep into the enemy's territory, you are bound to fail; but if you advance with great force to their periphery, you can wage war. This is why in warfare the light and the heavy forces are mutually connected. When camping overnight, take care over your weapons and armor. When marching, take care to maintain the rank and file. When fighting, take care in advancing and stopping.

7 In every case of war: If you are respectful, then the troops will be satisfied; if you lead, then the troops will follow. When orders are irksome, they will be taken lightly. When they are well thought out, they will be taken seriously. When the drum is beaten at a pace, [the troops] will move quickly.

When it is beaten with composure, they will move at a measured pace. When troops' uniforms are smart, they feel nimble. When the outfits take the eye, the troops will be steadfast.

8 Generally, if chariots are solid and the armor and weapons are advantageous, even a light force can be effective. If you prioritize equality [of the ranks], then victory will not be certain. If you prioritize taking charge, then many will die. If you prioritize survival, then many will have their doubts. If you prioritize death, then you will not be victorious.

9 Generally, men will die for love, out of anger, in fear of domination, for righteousness, and for profit.

10 In every case of war: When bound by teachings, men will take death lightly. When bound by the Way [Tao], men will perceive death to be honorable.

11 In every case of war: Whether you are victorious depends on whether or not the troops have [the victorious] spirit. Determine whether to take action in accordance with Heaven and men.[12]

12 In every case of war: The Three Armies' duties should not exceed three days; a company's watch should not exceed half a day; a single man's guard duty should not exceed one rest period.

---

12. This maxim highlights the need for commanders both to cultivate the spirit of victory and to take advantage of the seasons and the weather—something that has seemed impractical to many commentators.

司馬法 METHODS OF THE SIMA

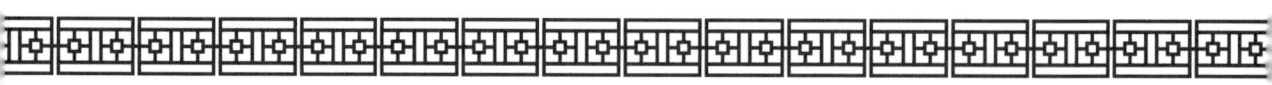

13 In general, those who are greatest use the roots, while their subsidiaries use the branches. Warfare is the implementation of strategies to preserve subtlety. The roots and branches are merely the manner of [exploiting the] balance of power.

14 Generally, regarding victory: When the Three Armies are united, every man is victorious.

15 Generally, regarding drums: There are drums for the flags and banners; for the chariots; for the horses; for the infantry; for the other troops; for the head; and to keep the feet in time to the beat.[13]

16 In every case of war: If your army is already solid, do not render it heavier. When making a major advance, do not exhaust all your resources, since squandering everything is generally dangerous.

17 In every case of war: It is not devising a formation that is difficult; it is making the men capable of getting into formation that is difficult. It is not making the men capable of getting into formation that is difficult; it is teaching the men to use the formation that is difficult. It is not knowledge [of what to do] but practice that is difficult. Men from all four corners have their own nature. That nature differs from region to region. Through teaching they develop their own [regional] customs. Customs differ from region to region too. It is the Way [Tao] that can transform customs.

---

13. The "drums for the head" refer to drums used to direct the attention of the troops to one side or the other.

嚴位 DISCIPLINED FORMATIONS

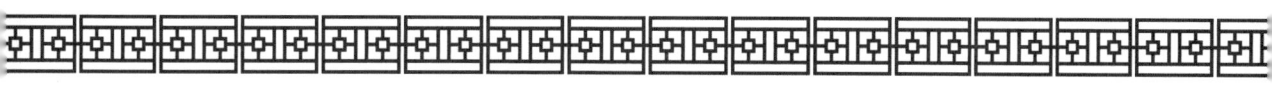

18 Generally, whether you have many troops or few, even if they have won, they should act as if they have not. Infantry should not brag about the sharpness of their weapons or the strength of their armor. Cavalrymen should not brag about the solidity of their chariots or the quality of their horses. Ultimately, a large army should not consider itself great, as this is no means of obtaining the Way [Tao].

19 In every case of war: If you are victorious, then share your achievements with your troops. If you are in command and about to recommence battle, then be generous with rewards and punishments. If your command does not lead to victory, hold yourself responsible for any failures. If you recommence battle, then promise to stay on the frontline yourself and do not repeat your initial strategy. Whether you are victorious or not, do not go against these methods. This is called the just principle.

20 Generally, regarding the people: Rescue them with benevolence; wage war with righteousness; make decisions with intelligence; enter battle with bravery; exercise command with trustworthiness; encourage troops through benefits; and gain victory through achievements. In this way benevolence lies within the heart and righteousness lies within practice. To rely on [the nature of] things is to be intelligent. To rely on the great is to be brave. To rely on long periods is to be trustworthy. Deference creates harmony so the men will be deferential themselves. If individuals accept responsibility for their failings, they will compete to be virtuous in conduct. If men take pleasure in their hearts, they will use their strength effectively.

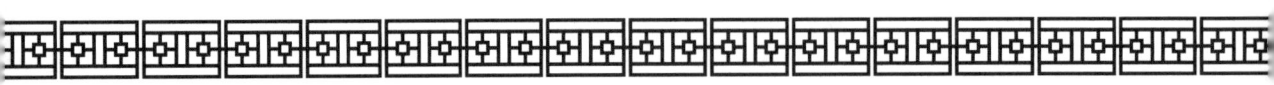

21 In every case of war: Attack what is weak and calm; avoid what is strong yet calm. Attack their men fatigued from labor; avoid those who are rested from leisure. Attack those who have great fears; avoid those with little fear. This has been the nature of governing [the army] since antiquity.

用眾
USING THE MASSES

1 In every case of war: A small group of troops must be solid; a large group must be well controlled. A small group benefits from taunting the enemy, while a large group benefits from using conventional tactics. When in large numbers, advance and stop. When in a small group, advance and retreat. If a large group encounters a small number of enemies, then surround them from afar but keep watch. [Conversely] divide your forces and take turns to attack—the few can still deal with large groups. If their masses are filled with doubt, then take advantage of their fear yourself. If you take the opportunity to make a gain, then put down your flags, turn [to retreat], and make a counter-attack. If the enemy are great in number, then collect together and let them surround you. If the enemy are few and fearful, avoid them and allow them through.

用眾 USING THE MASSES

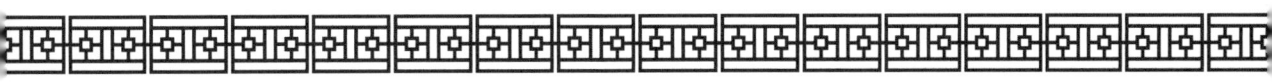

2. In every case of war: Keep the wind and the heights behind you. Keep the peaks to your right and narrow passes to your left. Pass through terrain, whether it is simply marshlands or if an embankment has been built. Travel at double pace, day or night, configured like a turtle's back.

3. In every case of war: Deploy the troops and observe the enemy's actions. Watch the enemy, then advance. If they are waiting [for you to attack], then act accordingly. Do not beat the drum [to advance] but wait for their masses to arise. If they attack, then assemble the troops and prepare for the attack.

4. In every case of war: Use large and small numbers to observe their [tactical] changes. Advance and retreat accordingly to observe their armies' solidity. Imperil them and observe their fears. Keep quiet and observe when they become slack. Maneuver your forces and observe their consternation. Attack by surprise and observe how they are managed. Attack where they have doubts; add to their haste; focus on what makes them submissive; ambush their plans and strategies; follow through when they are wounded; obstruct their designs; seize their minds; and prey on their fears.

5. When pursuing those who are fleeing, do not rest. If some of the enemy's men stop on the road, then be concerned.

6. When nearing the enemy's capital, you must have a road down which you can advance. When retreating, you must put some thought into how you will return.

7 In every case of war: If you move first, you will be at a disadvantage. If you move last, you may be fearful. If you rest, you will become lax, though if you do not rest, you will face exhaustion. Rest for a long time and the enemy may also become fearful. Writing to family with whom you have become separated [through war]: this is called anxiety over being cut off from the past. Selecting the élite and ranking the weapons: this is called increasing the strength of the men. Dropping the responsibilities [of office] and [taking only] limited rations: this is called enlightening the thoughts of the men. This has been the nature of government since antiquity.

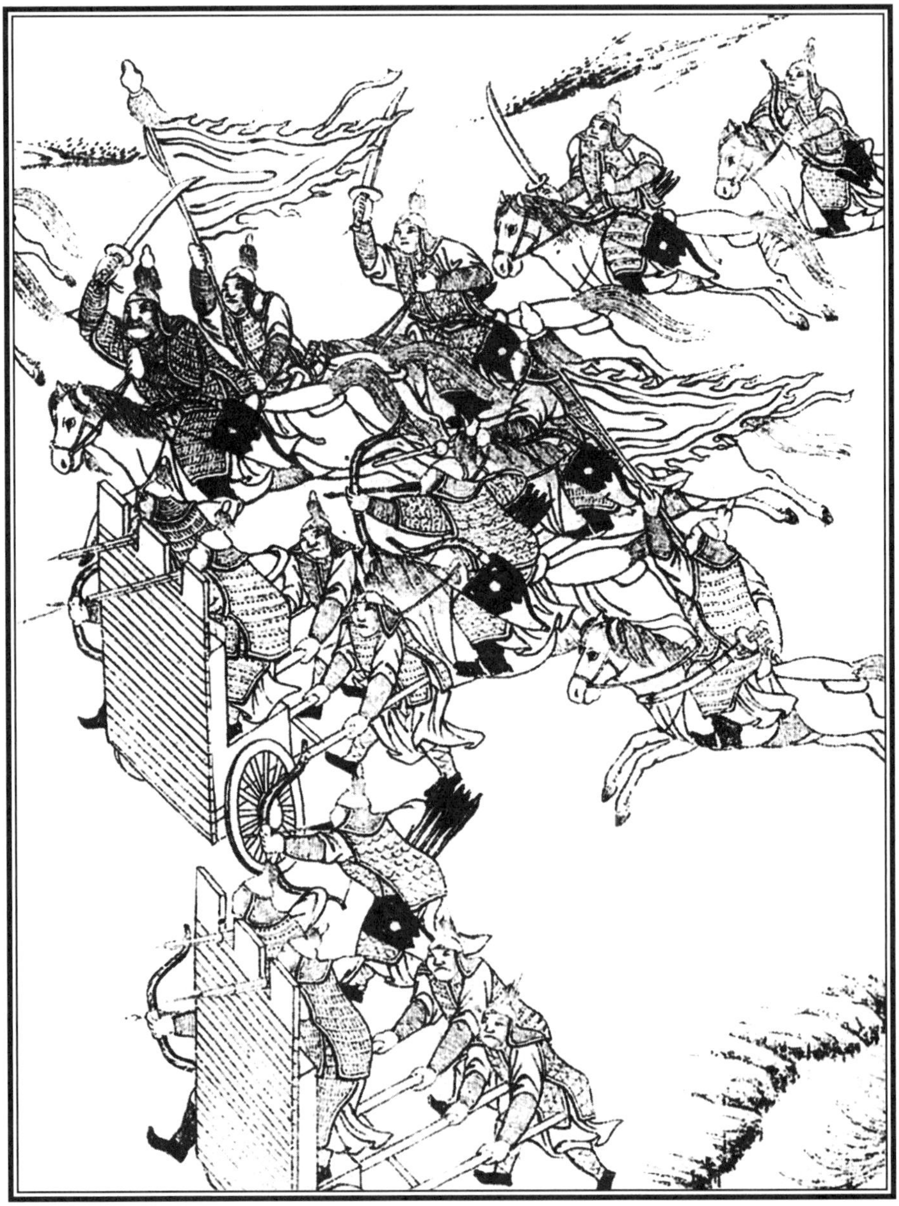

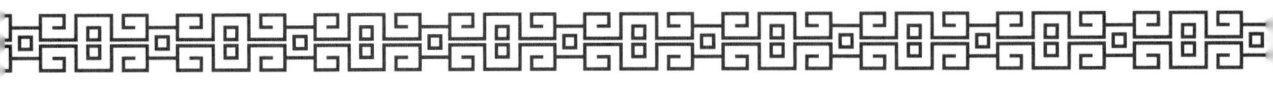

孫子兵法
THE ART OF WAR

SUN TZU

始計
LAYING PLANS

1 Sun Tzu said: The art of war is of vital importance to the State.

2 It is a matter of life and death, a road either to safety or to ruin. Hence it is a subject of inquiry which can on no account be neglected.

3 The art of war, then, is governed by five constant factors, to be taken into account in one's deliberations, when seeking to determine the conditions obtaining in the field.

4 These are:
(1) The Moral Law;
(2) Heaven;
(3) Earth;
(4) The Commander;
(5) Method and Discipline.

5 The Moral Law causes the people to be in complete accord with their ruler, so that they will follow him regardless of their lives, undismayed by any danger.

6 Heaven signifies night and day, cold and heat, times and seasons.

7 Earth comprises distances, great and small; danger and security; open ground and narrow passes; the chances of life and death.

8 The Commander stands for the virtues of wisdom, sincerity, benevolence, courage, and strictness.

9 By Method and Discipline are to be understood the marshaling of the army in its proper subdivisions, the graduations of rank among the officers, the maintenance of roads by which supplies may reach the army, and the control of military expenditure.

10 These five heads should be familiar to every general: he who knows them will be victorious; he who knows them not will fail.

11 Therefore, in your deliberations, when seeking to determine the military conditions, let them be made the basis of a comparison, in this wise:—

12 (1) Which of the two sovereigns is imbued with the Moral Law?
(2) Which of the two generals has most ability?
(3) With whom lie the advantages derived from Heaven and Earth?
(4) On which side is Discipline most rigorously enforced?
(5) Which army is stronger?
(6) On which side are officers and men more highly trained?

始計 LAYING PLANS

(7) In which army is there the greater constancy both in reward and punishment?

13 By means of these seven considerations I can forecast victory or defeat.

14 The general that hearkens to my counsel and acts upon it, will conquer: let such a one be retained in command! The general that hearkens not to my counsel nor acts upon it, will suffer defeat:—let such a one be dismissed!

15 While heeding the profit of my counsel, avail yourself also of any helpful circumstances over and beyond the ordinary rules.

16 According as circumstances are favorable, one should modify one's plans.

17 All warfare is based on deception.

18 Hence, when able to attack, we must seem unable; when using our forces, we must seem inactive; when we are near, we must make the enemy believe we are far away; when far away, we must make him believe we are near.

19 Hold out baits to entice the enemy. Feign disorder, and crush him.

20 If he is secure at all points, be prepared for him. If he is in superior strength, evade him.

21 If your opponent is of choleric temper, seek to irritate him. Pretend to be weak, that he may grow arrogant.

22 If he is taking his ease, give him no rest. If his forces are united, separate them.

23 Attack him where he is unprepared, appear where you are not expected.

24 These military devices, leading to victory, must not be divulged beforehand.

25 Now the general who wins a battle makes many calculations in his temple ere the battle is fought. The general who loses a battle makes but few calculations beforehand. Thus do many calculations lead to victory, and few calculations to defeat: how much more no calculation at all! It is by attention to this point that I can foresee who is likely to win or lose.

作戰
WAGING WAR

1 Sun Tzu said: In the operations of war, where there are in the field 1,000 swift chariots, as many heavy chariots, and 100,000 mail-clad soldiers, with provisions enough to carry them 1,000 li, the expenditure at home and at the front, including entertainment of guests, small items such as glue and paint, and sums spent on chariots and armor, will reach the total

作戰 WAGING WAR

of 1,000 ounces of silver per day. Such is the cost of raising an army of 100,000 men.

2 When you engage in actual fighting, if victory is long in coming, then men's weapons will grow dull and their ardor will be damped. If you lay siege to a town, you will exhaust your strength.

3 Again, if the campaign is protracted, the resources of the State will not be equal to the strain.

4 Now, when your weapons are dulled, your ardor damped, your strength exhausted, and your treasure spent, other chieftains will spring up to take advantage of your extremity. Then no man, however wise, will be able to avert the consequences that must ensue.

5 Thus, though we have heard of stupid haste in war, cleverness has never been seen associated with long delays.

6 There is no instance of a country having benefited from prolonged warfare.

7 It is only one thoroughly acquainted with the evils of war who can thoroughly understand the profitable way of carrying it on.

8 The skillful soldier does not raise a second levy, neither are his supply-wagons loaded more than twice.

9 Bring war material with you from home, but forage on the enemy. Thus the army will have food enough for its needs.

10 Poverty of the State Exchequer causes an army to be maintained by contributions from a distance. Contributing to maintain an army at a distance causes the people to be impoverished.

11 On the other hand, the proximity of an army causes prices to go up; and high prices cause the people's substance to be drained away.

12 When their substance is drained away, the peasantry will be afflicted by heavy exactions.

13 & 14 With this loss of substance and exhaustion of strength, the homes of the people will be stripped bare, and three-tenths of their income will be dissipated; while government expenses for broken chariots, worn-out horses, breast-plates and helmets, bows and arrows, spears and shields, protective mantles, draught-oxen and heavy wagons will amount to four-tenths of its total revenue.

15 Hence a wise general makes a point of foraging on the enemy. One cartload of the enemy's provisions is equivalent to 20 of one's own, and likewise a single *picul*[14] of his provender is equivalent to 20 from one's own store.

---

14. One *picul* weighs approximately 133 lb.

16 Now in order to kill the enemy, our men must be roused to anger; that there may be advantage from defeating the enemy, they must have their rewards.

17 Therefore in chariot fighting, when ten or more chariots have been taken, those should be rewarded who took the first. Our own flags should be substituted for those of the enemy, and the chariots mingled and used in conjunction with ours. The captured soldiers should be kindly treated and kept.

18 This is called using the conquered foe to augment one's own strength.

19 In war, then, let your great object be victory, not lengthy campaigns.

20 Thus it may be known that the leader of armies is the arbiter of the people's fate, the man on whom it depends whether the nation shall be in peace or in peril.

謀攻
ATTACK STRATAGEMS

1 Sun Tzu said: In the practical art of war, the best thing of all is to take the enemy's country whole and intact; to shatter and destroy it is not so good. So, too, it is better to capture an army entire than to destroy it, to capture a regiment, a detachment, or a company entire than to destroy them.

2   Hence to fight and conquer in all your battles is not supreme excellence; supreme excellence consists in breaking the enemy's resistance without fighting.

3   Thus the highest form of generalship is to balk the enemy's plans; the next best is to prevent the junction of the enemy's forces; the next in order is to attack the enemy's army in the field; and the worst policy of all is to besiege walled cities.

4   The rule is, not to besiege walled cities if it can possibly be avoided. The preparation of mantlets, movable shelters, and various implements of war, will take up three whole months; and the piling up of mounds against the walls will take three months more.

5   The general, unable to control his irritation, will launch his men to the assault like swarming ants, with the result that one-third of his men are slain, while the town still remains untaken. Such are the disastrous effects of a siege.

謀攻 ATTACK STRATAGEMS

6   Therefore the skillful leader subdues the enemy's troops without any fighting; he captures their cities without laying siege to them; he overthrows their kingdom without lengthy operations in the field.

7   With his forces intact he will dispute the mastery of the Empire, and thus, without losing a man, his triumph will be complete. This is the method of attacking by stratagem.

8   It is the rule in war, if our forces are ten to the enemy's one, to surround him; if five to one, to attack him; if twice as numerous, to divide our army into two.

9   If equally matched, we can offer battle; if slightly inferior in numbers, we can avoid the enemy; if quite unequal in every way, we can flee from him.

10 Hence, though an obstinate fight may be made by a small force, in the end it must be captured by the larger force.

11 Now the general is the bulwark of the State; if the bulwark is complete at all points, the State will be strong; if the bulwark is defective, the State will be weak.

12 There are three ways in which a ruler can bring misfortune upon his army:—

13 (1) By commanding the army to advance or to retreat, being ignorant of the fact that it cannot obey. This is called hobbling the army.

14 (2) By attempting to govern an army in the same way as he administers a kingdom, being ignorant of the conditions which obtain in an army. This causes restlessness in the soldiers' minds.

15 (3) By employing the officers of his army without discrimination, through ignorance of the military principle of adaptation to circumstances. This shakes the confidence of the soldiers.

16 But when the army is restless and distrustful, trouble is sure to come from the other feudal princes. This is simply bringing anarchy into the army, and flinging victory away.

17 Thus we may know that there are five essentials for victory:
(1) He will win who knows when to fight and when not to fight.
(2) He will win who knows how to handle both superior and inferior forces.
(3) He will win whose army is animated by the same spirit throughout all its ranks.
(4) He will win who, prepared himself, waits to take the enemy unprepared.
(5) He will win who has military capacity and is not interfered with by the sovereign.

18 Hence the saying: If you know the enemy and know yourself, you need not fear the result of a hundred battles. If you know yourself but not the enemy, for every victory gained you will also suffer a defeat. If you know neither the enemy nor yourself, you will succumb in every battle.

軍形
TACTICAL DISPOSITIONS

1 Sun Tzu said: The good fighters of old first put themselves beyond the possibility of defeat, and then waited for an opportunity of defeating the enemy.

2 To secure ourselves against defeat lies in our own hands, but the opportunity of defeating the enemy is provided by the enemy himself.

3 Thus the good fighter is able to secure himself against defeat, but cannot make certain of defeating the enemy.

4 Hence the saying: One may know how to conquer without being able to do it.

5 Security against defeat implies defensive tactics; ability to defeat the enemy means taking the offensive.

6 Standing on the defensive indicates insufficient strength; attacking, a superabundance of strength.

7 The general who is skilled in defense hides in the most secret recesses of the Earth; he who is skilled in attack flashes forth from the topmost heights of Heaven. Thus on the one hand we have the ability to protect ourselves; on the other, a victory that is complete.

8 To see victory only when it is within the ken of the common herd is not the acme of excellence.

9 Neither is it the acme of excellence if you fight and conquer and the whole Empire says: "Well done!"

10 To lift an autumn leaf is no sign of great strength; to see the sun and moon is no sign of sharp sight; to hear the noise of thunder is no sign of a quick ear.

11 What the ancients called a clever fighter is one who not only wins but excels in winning with ease.

12 Hence his victories bring him neither reputation for wisdom nor credit for courage.

13 He wins his battles by making no mistakes. Making no mistakes is what

軍形 TACTICAL DISPOSITIONS

establishes the certainty of victory, for it means conquering an enemy that is already defeated.

14 Hence the skillful fighter puts himself into a position which makes defeat impossible, and does not miss the moment for defeating the enemy.

15 Thus it is that in war the victorious strategist only seeks battle after the victory has been won, whereas he who is destined to defeat first fights and afterward looks for victory.

16 The consummate leader cultivates the Moral Law, and strictly adheres to method and discipline; thus it is in his power to control success.

17 In respect of military method, we have, firstly, Measurement; secondly, Estimation of quantity; thirdly, Calculation; fourthly, Balancing of chances; fifthly, Victory.

18 Measurement owes its existence to Earth; Estimation of quantity to Measurement; Calculation to Estimation of quantity; Balancing of chances to Calculation; and Victory to Balancing of chances.

19 A victorious army opposed to a routed one is as a pound weight placed in the scale against a single grain.

20   The onrush of a conquering force is like the bursting of pent-up waters into a chasm a thousand fathoms deep.

兵勢
ENERGY

1   Sun Tzu said: The control of a large force is the same principle as the control of a few men: it is merely a question of dividing up their numbers.

2   Fighting with a large army under your command is nowise different from fighting with a small one: it is merely a question of instituting signs and signals.

3   To ensure that your whole host may withstand the brunt of the enemy's attack and remain unshaken—this is effected by maneuvers direct and indirect.

4   That the impact of your army may be like a grindstone dashed against an egg—this is effected by the science of weak points and strong.

5   In all fighting, the direct method may be used for joining battle, but indirect methods will be needed in order to secure victory.

6   Indirect tactics, efficiently applied, are inexhaustible as Heaven and Earth, unending as the flow of rivers and streams; like the sun and moon, they end but to begin anew; like the four seasons, they pass away to return once more.

7 There are not more than five musical notes, yet the combinations of these five give rise to more melodies than can ever be heard.

8 There are not more than five primary colors (blue, yellow, red, white, and black), yet in combination they produce more hues than can ever be seen.

9 There are not more than five cardinal tastes (sour, acrid, salt, sweet, and bitter), yet combinations of them yield more flavors than can ever be tasted.

10 In battle, there are not more than two methods of attack—the direct and the indirect; yet these two in combination give rise to an endless series of maneuvers.

11 The direct and the indirect lead on to each other in turn. It is like moving in a circle—you never come to an end. Who can exhaust the possibilities of their combination?

12 The onset of troops is like the rush of a torrent which will even roll stones along in its course.

13 The quality of decision is like the well-timed swoop of a falcon which enables it to strike and destroy its victim.

14 Therefore the good fighter will be terrible in his onset, and prompt in his decision.

15 Energy may be likened to the bending of a crossbow; decision, to the releasing of a trigger.

16 Amid the turmoil and tumult of battle, there may be seeming disorder and yet no real disorder at all; amid confusion and chaos, your array may be without head or tail, yet it will be proof against defeat.

17 Simulated disorder postulates perfect discipline, simulated fear postulates courage; simulated weakness postulates strength.

18 Hiding order beneath the cloak of disorder is simply a question of subdivision; concealing courage under a show of timidity presupposes a fund of latent energy; masking strength with weakness is to be effected by tactical dispositions.

19 Thus one who is skillful at keeping the enemy on the move maintains deceitful appearances, according to which the enemy will act. He sacrifices something, that the enemy may snatch at it.

20 By holding out baits, he keeps him on the march; then with a body of picked men he lies in wait for him.

21 The clever combatant looks to the effect of combined energy, and does not require too much from individuals. Hence his ability to pick out the right men and utilize combined energy.

22 When he utilizes combined energy, his fighting men become as it were like unto rolling logs or stones. For it is the nature of a log or stone to remain motionless on level ground, and to move when on a slope; if four-cornered, to come to a standstill, but if round-shaped, to go rolling down.

23 Thus the energy developed by good fighting men is as the momentum of a round stone rolled down a mountain thousands of feet in height. So much on the subject of energy.

虛實
WEAK POINTS AND STRONG

1 Sun Tzu said: Whoever is first in the field and awaits the coming of the enemy will be fresh for the fight; whoever is second in the field and has to hasten to battle will arrive exhausted.

2 Therefore the clever combatant imposes his will on the enemy, but does not allow the enemy's will to be imposed on him.

3 By holding out advantages to him, he can cause the enemy to approach of his own accord; or, by inflicting damage, he can make it impossible for the enemy to draw near.

4. If the enemy is taking his ease, he can harass him; if well supplied with food, he can starve him out; if quietly encamped, he can force him to move.

5. Appear at points which the enemy must hasten to defend; march swiftly to places where you are not expected.

6. An army may march great distances without distress, if it marches through country where the enemy is not.

7. You can be sure of succeeding in your attacks if you only attack places which are undefended. You can ensure the safety of your defense if you only hold positions that cannot be attacked.

8. Hence that general is skillful in attack whose opponent does not know what to defend; and he is skillful in defense whose opponent does not know what to attack.

9. O divine art of subtlety and secrecy! Through you we learn to be invisible, through you inaudible; and hence we can hold the enemy's fate in our hands.

10. You may advance and be absolutely irresistible, if you make for the enemy's

虛實 WEAK POINTS AND STRONG

weak points; you may retire and be safe from pursuit if your movements are more rapid than those of the enemy.

11 If we wish to fight, the enemy can be forced to an engagement even though he be sheltered behind a high rampart and a deep ditch. All we need do is attack some other place that he will be obliged to relieve.

12 If we do not wish to fight, we can prevent the enemy from engaging us even though the lines of our encampment be merely traced out on the ground. All we need do is to throw something odd and unaccountable in his way.

13 By discovering the enemy's dispositions and remaining invisible ourselves, we can keep our forces concentrated, while the enemy's must be divided.

14 We can form a single united body, while the enemy must split up into fractions. Hence there will be a whole pitted against separate parts of a whole, which means that we shall be many to the enemy's few.

15 And if we are able thus to attack an inferior force with a superior one, our opponents will be in dire straits.

16 The spot where we intend to fight must not be made known; for then the enemy will have to prepare against a possible attack at several different points; and his forces being thus distributed in many directions, the numbers we shall have to face at any given point will be proportionately few.

17 For should the enemy strengthen his van, he will weaken his rear; should he strengthen his rear, he will weaken his van; should he strengthen his left, he will weaken his right; should he strengthen his right, he will weaken his left. If he sends reinforcements everywhere, he will everywhere be weak.

18 Numerical weakness comes from having to prepare against possible attacks; numerical strength, from compelling our adversary to make these preparations against us.

19 Knowing the place and the time of the coming battle, we may concentrate from the greatest distances in order to fight.

20 But if neither time nor place be known, then the left wing will be impotent to succor the right, the right equally impotent to succor the left, the van unable to relieve the rear, or the rear to support the van. How much more so if the furthest portions of the army are anything under a hundred li apart, and even the nearest are separated by several li!

21 Though according to my estimate the soldiers of Yueh exceed our own in number, that shall advantage them nothing in the matter of victory. I say then that victory can be achieved.

22 Though the enemy be stronger in numbers, we may prevent him from fighting. Scheme so as to discover his plans and the likelihood of their success.

23 Rouse him, and learn the principle of his activity or inactivity. Force him to reveal himself, so as to find out his vulnerable spots.

24 Carefully compare the opposing army with your own, so that you may know where strength is superabundant and where it is deficient.

25 In making tactical dispositions, the highest pitch you can attain is to conceal them; conceal your dispositions, and you will be safe from the prying of the subtlest spies, from the machinations of the wisest brains.

26 How victory may be produced for them out of the enemy's own tactics— that is what the multitude cannot comprehend.

27 All men can see the tactics whereby I conquer, but what none can see is the strategy out of which victory is evolved.

28 Do not repeat the tactics which have gained you one victory, but let your methods be regulated by the infinite variety of circumstances.

29 Military tactics are like unto water; for water in its natural course runs away from high places and hastens downwards.

30 So in war, the Way [Tao] is to avoid what is strong and to strike at what is weak.

31 Water shapes its course according to the nature of the ground over which it flows; the soldier works out his victory in relation to the foe whom he is facing.

32 Therefore, just as water retains no constant shape, so in warfare there are no constant conditions.

33 He who can modify his tactics in relation to his opponent and thereby succeed in winning, may be called a Heaven-born captain.

34 The five elements (water, fire, wood, metal, earth) are not always equally predominant; the four seasons make way for each other in turn. There are short days and long; the moon has its periods of waning and waxing.

軍爭
MANEUVERING

1 Sun Tzu said: In war, the general receives his commands from the sovereign.

2 Having collected an army and concentrated his forces, he must blend and harmonize the different elements thereof before pitching his camp.

3 After that, comes tactical maneuvering, than which there is nothing more difficult. The difficulty of tactical maneuvering consists in turning the devious into the direct, and misfortune into gain.

4 Thus, to take a long and circuitous route, after enticing the enemy out of the way, and though starting after him, to contrive to reach the goal before him, shows knowledge of the artifice of deviation.

5 Maneuvering with an army is advantageous; with an undisciplined multitude, most dangerous.

6 If you set a fully equipped army in march in order to snatch an advantage, the chances are that you will be too late. On the other hand, to detach a flying column for the purpose involves the sacrifice of its baggage and stores.

7   Thus, if you order your men to roll up their buff-coats, and make forced marches without halting day or night, covering double the usual distance at a stretch, doing 100 li in order to wrest an advantage, the leaders of all your three divisions will fall into the hands of the enemy.

8   The stronger men will be in front, the jaded ones will fall behind, and on this plan only one-tenth of your army will reach its destination.

9   If you march 50 li in order to outmaneuver the enemy, you will lose the leader of your first division, and only half your force will reach the goal.

10   If you march 30 li with the same object, two-thirds of your army will arrive.

11   We may take it then that an army without its baggage-train is lost; without provisions it is lost; without bases of supply it is lost.

12   We cannot enter into alliances until we are acquainted with the designs of our neighbors.

13   We are not fit to lead an army on the march unless we are familiar with the face of the country—its mountains and forests, its pitfalls and precipices, its marshes and swamps.

軍爭 MANEUVERING

14 We shall be unable to turn natural advantage to account unless we make use of local guides.

15 In war, practice dissimulation, and you will succeed.

16 Whether to concentrate or to divide your troops must be decided by circumstances.

17 Let your rapidity be that of the wind, your compactness be that of the forest.

18 In raiding and plundering be like fire, in immovability like a mountain.

19 Let your plans be dark and impenetrable as night, and when you move, fall like a thunderbolt.

20 When you plunder a countryside, let the spoil be divided among your men; when you capture new territory, cut it up into allotments for the benefit of the soldiery.

21 Ponder and deliberate before you make a move.

22 He will conquer who has learnt the artifice of deviation. Such is the art of maneuvering.

23 The Book of Army Management says: On the field of battle, the spoken word does not carry far enough: hence the institution of gongs and drums. Nor can ordinary objects be seen clearly enough: hence the institution of banners and flags.

24 Gongs and drums, banners and flags, are means whereby the ears and eyes of the host may be focused on one particular point.

25 The host thus forming a single united body, it is impossible either for the brave to advance alone, or for the cowardly to retreat alone. This is the art of handling large masses of men.

26 In night-fighting, then, make much use of signal-fires and drums, and in fighting by day, of flags and banners, as a means of influencing the ears and eyes of your army.

27 A whole army may be robbed of its spirit; a commander-in-chief may be robbed of his presence of mind.

28 Now a soldier's spirit is keenest in the morning; by noonday it has begun to flag; and in the evening, his mind is bent only on returning to camp.

29 A clever general, therefore, avoids an army when its spirit is keen, but attacks it when it is sluggish and inclined to return. This is the art of studying moods.

軍爭 MANEUVERING

30 Disciplined and calm, to await the appearance of disorder and hubbub among the enemy:—this is the art of retaining self-possession.

31 To be near the goal while the enemy is still far from it, to wait at ease while the enemy is toiling and struggling, to be well-fed while the enemy is famished:—this is the art of husbanding one's strength.

32 To refrain from intercepting an enemy whose banners are in perfect order, to refrain from attacking an army drawn up in calm and confident array:—this is the art of studying circumstances.

33 It is a military axiom not to advance uphill against the enemy, nor to oppose him when he comes downhill.

34 Do not pursue an enemy who simulates flight; do not attack soldiers whose temper is keen.

35 Do not swallow bait offered by the enemy. Do not interfere with an army that is returning home.

36 When you surround an army, leave an outlet free. Do not press a desperate foe too hard.

37 Such is the art of warfare.

九變
VARIATION IN TACTICS

1 Sun Tzu said: In war, the general receives his commands from the sovereign, collects his army, and concentrates his forces.

2 When in difficult country, do not encamp. In country where high roads intersect, join hands with your allies. Do not linger in dangerously isolated positions. In hemmed-in situations, you must resort to stratagem. In desperate positions, you must fight.

3 There are roads which must not be followed, armies which must not be attacked, towns which must not be besieged, positions which must not be contested, commands of the sovereign which must not be obeyed.

4 The general who thoroughly understands the advantages that accompany variation of tactics knows how to handle his troops.

5 The general who does not understand these, may be well acquainted with the configuration of the country, yet he will not be able to turn his knowledge to practical account.

6 So, the student of war who is unversed in the art of war of varying his plans, even though he be acquainted with the Five Advantages, will fail to make the best use of his men.

九變 VARIATION IN TACTICS

7 Hence in the wise leader's plans, considerations of advantage and of disadvantage will be blended together.

8 If our expectation of advantage be tempered in this way, we may succeed in accomplishing the essential part of our schemes.

9 If, on the other hand, in the midst of difficulties we are always ready to seize an advantage, we may extricate ourselves from misfortune.

10 Reduce the hostile chiefs by inflicting damage on them; and make trouble for them, and keep them constantly engaged; hold out specious allurements, and make them rush to any given point.

11 The art of war teaches us to rely not on the likelihood of the enemy's not coming, but on our own readiness to receive him; not on the chance of his not attacking, but rather on the fact that we have made our position unassailable.

12 There are five dangerous faults which may affect a general:
    (1) recklessness, which leads to destruction;
    (2) cowardice, which leads to capture;
    (3) a hasty temper, which can be provoked by insults;
    (4) a delicacy of honor which is sensitive to shame;
    (5) over-solicitude for his men, which exposes him to worry and trouble.

13 These are the five besetting sins of a general, ruinous to the conduct of war.

14 When an army is overthrown and its leader slain, the cause will surely be found among these five dangerous faults. Let them be a subject of meditation.

行軍
THE ARMY ON THE MARCH

1. Sun Tzu said: We come now to the question of encamping the army, and observing signs of the enemy. Pass quickly over mountains, and keep in the neighborhood of valleys.

2. Camp in high places, facing the sun. Do not climb heights in order to fight. So much for mountain warfare.

3. After crossing a river, you should get far away from it.

4. When an invading force crosses a river on its onward march, do not advance to meet it in midstream. It will be best to let half the army get across, and then deliver your attack.

5. If you are anxious to fight, you should not go to meet the invader near a river which he has to cross.

6. Moor your craft higher up than the enemy, and facing the sun. Do not move upstream to meet the enemy. So much for river warfare.

7. In crossing salt-marshes, your sole concern should be to get over them quickly, without any delay.

8 If forced to fight in a salt-marsh, you should have water and grass near you, and get your back to a clump of trees. So much for operations in salt-marshes.

9 In dry, level country, take up an easily accessible position with rising ground to your right and on your rear, so that the danger may be in front, and safety lie behind. So much for campaigning in flat country.

10 These are the four useful branches of military knowledge which enabled the Yellow Emperor to vanquish four other sovereigns.

11 All armies prefer high ground to low and sunny places to dark.

12 If you are careful of your men, and camp on hard ground, the army will be free from disease of every kind, and this will spell victory.

13 When you come to a hill or a bank, occupy the sunny side, with the slope on your right rear. Thus you will at once act for the benefit of your soldiers and utilize the natural advantages of the ground.

14 When, in consequence of heavy rains up-country, a river which you wish to ford is swollen and flecked with foam, you must wait until it subsides.

15 Country in which there are precipitous cliffs with torrents running between, deep natural hollows, confined places, tangled thickets, quagmires and crevasses, should be left with all possible speed and not approached.

行軍 THE ARMY ON THE MARCH

16 While we keep away from such places, we should get the enemy to approach them; while we face them, we should let the enemy have them on his rear.

17 If in the neighborhood of your camp there should be any hilly country, ponds surrounded by aquatic grass, hollow basins filled with reeds, or woods with thick undergrowth, they must be carefully routed out and searched; for these are places where men in ambush or insidious spies are likely to be lurking.

18 When the enemy is close at hand and remains quiet, he is relying on the natural strength of his position.

19 When he keeps aloof and tries to provoke a battle, he is anxious for the other side to advance.

20 If his place of encampment is easy of access, he is tendering a bait.

21 Movement among the trees of a forest shows that the enemy is advancing. The appearance of a number of screens in the midst of thick grass means that the enemy wants to make us suspicious.

22 The rising of birds in their flight is the sign of an ambuscade. Startled beasts indicate that a sudden attack is coming.

23 When there is dust rising in a high column, it is the sign of chariots advancing; when the dust is low, but spread over a wide area, it betokens the approach of infantry. When it branches out in different directions, it shows that parties have been sent to collect firewood. A few clouds of dust moving to and fro signify that the army is encamping.

24 Humble words and increased preparations are signs that the enemy is about to advance. Violent language and driving forward as if to the attack are signs that he will retreat.

25 When the light chariots come out first and take up a position on the wings, it is a sign that the enemy is forming for battle.

26 Peace proposals unaccompanied by a sworn covenant indicate a plot.

27 When there is much running about and the soldiers fall into rank, it means that the critical moment has come.

28 When some are seen advancing and some retreating, it is a lure.

29 When the soldiers stand leaning on their spears, they are faint from want of food.

30 If those who are sent to draw water begin by drinking themselves, the army is suffering from thirst.

行軍 THE ARMY ON THE MARCH

31 If the enemy sees an advantage to be gained and makes no effort to secure it, the soldiers are exhausted.

32 If birds gather on any spot, it is unoccupied. Clamor by night betokens nervousness.

33 If there is disturbance in the camp, the general's authority is weak. If the banners and flags are shifted about, sedition is afoot. If the officers are angry, it means that the men are weary.

34 When an army feeds its horses with grain and kills its cattle for food, and when the men do not hang their cooking-pots over the camp-fires, showing that they will not return to their tents, you may know that they are determined to fight to the death.

35 The sight of men whispering together in small knots or speaking in subdued tones points to disaffection among the rank and file.

36 Too frequent rewards signify that the enemy is at the end of his resources; too many punishments betray a condition of dire distress.

37 To begin by bluster, but afterward to take fright at the enemy's numbers, shows a supreme lack of intelligence.

38 When envoys are sent with compliments in their mouths, it is a sign that the enemy wishes for a truce.

39 If the enemy's troops march up angrily and remain facing ours for a long time without either joining battle or taking themselves off again, the situation is one that demands great vigilance and circumspection.

40 If our troops are no more in number than the enemy, that is amply sufficient; it only means that no direct attack can be made. What we can do is simply to concentrate all our available strength, keep a close watch on the enemy, and obtain reinforcements.

41 He who exercises no forethought but makes light of his opponents is sure to be captured by them.

42 If soldiers are punished before they have grown attached to you, they will not prove submissive; and, unless submissive, they will be practically useless. If, when the soldiers have become attached to you, punishments are not enforced, they will still be useless.

43 Therefore soldiers must be treated in the first instance with humanity, but kept under control by means of iron discipline. This is a certain road to victory.

44 If in training soldiers commands are habitually enforced, the army will be well-disciplined; if not, its discipline will be bad.

45 If a general shows confidence in his men but always insists on his orders being obeyed, the gain will be mutual.

地形
TERRAIN

1 Sun Tzu said: We may distinguish six kinds of terrain, to wit:

(1) accessible ground;

(2) entangling ground;

(3) temporizing ground;

(4) narrow passes;

(5) precipitous heights;

(6) positions at a great distance from the enemy.

2 Ground which can be freely traversed by both sides is called accessible.

3 With regard to ground of this nature, be before the enemy in occupying the raised and sunny spots, and carefully guard your line of supplies. Then you will be able to fight with advantage.

4 Ground which can be abandoned but is hard to reoccupy is called entangling.

5 From a position of this sort, if the enemy is unprepared, you may sally forth and defeat him. But if the enemy is prepared for your coming, and you fail to defeat him, then, return being impossible, disaster will ensue.

6 When the position is such that neither side will gain by making the first move, it is called temporizing ground.

7 In a position of this sort, even though the enemy should offer us an attractive bait, it will be advisable not to stir forth, but rather to retreat, thus enticing the enemy in his turn; then, when part of his army has come out, we may deliver our attack with advantage.

8 With regard to narrow passes, if you can occupy them first, let them be strongly garrisoned and await the advent of the enemy.

9 Should the army forestall you in occupying a pass, do not go after him if the pass is fully garrisoned, but only if it is weakly garrisoned.

10 With regard to precipitous heights, if you are beforehand with your adversary, you should occupy the raised and sunny spots, and there wait for him to come up.

11 If the enemy has occupied them before you, do not follow him, but retreat and try to entice him away.

地形 TERRAIN

12 If you are situated at a great distance from the enemy, and the strength of the two armies is equal, it is not easy to provoke a battle, and fighting will be to your disadvantage.

13 These six are the principles connected with Earth. The general who has attained a responsible post must be careful to study them.

14 Now an army is exposed to six calamities, not arising from natural causes, but from faults for which the general is responsible. These are:

    (1) flight;
    (2) insubordination;
    (3) collapse;
    (4) ruin;
    (5) disorganization;
    (6) rout.

15 Other conditions being equal, if one force is hurled against another ten times its size, the result will be the flight of the former.

16 When the common soldiers are too strong and their officers too weak, the result is insubordination. When the officers are too strong and the common soldiers too weak, the result is collapse.

17 When the higher officers are angry and insubordinate, and on meeting the enemy give battle on their own account from a feeling of resentment, before the commander-in-chief can tell whether or not he is in a position to fight, the result is ruin.

18 When the general is weak and without authority; when his orders are not clear and distinct; when there are no fixed duties assigned to officers and men, and the ranks are formed in a slovenly haphazard manner, the result is utter disorganization.

19 When a general, unable to estimate the enemy's strength, allows an inferior force to engage a larger one, or hurls a weak detachment against a powerful one, and neglects to place picked soldiers in the front rank, the result must be a rout.

20 These are six ways of courting defeat, which must be carefully noted by the general who has attained a responsible post.

21 The natural formation of the country is the soldier's best ally; but a power of estimating the adversary, of controlling the forces of victory, and of shrewdly calculating difficulties, dangers, and distances, constitutes the test of a great general.

22 He who knows these things, and in fighting puts his knowledge into practice, will win his battles. He who knows them not, nor practices them, will surely be defeated.

地形 TERRAIN

23 If fighting is sure to result in victory, then you must fight, even though the ruler forbids it; if fighting will not result in victory, then you must not fight, even at the ruler's bidding.

24 The general who advances without coveting fame and retreats without fearing disgrace, whose only thought is to protect his country and do good service for his sovereign, is the jewel of the kingdom.

25 Regard your soldiers as your children, and they will follow you into the deepest valleys; look upon them as your own beloved sons, and they will stand by you even unto death.

26 If, however, you are indulgent, but unable to make your authority felt; kind-hearted, but unable to enforce your commands; and incapable, moreover, of quelling disorder: then your soldiers must be likened to spoilt children; they are useless for any practical purpose.

27 If we know that our own men are in a condition to attack, but are unaware that the enemy is not open to attack, we have gone only halfway toward victory.

28 If we know that the enemy is open to attack, but are unaware that our own men are not in a condition to attack, we have gone only halfway toward victory.

29 If we know that the enemy is open to attack, and also know our men are in a condition to attack, but are unaware that the nature of the ground makes fighting impracticable, we have still gone only halfway toward victory.

30 Hence the experienced soldier, once in motion, is never bewildered; once he has broken camp, he is never at a loss.

31 Hence the saying: If you know the enemy and know yourself, your victory will not stand in doubt; if you know Heaven and know Earth, you may make your victory complete.

九地
THE NINE SITUATIONS

1 Sun Tzu said: The art of war recognizes nine varieties of ground:

(1) dispersive ground;

(2) facile ground;

(3) contentious ground;

(4) open ground;

(5) ground of intersecting highways;

(6) serious ground;

(7) difficult ground;

(8) hemmed-in ground;

(9) desperate ground.

九地 THE NINE SITUATIONS

2 When a chieftain is fighting in his own territory, it is dispersive ground.

3 When he has penetrated into hostile territory, but to no great distance, it is facile ground.

4 Ground the possession of which imports great advantage to either side, is contentious ground.

5 Ground on which each side has liberty of movement is open ground.

6 Ground which forms the key to three contiguous states, so that he who occupies it first has most of the Empire at his command, is a ground of intersecting highways.

7 When an army has penetrated into the heart of a hostile country, leaving a number of fortified cities in its rear, it is serious ground.

8 Mountain forests, rugged steeps, marshes, and fens—all country that is hard to traverse: this is difficult ground.

9 Ground which is reached through narrow gorges, and from which we can only retire by tortuous paths, so that a small number of the enemy would suffice to crush a large body of our men: this is hemmed-in ground.

10 Ground on which we can only be saved from destruction by fighting without delay, is desperate ground.

11 On dispersive ground, therefore, fight not. On facile ground, halt not. On contentious ground, attack not.

12 On open ground, do not try to block the enemy's way. On the ground of intersecting highways, join hands with your allies.

13 On serious ground, gather in plunder. In difficult ground, keep steadily on the march.

14 On hemmed-in ground, resort to stratagem. On desperate ground, fight.

15 Those who were called skillful leaders of old knew how to drive a wedge between the enemy's front and rear; to prevent co-operation between his large and small divisions; to hinder the good troops from rescuing the bad, the officers from rallying their men.

九地 THE NINE SITUATIONS

16 When the enemy's men were united, they managed to keep them in disorder.

17 When it was to their advantage, they made a forward move; when otherwise, they stopped still.

18 If asked how to cope with a great host of the enemy in orderly array and on the point of marching to the attack, I should say: "Begin by seizing something which your opponent holds dear; then he will be amenable to your will."

19 Rapidity is the essence of war: take advantage of the enemy's unreadiness, make your way by unexpected routes, and attack unguarded spots.

20 The following are the principles to be observed by an invading force: The farther you penetrate into a country, the greater will be the solidarity of your troops, and thus the defenders will not prevail against you.

21 Make forays in fertile country in order to supply your army with food.

22 Carefully study the well-being of your men, and do not overtax them. Concentrate your energy and hoard your strength. Keep your army continually on the move, and devise unfathomable plans.

23 Throw your soldiers into positions whence there is no escape, and they will prefer death to flight. If they will face death, there is nothing they may not achieve. Officers and men alike will put forth their uttermost strength.

24 Soldiers when in desperate straits lose the sense of fear. If there is no place of refuge, they will stand firm. If they are in hostile country, they will show a stubborn front. If there is no help for it, they will fight hard.

25 Thus, without waiting to be marshaled, the soldiers will be constantly on the qui vive; without waiting to be asked, they will do your will; without restrictions, they will be faithful; without giving orders, they can be trusted.

26 Prohibit the taking of omens, and do away with superstitious doubts. Then, until death itself comes, no calamity need be feared.

27 If our soldiers are not overburdened with money, it is not because they have a distaste for riches; if their lives are not unduly long, it is not because they are disinclined to longevity.

28 On the day they are ordered out to battle, your soldiers may weep, those sitting up bedewing their garments, and those lying down letting the tears run down their cheeks. But let them once be brought to bay, and they will display the courage of a Chu or a Kuei.

29 The skillful tactician may be likened to the *shuai-jan*. Now the *shuai-jan* is a snake that is found in the Ch'ang mountains. Strike at its head, and you will be attacked by its tail; strike at its tail, and you will be attacked by its head; strike at its middle, and you will be attacked by head and tail both.

30 Asked if an army can be made to imitate the *shuai-jan*, I should answer, "Yes." For the men of Wu and the men of Yueh are enemies; yet if they are crossing a river in the same boat and are caught by a storm, they will come to each other's assistance just as the left hand helps the right.

31 Hence it is not enough to put one's trust in the tethering of horses, and the burying of chariot wheels in the ground.

32 The principle on which to manage an army is to set up one standard of courage which all must reach.

33 How to make the best of both strong and weak, that is a question involving the proper use of ground.

34 Thus the skillful general conducts his army just as though he were leading a single man, willy-nilly, by the hand.

35 It is the business of a general to be quiet and thus ensure secrecy; upright and just, and thus maintain order.

36 He must be able to mystify his officers and men by false reports and appearances, and thus keep them in total ignorance.

37 By altering his arrangements and changing his plans, he keeps the enemy without definite knowledge. By shifting his camp and taking circuitous routes, he prevents the enemy from anticipating his purpose.

38 At the critical moment, the leader of an army acts like one who has climbed up a height and then kicks away the ladder behind him. He carries his men deep into hostile territory before he shows his hand.

39 He burns his boats and breaks his cooking-pots; like a shepherd driving a flock of sheep, he drives his men this way and that, and nothing knows whither he is going.

40 To muster his host and bring it into danger:—this may be termed the business of the general.

41 The different measures suited to the nine varieties of ground; the expediency of aggressive or defensive tactics; and the fundamental laws of human nature: these are things that must most certainly be studied.

42 When invading hostile territory, the general principle is that penetrating deeply brings cohesion; penetrating but a short way means dispersion.

九地 THE NINE SITUATIONS

43 When you leave your own country behind, and take your army across neighborhood territory, you find yourself on critical ground. When there are means of communication on all four sides, the ground is one of intersecting highways.

44 When you penetrate deeply into a country, it is serious ground. When you penetrate but a little way, it is facile ground.

45 When you have the enemy's strongholds in your rear, and narrow passes in front, it is hemmed-in ground. When there is no place of refuge at all, it is desperate ground.

46 Therefore, on dispersive ground, I would inspire my men with unity of purpose. On facile ground, I would see that there is close connection between all parts of my army.

47 On contentious ground, I would hurry up my rear.

48 On open ground, I would keep a vigilant eye on my defences. On ground of intersecting highways, I would consolidate my alliances.

49 On serious ground, I would try to ensure a continuous stream of supplies. On difficult ground, I would keep pushing on along the road.

50 On hemmed-in ground, I would block any way of retreat. On desperate ground, I would proclaim to my soldiers the hopelessness of saving their lives.

51 For it is the soldier's disposition to offer an obstinate resistance when surrounded, to fight hard when he cannot help himself, and to obey promptly when he has fallen into danger.

52 We cannot enter into alliance with neighboring princes until we are acquainted with their designs. We are not fit to lead an army on the march unless we are familiar with the face of the country—its mountains and forests, its pitfalls and precipices, its marshes and swamps. We shall be unable to turn natural advantages to account unless we make use of local guides.

53 To be ignorant of any one of the following four or five principles does not befit a warlike prince.

54 When a warlike prince attacks a powerful state, his generalship shows itself in preventing the concentration of the enemy's forces. He overawes his opponents, and their allies are prevented from joining against him.

55 Hence he does not strive to ally himself with all and sundry, nor does he foster the power of other states. He carries out his own secret designs, keeping his antagonists in awe. Thus he is able to capture their cities and overthrow their kingdoms.

56 Bestow rewards without regard to rule, issue orders without regard to previous arrangements; and you will be able to handle a whole army as though you had to do with but a single man.

57 Confront your soldiers with the deed itself; never let them know your design. When the outlook is bright, bring it before their eyes; but tell them nothing when the situation is gloomy.

58 Place your army in deadly peril, and it will survive; plunge it into desperate straits, and it will come off in safety.

59 For it is precisely when a force has fallen into harm's way that it is capable of striking a blow for victory.

60 Success in warfare is gained by carefully accommodating ourselves to the enemy's purpose.

61 By persistently hanging on the enemy's flank, we shall succeed in the long run in killing the commander-in-chief.

62 This is called the ability to accomplish a thing by sheer cunning.

63 On the day that you take up your command, block the frontier passes, destroy the official tallies, and stop the passage of all emissaries.

64 Be stern in the council-chamber, so that you may control the situation.

65 If the enemy leaves a door open, you must rush in.

66 Forestall your opponent by seizing what he holds dear, and subtly contrive to time his arrival on the ground.

67 Walk in the path defined by rule, and accommodate yourself to the enemy until you can fight a decisive battle.

68 At first, then, exhibit the coyness of a maiden, until the enemy gives you an opening; afterward emulate the rapidity of a running hare, and it will be too late for the enemy to oppose you.

火攻
ATTACK BY FIRE

1 Sun Tzu said: There are five ways of attacking with fire. The first is to burn soldiers in their camp; the second is to burn stores; the third is to burn baggage trains; the fourth is to burn arsenals and magazines; the fifth is to hurl dropping fire among the enemy.

2 In order to carry out an attack, we must have means available. The material for raising fire should always be kept in readiness.

3 There is a proper season for making attacks with fire, and there are special days for starting a conflagration.

4 The proper season is when the weather is very dry; the special days are those when the moon is in the constellations of the Sieve, the Wall, the Wing, or the Cross-bar; for these four are all days of rising wind.

5 In attacking with fire, one should be prepared to meet five possible developments:

6 (1) When fire breaks out inside the enemy's camp, respond at once with an attack from without.

7 (2) If there is an outbreak of fire, but the enemy's soldiers remain quiet, bide your time and do not attack.

8 (3) When the force of the flames has reached its height, follow it up with an attack, if that is practicable; if not, stay where you are.

9 (4) If it is possible to make an assault with fire from without, do not wait for it to break out within, but deliver your attack at a favorable moment.

10 (5) When you start a fire, be to windward of it. Do not attack from the leeward.

11 A wind that rises in the daytime lasts long, but a night breeze soon falls.

12 In every army, the five developments connected with fire must be known, the movements of the stars calculated, and a watch kept for the proper days.

13 Hence those who use fire as an aid to the attack show intelligence; those who use water as an aid to the attack gain an accession of strength.

14 By means of water, an enemy may be intercepted, but not robbed of all his belongings.

15 Unhappy is the fate of one who tries to win his battles and succeed in his attacks without cultivating the spirit of enterprise; for the result is waste of time and general stagnation.

16 Hence the saying: The enlightened ruler lays his plans well ahead; the good general cultivates his resources.

17 Move not unless you see an advantage; use not your troops unless there is something to be gained; fight not unless the position is critical.

18 No ruler should put troops into the field merely to gratify his own spleen; no general should fight a battle simply out of pique.

19 If it is to your advantage, make a forward move; if not, stay where you are.

20 Anger may in time change to gladness; vexation may be succeeded by content.

21 But a kingdom that has once been destroyed can never come again into being; nor can the dead ever be brought back to life.

22 Hence the enlightened ruler is heedful, and the good general full of caution. This is the Way [Tao] to keep a country at peace and an army intact.

用間
THE USE OF SPIES

1 Sun Tzu said: Raising a host of 100,000 men and marching them great distances entails heavy loss on the people and a drain on the resources of the State. The daily expenditure will amount to 1,000 ounces of silver. There will be commotion at home and abroad, and men will drop down exhausted on the highways. As many as 700,000 families will be impeded in their labor.

2 Hostile armies may face each other for years, striving for the victory which is decided in a single day. This being so, to remain in ignorance of the enemy's condition simply because one grudges the outlay of 100 ounces of silver in honors and emoluments, is the height of inhumanity.

3 One who acts thus is no leader of men, no present help to his sovereign, no master of victory.

4 Thus, what enables the wise sovereign and the good general to strike and conquer, and achieve things beyond the reach of ordinary men, is foreknowledge.

5 Now this foreknowledge cannot be elicited from spirits; it cannot be obtained inductively from experience, nor by any deductive calculation.

用間 THE USE OF SPIES

6 Knowledge of the enemy's dispositions can only be obtained from other men.

7 Hence the use of spies, of whom there are five classes:
(1) local spies;
(2) inward spies;
(3) converted spies;
(4) doomed spies;
(5) surviving spies.

8 When these five kinds of spy are all at work, none can discover the secret system. This is called "divine manipulation of the threads." It is the sovereign's most precious faculty.

9 Having local spies means employing the services of the inhabitants of a district.

10 Having inward spies, means making use of officials of the enemy.

11 Having converted spies, means getting hold of the enemy's spies and using them for our own purposes.

12 Having doomed spies, means doing certain things openly for purposes of deception, and allowing our spies to know of them and report them to the enemy.

13 Surviving spies, finally, are those who bring back news from the enemy's camp.

14 Hence it is that with none in the whole army are more intimate relations to be maintained than with spies. None should be more liberally rewarded. In no other business should greater secrecy be preserved.

15 Spies cannot be usefully employed without a certain intuitive sagacity.

16 They cannot be properly managed without benevolence and straightforwardness.

17 Without subtle ingenuity of mind, one cannot make certain of the truth of their reports.

18 Be subtle! Be subtle! and use your spies for every kind of business.

19 If a secret piece of news is divulged by a spy before the time is ripe, he must be put to death together with the man to whom the secret was told.

用間 THE USE OF SPIES

20 Whether the object be to crush an army, to storm a city, or to assassinate an individual, it is always necessary to begin by finding out the names of the attendants, the aides-de-camp, and door-keepers and sentries of the general in command. Our spies must be commissioned to ascertain these.

21 The enemy's spies who have come to spy on us must be sought out, tempted with bribes, led away, and comfortably housed. Thus they will become converted spies and available for our service.

22 It is through the information brought by the converted spy that we are able to acquire and employ local and inward spies.

23 It is owing to his information, again, that we can cause the doomed spy to carry false tidings to the enemy.

24 Lastly, it is by his information that the surviving spy can be used on appointed occasions.

25 The end and aim of spying in all its five varieties is knowledge of the enemy; and this knowledge can only be derived, in the first instance, from the converted spy. Hence it is essential that the converted spy be treated with the utmost liberality.

26 Of old, the rise of the Yin dynasty was due to I Chih, who had served under the Hsia. Likewise, the rise of the Chou dynasty was due to Lu Ya, who had served under the Yin.

27 Hence it is only the enlightened ruler and the wise general who will use the highest intelligence of the army for purposes of spying and thereby they achieve great results. Spies are a most important element in warfare, because on them depends an army's ability to move.

康熙乾隆年间

吴子
WUZI

Translated by George Fleming in association
with First Edition Translations Ltd.

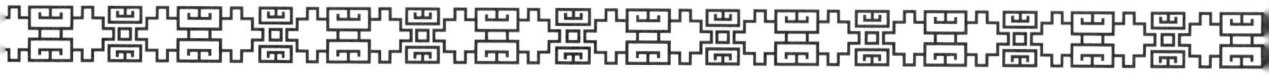

圖國
GOVERNING THE STATE

1 Wu Qi, wearing Confucian official dress, met with Marquess Wen of Wei[15] to discuss military strategy. Marquess Wen said: "I have no interest in military affairs."

Wu Qi replied: "The evidence of my own eyes suggests otherwise, my lord. To judge from what I have seen in the past, I might say you are not speaking entirely honestly. All throughout the year, you have ordered wild beasts killed and their hides collected; you have painted them [the hides] with cinnabar and lacquered them in vermilion, and then emblazoned them with rhinoceros and elephant designs. If you were to use such hides for clothing, they would not keep you warm in winter, nor would they keep you cool in summer. You have had a 2 *zhang*, 4 chi [24-ft]-long trident and a shorter, 1 *zhang*, 2 chi [12-ft]-long trident manufactured. You have used these animal hides to protect your chariots and reinforce their wheels. These vehicles are nothing beautiful to look at, and will be rather cumbersome should you go hunting in the wild. What possible purpose can they serve?

"If you intend to wage war but do not find someone capable of driving them, your effort will be like a nesting hen fighting a wild cat, or a puppy fighting a tiger. Even if it were very fierce, it would soon die.

---

15. Born Wei Si, died c.396 BCE.

"There was once a leader of the Chengsang clan who devoted his attention to civil affairs, but neglected his military. The result was the destruction of his kingdom. There was once a ruler of the Hu clan who relied on his large army and loved warfare, but forgot about civilization—his actions ended his dynasty. A wise ruler would learn from these examples from history: he would surely cultivate the arts at home while preparing for military conflicts abroad. Thus, a ruler who does not attack the enemy does not live up to the standard of righteousness. If he simply laments the loss of his own men in battle without doing anything more, then he is not a benevolent man."

Marquess Wen personally laid out a banquet place for Wu Qi, and his wife served Wu Qi wine. At a ceremony in the ancestral temple, Wen made Wu Qi one of his top generals and placed him in charge of the Xihe command. Wu Qi went on to serve in 76 large battles. In 64 of these, he achieved a complete victory. The rest were stalemates. The expansion of the territory of Wei 1,000 li in all directions was all the work of Wu Qi.

2 Wu Qi said: "In the past, those in power put the common people first. Only then could they win over the populace. There are four taboos in strategy: never send out the army if the state is not united; never go into battle unless your army is united; never advance unless you have a cohesive battle formation; and ensure your army fights as one unit—otherwise, victory will elude your grasp. For this reason, a wise ruler will always take care to unite his army before sending it to war. They will not take private counsel lightly; they will ask for advice in the ancestral temple and ask the holy turtles there

圖國 GOVERNING THE STATE

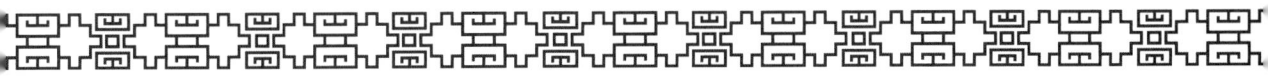

to divine the future. Such a ruler will only take military action after Heaven has issued a positive omen. When the people know that their ruler truly cares about whether they live or die, then when their lord leads them on the battlefield, soldiers will see death as honorable and retreat as dishonorable."

3 Wu Qi said: "The Way [Tao] is the means by which everything returns to its original state. Righteousness motivates people to serve and distinguish themselves. Strategy is a means to self-preservation and profit. Key principles allow us to preserve the state and our gains. If a ruler does not act in accordance with the Way [Tao], and is not righteous but sets himself above the people, then disaster is not far off. This is why the wise rulers of old maintained peace throughout their realms by observing the Way [Tao]. They ruled righteously, and inspired the people through the ritual codes. They reassured the people with their personal virtue. When a ruler pays attention to these four areas, his kingdom will prosper. If he does not, the opposite is true.

"When Tang of Shang rose up against the tyrant King Jie of Xia, the ordinary people were overjoyed; when Duke Wu of Zhou attacked the evil King Zhou of Shang, the people of the Shang capital Yin did not protest. As long as a ruler's actions follow the laws of Heaven and the will of the people, then they will find a smooth road ahead."

4 Wu Qi said: "In order to control your state and your army, you must use rituals to give order to people's behavior, inspire them with the ideal of righteousness, and limit their actions through a sense of honor. When a man has a sense of honor, he can both fight in battle and control himself in private. However, winning a battle is easy; keeping your gains is not. Therefore, consider: a state that defeats its enemies in five battles invites trouble; a state that does so in four battles wears itself out. A state that defeats its enemies after three battles holds its own. A state that defeats its enemies after two battles asserts its claim to an empire, while the state that seizes total victory in a single battle creates an empire. There are few examples of a single state managing to defeat all of its enemies after many battles and still forging an empire. Most states will be destroyed in the attempt."

5 Wu Qi said: "There are five causes of war: the pursuit of fame, wealth, revenge, rebellion, and famine. There are also five types of army: strong, violent, determined, righteous, and treacherous. A strong army refers to the reliance on numbers to subdue the enemy; a violent army is one that understands only money and has no understanding of the rituals; a determined army is the sort raised in anger; a righteous army refers to those that quell a rebellion; lastly, a treacherous army is raised by those who take advantage of an unstable situation in the state to encourage the people to revolt. Dealing with each type of army requires a different strategy. The righteous army will submit only to reason; the strong army must be appeased; the determined army must be persuaded; the violent must be tricked; and the treacherous must be dealt with by force."

圖國 GOVERNING THE STATE

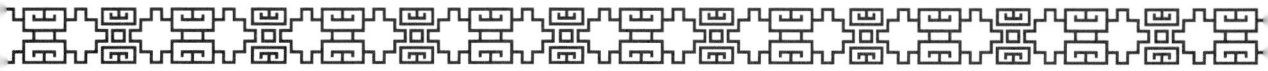

6 Marquess Wu of Wei[16] said: "Pray tell us about governing an army, assigning soldiers, and keeping the state intact."

Wu Qi replied: "The wise princes of old made sure to approach their ministers in the manner prescribed by the ritual codes, and treated all their subjects with the proper ceremony. They united and pacified the officials and the public. These rulers would set an example while following local custom, and would seek out the best talent in order to keep the state well defended against any threat. For example, Huan of Qi gathered 50,000 soldiers to his command, with which he asserted his supremacy over the other lords. King Wen of Jin recruited 40,000 frontline troops, with which he realized his ambitions. King Miu of Qin created a force of 30,000 shock troops, allowing Qin to subdue its enemies. Therefore, a ruler of a strong state must understand their population in order to recruit the best talent. All those who are bold and strong should be organized into one unit; those keen to prove their loyalty and bravery into another. Soldiers who can climb to great heights and cover great distances on foot, should be gathered together. All those dukes or ministers who have lost their positions and need to prove their worth in the eyes of their ruler should be placed in another unit. Former deserters who want to make amends should be placed in a unit. These five different units are the heart of a powerful army. With 3,000 such men, you can break any siege at home, and raze any city abroad."

---

16. Born Wei Ji, the son of Marquess Wen. Died c.370 BCE.

7 Marquess Wu said: "Please tell me how to create a strong battle line, tight defense, and win any battle."

Wu Qi replied: "It is better for me to show you than to tell you. As long as you promote the talented and worthy and disregard the mediocre, then you will have created a strong formation. A strong defense requires the people to keep to their fields and residences, and obey the officials. When all the ordinary people support you, and oppose the enemy, then victory is assured."

8 Marquess Wu was discussing martial affairs and found that none of his ministers could match his talent. The Marquess dismissed the court, looking pleased. Wu Qi stepped forward and said: "There was an occasion in the past when Prince Zhuang of Chu was also discussing matters. He too was unrivaled by his ministers, but when he withdrew from court, he looked worried. Master Shen asked: 'What troubles you, my lord?' Prince Zhuang replied: 'I have heard that there are many wise rulers in other states, and worthy advisors to serve them too. If I could learn from such advisors, then Chu would become strong enough to assert itself among its neighbors. If I had such men as my friends, I could accomplish even greater things. I am a man of limited ability, and not even my own ministers are better than me. Our country is in great peril!'" Wu Qi explained: "Your behavior is exactly what Prince Zhuang was worried about that day, my lord—and yet you seem to think it is cause for celebration. This terrifies me." The Marquess was left looking ashamed.

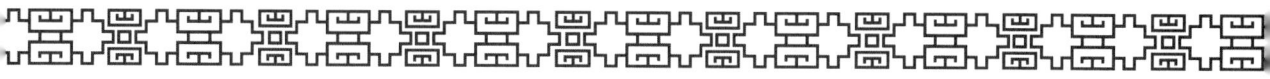

料敵
UNDERSTANDING THE ENEMY

1 Marquess Wu asked Wu Qi: "Currently, I am threatened by Qin to the west, Chu in the south, Zhao across my northern border, and Qi to the east. Yan blocks my escape in one direction, Han in the other. The six states have us surrounded. I am in an extremely unfavorable position. I am very concerned. What is to be done?"

Wu Qi replied: "The first and most important step to securing your state is to be ready. You have already done this, so you are safe from immediate danger. Allow me to summarize the situation of your six neighbors. Qi's army is large, but weak. Qin's army is broken up into many small regiments, but each of these is a powerful fighting unit. Chu has orderly battle lines but cannot withstand a sustained assault. Yan's army can defend itself but is inflexible. The armies of Yan and Zhao are orderly but no use in battle.

"The people of Qi are hardy and determined, and their state is wealthy. The ruling class are given to extravagance and arrogance, and treat their people with contempt. Their orders carry little weight and there is great disparity in income. Qi's army is not united. The troops are strong only at the front, so the army is large but weak as a whole. The strategy to defeat Qi is to divide your army into three, and attack their flanks. You can then use the remaining part of your force to assault the center of their formation. This strategy should result in their ranks breaking.

"Qin is a resilient state set in mountainous terrain. The state has a rigorous system with well-established rewards and punishments. Qin's soldiers are more than ready to fight and can hold their own as individuals in battle. The key to defeating Qin is to undermine them through lucrative bribes. This will cause the soldiers to abandon their commanders. Take advantage of the disorder in their ranks and attack. If you lay ambushes and wait for the opportunity, you can capture Qin's generals.

"Chu is a weak, large country. Its government is disorganized in its edicts and the people are tired. This is why Chu has neat formations but cannot withstand a sustained assault. In order to defeat Chu, bring its garrisons into disarray with attacks and break their spirit. Wear them down with lightning raids. Its army can be defeated without the need for a single pitched battle.

"Yan is an honest state whose people are careful and who value the brave and good. They are not good at deception or intrigue, so they hold their ground and have no skill in seizing opportunities. The strategy for defeating Yan should be as follows. Make an initial attack that harries their army, then maneuver around behind them. This strategy will sow doubts in the King of Yan's mind, and his subjects will be filled with fear. Next, deploy your chariots and cavalry along the route that Yan's army would have to follow to retreat. This will allow your army to capture their generals. The States of the Central Plains, namely Zhao and Han, are inclined to peace. Their systems of government reflect this. Their people are tired of warfare: they are battle-hardened but look on generals with contempt and resent their handsome salaries. The rank and file have no desire to die on the battlefield. Overall, they are disciplined but not experienced. They have orderly formations but they are not effective. The strategy to defeat the States of the Central Plains

料敵 UNDERSTANDING THE ENEMY

is to break through their lines with strong formations. If they attack, then repulse them; when they withdraw, pursue them. This strategy will wear them down. That concludes my report on the six neighboring states.

"Within your army, you will find fierce fighters strong enough to lift a huge tripod, or who can run faster than a warhorse. You must recruit such talented soldiers who can capture the standards of the enemy and kill their generals. Those with such military prowess should be separated from the rank and file, and promoted: such men should be the crack troops of an army. Those soldiers who can use all kinds of weapons, who are healthy and nimble, and determined to destroy the enemy, should be promoted. With such men, you are sure of victory. Treat their parents, wives, and sons well, and motivate them with rewards and punishments in equal measure. Such hardened soldiers will be able to fight for sustained periods. As long as you can understand these issues, then you will be able to defeat enemies who outnumber you many times."

Marquess Wu replied: "Very well."

2 Wu Qi said: "There are eight scenarios in which you may join battle without needing to use divination.

(1) If a fierce wind is blowing or it is very cold, then march by night and cross rivers on rafts. Do not worry about a little hardship on the way;

(2) In the fiercest heat of summer, set out late in the day and then move quickly without resting throughout the night. March without eating or drinking to cover more ground;

(3) When the army has run out of rations, the locals are discontented,

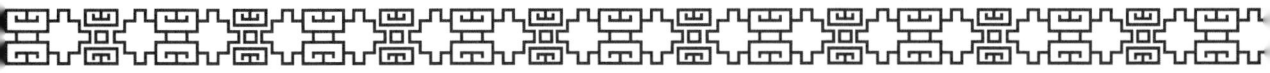

rumors have begun to spread, and the army's leaders cannot control the situation;

(4) If the army's supplies are exhausted and it is low on firewood or hay, and the weather is overcast or rainy, the army has no place to raid;

(5) When the army has few men, the terrain is inhospitable, the men and horses are tired and ill, and they are some distance away from any relieving army;

(6) When they have traveled far and it is nearing sunset, the soldiers are tired and afraid, and have not eaten, so they have taken off their armor and are at rest;

(7) When the commanders or officials do not have any authority, the soldiers are unruly, the army as a whole is nervous, and has no relief force nearby;

(8) When the army only has unstable formations, the camp is not yet set up for the night, or when the army is moving across a slope or mountain pass, and is half exposed.

In all of the above situations, you must attack at once.

There are six scenarios in which you should retreat without any need to use divination:

(1) In large countries with large populations;

(2) Where the ruler loves his subjects and the people are widely blessed;

(3) Where the government's policies are authoritative and justice is transparent, and orders are swiftly obeyed;

(4) Where lower-ranking soldiers can distinguish themselves and move to the top of the army, and where the ruler employs wise advisors;

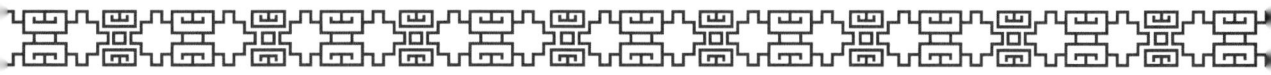

(5) Where there are large armies full of well-equipped crack troops;

(6) Where the state in question has allies all around and the support of a greater state.

In all of the above situations, you are no match for the enemy. You must retreat without question. To handle these situations, you must know how to advance or retreat according to your strength relative to the enemy's."

3 Marquess Wu said: "Can you tell me how to observe the enemy to understand their inner workings; to observe their movements in order to understand how to stop and defeat them?"

Wu Qi replied: "If the enemy comes in a huge, disorganized mass, their chain of command will be in chaos and they will not be in control of their men and horses. One of your soldiers will be equal to ten of theirs in battle—we can catch them at a disadvantage. When your enemies have not had time to assemble their forces, or to reach a consensus between the ruler and his ministers, to dig defensive ditches and raise ramparts, or to give out the required orders, their army will be in disarray. They will be unable to advance or retreat. At this point, if you attack them, even with half their number, victory is assured."

4 Marquess Wu asked: "When must an enemy be attacked?"

Wu Qi replied, "In warfare, you must assess the strengths and weaknesses of the enemy, and then attack their vulnerable points. You should attack in the following situations: When the enemy has just arrived after a long journey and they have not assumed the proper formations; when the enemy has finished a meal and their guard is down; when they are on the run; when they are tired; when they do not have an advantageous position; when the weather is not in their favor; when they are in disarray; when they have just traveled a long way and have had no time to rest; when they are in the middle of crossing a river; when they are in a mountain pass or narrow road; when they are forming up; when their commanders have become separated from the rank and file; and when they are afraid. In the above situations, you should charge the enemy with your best troops, divide your men, and pursue the fleeing enemy. A swift attack is absolutely necessary."

治兵
ARMY DISCIPLINE

1 Marquess Wu asked: "What is the most important principle of advancing?"

Wu Qi replied: "First, you must understand how to simplify things for your armies, the importance of incentives and punishments, and establishing your authority."

The Marquess asked: "What is your meaning?"

Wu Qi answered: "Make sure the land you use is suitable for your horses; for your horses to pull the chariots; for the chariots to carry your soldiers; and then your soldiers can concentrate on fighting. You must understand

治兵 ARMY DISCIPLINE

the lie of the land in order to follow the best path for your horses. Feed your horses regularly, and then they will easily pull your chariots. Keep the axles of your chariots well greased, and your chariots will have no problem transporting your men. Make sure your soldiers have sharp weapons and tough armor, so that they will be prepared for battle. Give powerful incentives to keep the army advancing, and punish those who fall back. Implement the system of punishments and rewards thoroughly to establish your authority. Once your army system is well established, victory will be within your grasp."

2 Marquess Wu asked: "How does an army gain victory?"

Wu Qi replied: "Discipline is the key."

Marquess Wu asked: "Won't the larger army always win?"

Wu Qi said: "If the army's directives and orders are unclear; when the system of punishments and rewards has no authority; when you cannot get your troops to stop at the sound of the gong, or to advance at the sound of the drums, then it will not matter even if you have 1,000,000 men—your army will be of no use. Army discipline means the following: In the camp, the men observe the rituals; on the march, they inspire awe; when the army advances, it cannot be stopped; when the army advances or withdraws, it does so in an orderly fashion; and the army follows its orders when changing direction. Even in the tightest spot, a disciplined army will keep its formation; even if it is dispersed, such an army will keep its ranks. Whether safe or in danger, a disciplined army will retain its cohesion; it can fight continually without tiring, and wherever it is sent, it will advance without hindrance. Such an army's bonds are as strong as those of father and son."

3. Wu Qi said: "An army on the march should keep a measured pace, consume food and drink appropriately, and not exhaust the men and horses. Observation of these three principles is necessary if an army is to remain strong and ready to follow a commander's orders. If the army covers too much ground at once, consumes too much or too little, or does not rest when the men and horses are tired, then it will be unable to carry out orders. When military orders are rendered useless, an army will be disorganized in the camp and will be defeated on the battlefield."

4. Wu Qi said: "Wherever two armies do battle, death awaits. Those that fight to the death survive; those that hope to survive die. Excellent commanders give their armies the urgency of someone on a sinking ship, or trapped in a burning house. There is no time to make cunning plans, or for the brave to summon their courage: they can only go straight into the fight ahead. This is why it is said: 'The most damaging behavior in warfare is hesitation; the worst disasters to befall an army are caused by indecision and doubt on the part of commanders.'"

治兵 ARMY DISCIPLINE

5 Wu Qi said: "Soldiers die because they lack the right skills; they are defeated because they have not honed the proper strategy. Therefore, training is an essential part of commanding an army. If 1 man can learn how to fight, he can train 10 others. If 10 learn, they can train 100. A hundred can train 1,000; 1,000 can train 10,000. If 10,000 learn how to fight, they can train an entire army. March only a short distance to meet an enemy who has just marched a long way; meet them when you are well rested and the enemy is tired; and attack with full stomachs while the enemy is hungry. If your troops are in a round formation, force them to assume a square one; if they are sitting down, force them to stand up; if they are on the move, practice stopping; if they move to the left, make them move to the right; if they advance, make them retreat; if your troops are divided into smaller blocks, make them maneuver into one block; and if they are a cohesive force, break them up. Commanders should train their troops to adapt to every situation before beginning weapons training. This is how an army is educated."

6 Wu Qi said: "Train your shorter men to use spears and ji halberds, and make the taller ones bowmen and crossbowmen. Make the able-bodied standard-bearers. Make courageous men drummers and gong-men, and place the weak in charge of food provision. Select intelligent men as strategic advisors. Place recruits from the same hometown together, and form groups of five and ten men to be responsible for one another. One roll of the drums means everyone should take up arms, two indicates a training drill, three that it is time for a meal, four that everybody should be dressed and ready to set out, and five to form ranks. When the drums sound together, the army should raise the flags and set forth."

7 Marquess Wu asked: "On what principle should you advance and halt?"

Wu Qi replied: "Do not make camp at a 'Stove of Heaven' or a 'Head of the Dragon.' By 'Stove of Heaven,' I mean the entrance to a valley. 'Head of the Dragon' refers to the summit of a large hill. An army should display the Azure Dragon flag on the left flank and the White Tiger flag on the right flank. The vanguard should display the Vermilion Bird, and at the rear should be the flag of Xuan Wu. The center of the army should display the main flag, and the army should follow its directions. On the eve of battle, pay attention to the direction of the wind. If you are facing downwind, attack; if you are going upwind, strengthen your formations and wait it out."

8 Marquess Wu asked: "What sort of method should be used to tame and train cavalry horses?"

Wu Qi replied: "Horses require safe shelter, sufficient water and fodder, and a controlled diet. Provide them with heat in winter, and a cool shady shelter in summer. Shave their manes regularly, and take care to make sure to protect their hooves. Accustom horses to all sorts of sights and sounds so that they do not panic in new situations. Train your horses to gallop and make sure they know how to stop. The horses should become comfortable with humans before they can be put to use. Make absolutely sure all the cavalry equipment, such as saddles, reins, bits, and bridles, is in good order. Horses are normally injured either at the start or at the end of their training. They can suffer from both hunger and an excess of food. At the end of the day when there is still a long journey to complete, riders should dismount for a time to give the horses a rest. It is better to have tired men than exhausted horses. It is important to make sure the horses have some energy left to prevent being overwhelmed by an enemy attack. A ruler who understands these principles can sweep across the land unmatched."

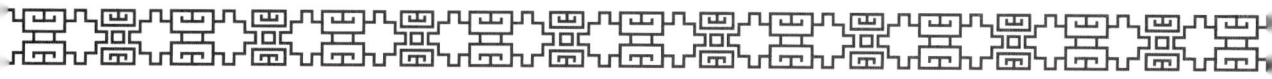

論將
CHOOSING GENERALS

1 Wu Qi said: "A general should be not only a skilled warrior, but also a man of letters. Warfare is about combining force and flexibility. Normally, when people discuss what makes a good general, they think only of courage. However, courage is only one of the qualities required. A commander who is merely brave will be reckless in battle without considering the most crucial issues—this is not good enough. Therefore, generals should pay attention to the following principles: order, foresight, resolution, caution, and simplicity. To be specific, order means observing the same rules when dealing with a larger army as one would when running a smaller one. Foresight refers to the mental state of preparation that an army should observe, equally whether on the march or in battle. Resolution refers to the unwavering attitude an army should have on the eve of battle. Caution means that having won a battle, an army should remain on its guard, just as it did beforehand. Simplicity refers to command without redundancy.

A general should respect every order given, and keep the army on standby until the enemy has been defeated. Observing these principles, from the moment an army is deployed, a general must be prepared to win glory in death—and never dishonor himself with cowardly survival."

2 Wu Qi said: "There are four key areas of warfare: morale, geography, intrigue, and fundamentals. The commander must be responsible for his entire force and inspire his troops' morale. The right narrow path, steep slope, or great mountain pass can be held successfully by 10 men against the assault of 1,000. Intrigue involves the sending of spies to cause defections, sallies by auxiliary troops to break up the enemy ranks and thereby sow discord between an enemy ruler and his ministers, and setting the senior and junior levels of an enemy hierarchy against each other. Making sure that your chariots and their axles and bolts are sturdy, that the oars and paddles for the boats are suitable, that the men know their battle formations, and the horses can easily gallop and pursue the enemy—these together constitute the fundamentals of the army. Only a soldier who understands these four key areas can become a general. However, he must inspire sufficient awe, and be a virtuous, humane, and brave man. These qualities will allow him to inspire obedience in his subordinates, in the rank and file, and fear in the enemy so that victory is assured. A commander whose orders are never disobeyed will receive no challenge from the enemy, wherever he goes. For a state to gain such a man is to assure its own strength; to lose him is to assure its decline and destruction. Someone who embodies these qualities is a noble general indeed."

3 Wu Qi said: "The *pi* and *gu* drums, the gong, and the bell are used to transmit orders for the ears. The different flags, pennants, and banners do the same for the eyes. Orders and punishments are used to enforce discipline. Soldiers listen for instructions, so they need to be able to distinguish between different sounds clearly. The different flags and banners should be in clearly different colors so that the soldiers can tell which order is being given. When a man is afraid of punishment, he will behave himself. If there is no system of instruments, flags, and punishments, then even a united country will be defeated by its enemies. This is why I say: 'When a commander gives the word, all obey; when a general points, the soldiers advance with all their might.'"

4 Wu Qi said: "In battle, a major consideration is to locate the enemy commander and make a thorough assessment of his character. If you adapt your strategy depending on the type of enemy you face, you should be able to win the battle without too much effort. If the enemy general is foolish and gullible, he can be tricked and drawn from his position. If he is a greedy and unscrupulous man, he can be bought with gifts. An enemy commander who is unable to adapt his strategy to the circumstances can be worn down gradually. When your enemy is led by rich, boorish commanders and manned by poor, resentful troops of the rank and file, you can exploit these differences. If the enemy is undecided as to whether to advance or retreat, you can frighten them into a rout. When the soldiers of an enemy army despise their commanders and think of defecting, you should block the normal accessible roads and leave the steep passes open.

In this way, you can lead the enemy into the passes and destroy them. In an area where it is easier to advance than retreat, the enemy can be drawn in. In places where it is difficult to advance and easier to retreat, the enemy can be pursued. When an enemy army is in a low-lying, wetland position with no way for the water to drain away, and there is heavy rain, you should drown them by flooding the area. If your enemy is camped in a wasteland or bog, where the grass is thick and secluded, then when the wind picks up you can set a fire and burn the enemy to death. When the enemy has not moved for a while, and their commanders and troops are off their guard, you can take advantage of their ill-preparedness and launch a surprise attack."

5 Marquess Wu asked: "If our two armies are facing one another and I do not know how skilled the enemy commander is, what should I do?"

Wu Qi replied: "Choose a brave, lower-ranking soldier to lead an attack of light troops on the enemy to test them. Retreat rather than pursue the enemy troops and observe how they react. If they appear well disciplined and move in unison, and pretend not to be able to keep up the pursuit, or do not press their advantage when there is one, then such a force must be led by a competent general. Do not engage such a force. If on the other hand, your enemy is a loud rabble, with uncoordinated flags, and troops who move about as they please, use an odd assortment of weapons, and rush to pursue or fall upon any possible target, then you know that their leader is a fool and no number of soldiers will be enough to save him from capture."

應變
ADAPTING IN THE FIELD

1 Marquess Wu asked: "What if my army, with chariots in good order, quality horses, brave commanders, and strong soldiers, is suddenly attacked by the enemy and breaks formation?"

Wu Qi replied: "The Way [Tao] you bring order to a battle is by the system of flags and banners in daylight, and by the gongs, drums, and *jia* and *di* flutes at night. When you order the army to go left, they go left. When you order the army to go right, they go right. Signal an advance by beating the drums, and signal a halt by sounding the gong. The first sound of the flutes means advance; the second means gather together. Anyone who disobeys an order is to be executed. When your armies are disciplined, and all the soldiers (from *shi* to *zu*) fight with every ounce of their strength, then you will find no enemy or formation that can withstand you."

2 Marquess Wu asked: "What should I do if I am outnumbered?"

Wu Qi replied: "Retreat from accessible ground; draw the enemy into a narrow pass. Therefore, it is said that for 1 man to defeat 10, there is no better place than a mountain pass. The same is true for 10 against 100, or 1,000 against 10,000. Even a very small force of men can cause fear in the hearts of every one of their enemies, when they beat gongs and drums in a narrow, cut-off area. When you have large forces, make use of open ground; when you have only a limited number, take to the narrow paths."

3 Marquess Wu said: "Imagine there is a huge army of well-trained, brave men. The army backs onto narrow trails, with mountains on one side and a river on the other. There is a deep gully defended by the enemy's powerful crossbowmen. Retreat is a safe option; to advance would be to enter a storm. The enemy is well supplied with food. A prolonged struggle is unrealistic."

Wu Qi replied: "Quite a challenging scenario! This sort of situation requires more than just cavalry and chariots; it demands Sage-like strategy. You would need a huge force, with thousands of chariots and cavalry, as well as infantry. Divide your army into five smaller forces and send each in a different direction. When the enemy sees this, they will be caught off guard and confused. If the enemy keeps to their position to shore up their defenses, send out emissaries to find out the enemy's intentions. If they are willing to withdraw, then your side should do the same. If the enemy does not listen, kills your messenger, and burns his letter, then attack at once with your five divisions. If you win the battle, do not give chase. If the tide is against you, retreat with all speed. In order to feign a retreat, move one division forward in an orderly fashion before engaging the enemy in a sudden attack. Use another two divisions to engage the enemy in front and cut off their retreat. The last two divisions should make a surprise attack on the enemy's positions from their flanks. When all five divisions attack at once, they will have a great impact. This is how one can assault a strong enemy."

應變 ADAPTING IN THE FIELD

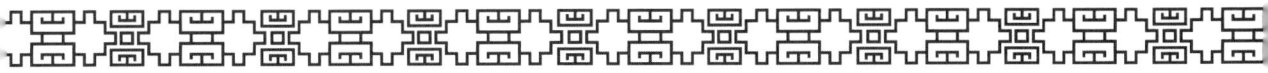

4 Marquess Wu asked: "Imagine the enemy attacks my forces at close range. I have no means of escape and my troops are filled with fear. What should I do?"

Wu Qi replied: "If I had the larger force, I would split my troops and attack from different directions. In the reverse situation, I would concentrate my troops and attack repeatedly. Faced with such an unremitting onslaught, even an enemy that outnumbers you can be defeated."

5 Marquess Wu asked: "Imagine the enemy surprises my army in a ravine. There are steep hills on either side, and the enemy outnumbers me. What should I do?"

Wu Qi replied: "Never tarry in the following places: hilly areas, forests and valleys, deep in the mountains, or in large swampy areas. Get out as soon as possible. If you are attacked by an enemy in a ravine, drum up a great sound and engage the enemy head-on. Send your bowmen and crossbowmen to the front, and keep them ready while you consider the next step. Probe the enemy's position, and at the first sign of disorder, attack."

6 Marquess Wu asked: "Imagine I have high mountains on my left and right. The path is narrow and cramped. Suddenly, I am attacked by the enemy. I do not have the force to repel them and no means of escape. What should I do?"

Wu Qi replied: "This is what I call 'Valley Warfare.' In this situation, no number of extra troops can help you. Select the best of your troops to fight the enemy. Place the swift of foot at the front of your battle lines armed with sharp weapons. Hide your chariots and cavalry several miles away, spread out in all directions. Unable to see all of your army, the enemy will strengthen their lines and be unwilling to risk moving from their position. At this moment, send out part of your force from the valley. The enemy will be confused. Harry them with your chariots and cavalry and do not give them any respite. This is my strategy for Valley Warfare."

7 Marquess Wu asked: "Imagine I run into the enemy in a low-lying area by a fast-flowing river, the water engulfs our chariots up to the yoke and wheels, and our cavalry is in danger of drowning. We have no boats. We cannot advance or withdraw: what should we do?"

Wu Qi replied: "This is what I call 'River Warfare.' Do not use your chariots and cavalry; stay on the bank. Find a vantage point and look all around until you can understand the dynamics of the river. Once you have figured out the different widths and depths at different points along the river, you will be in a position to defeat your enemy. If they try to cross to your side, attack them as they are halfway across."

8 Marquess Wu asked: "It has been raining for days on end. The horses are having difficulty trotting through the mud and the chariots cannot go anywhere. I am surrounded by the enemy on all sides. My troops are shaken. What should I do?"

Wu Qi replied: "Chariots can only be used in battle in dry, warm terrain. They will not work in wet areas. You should seek the high ground and avoid lower lying areas in order to put your chariots to good use. Always travel along proper roads so that you can move easily, whether advancing or withdrawing. If your enemies also use chariots, make use of the tracks they leave behind."

9 Marquess Wu asked: "If the enemy suddenly attacks my fields and pastures, stealing my cattle and sheep, how should I respond?"

10 Wu Qi replied: "When faced with bandit raids, do not underestimate their strength. Make good your defenses, but do not counterattack. When the raiders retreat at dusk, they will be laden down with their spoils. At night, they will be afraid. They will want to withdraw as quickly as possible and may become separated and isolated from one another. If you pursue them, you can rout your enemy."

11 Wu Qi said: "Let us talk about strategies for besieging a city. After you have taken the walls, enter their government offices and make yourself the new leader of their officials. Wherever your army goes, forbid the men from cutting down trees, destroying houses, pillaging food, killing livestock, or setting light to storehouses. This will demonstrate to the local population that you have no intention of violence. If anyone seeks surrender, accept and shelter them."

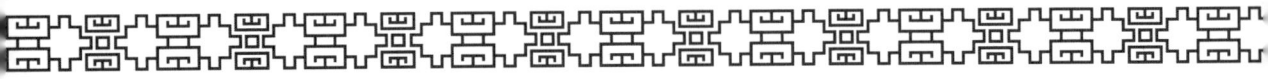

勵士
INSPIRING THE MEN

1 Marquess Wu asked: "Are strict punishments and handsome rewards sufficient to ensure victory?"

Wu Qi replied: "There is too much to say on this point. They are very important, but one cannot rely solely on punishments and rewards. What you should concentrate on, my lord, is ensuring that your soldiers obey orders gladly, that they fight willingly when the army goes into battle, and that they are willing to give their lives in the heat of battle."

2 Marquess Wu asked: "How can I achieve this?"

Wu Qi replied: "By promoting those who have done great deeds and inviting them to a banquet, and thereby encouraging those who have not yet distinguished themselves."

3 Marquess Wu proceeded to hold a banquet at the ancestral temple for three ranks of decorated soldier. The most decorated sat in the front row, on the finest mats, using the best tableware, and consumed all three sacrificial meats.[17] The next most decorated sat in the middle row, using less remarkable mats and tableware. The third rank of soldier, who had no particular distinction, sat in the back row and without any special tableware. After the banquet, the Marquess also rewarded the parents, wives, and

---

17. The three sacrificial meats were pork, beef, and lamb.

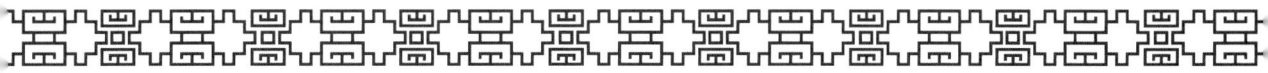

sons of those who had distinguished themselves outside the gate of the temple, with the size of the reward depending on the merit of the soldier in question. Parents who had lost a son on the battlefield received gifts every year and were visited by a representative of the government as a way of commemorating the deeds of their sons. Three years after Wei began to operate this system, the State of Qin raised an army and reached the borders of Xihe. When the soldiers in the State of Wei heard the news, there was no need for officials to issue any order—tens of thousands donned their armor and prepared to fight the invaders.

4 Marquess Wu summoned Wu Qi: "Now I can see how effective everything you have taught me is."

Wu Qi replied: "Every person has his own strengths and weaknesses; momentum comes and goes. I suggest, my lord, that you send out 50,000 ordinary men who have as yet no particular distinction. Let me lead them into battle. If we fail, then I become a laughing stock among all the other lords and lose my authority throughout the land. To use an analogy: imagine a bandit who has been condemned to death hiding out in the vast wilderness. Even if 1,000 men are hunting him down, each of those men will be looking over his shoulder. Do you know why? Because he is afraid the outlaw will suddenly strike him down. By the same token, when a man commits his whole being to the fight, he can make 1,000 quail. The 50,000 I plan to lead today will be like the bandit. If I lead such men against Qin's army, they will find it difficult to stop us."

5 So, the Marquess agreed to Wu Qi's plan. Wu Qi also took with him 500 chariots and 3,000 cavalry, crushing Qin's army of 500,000. Such a feat is a lesson in inspiration indeed.

6 One day before the battle, Wu Qi had issued a command to his forces: "All of you are to follow this order. If the chariot division, cavalry, and infantry cannot capture their equivalents in the enemy army, then no one will receive any reward—even if you manage to break the enemy lines."

On the day of the battle, Wu gave very few orders and yet ended up making his mark for miles with the victory.

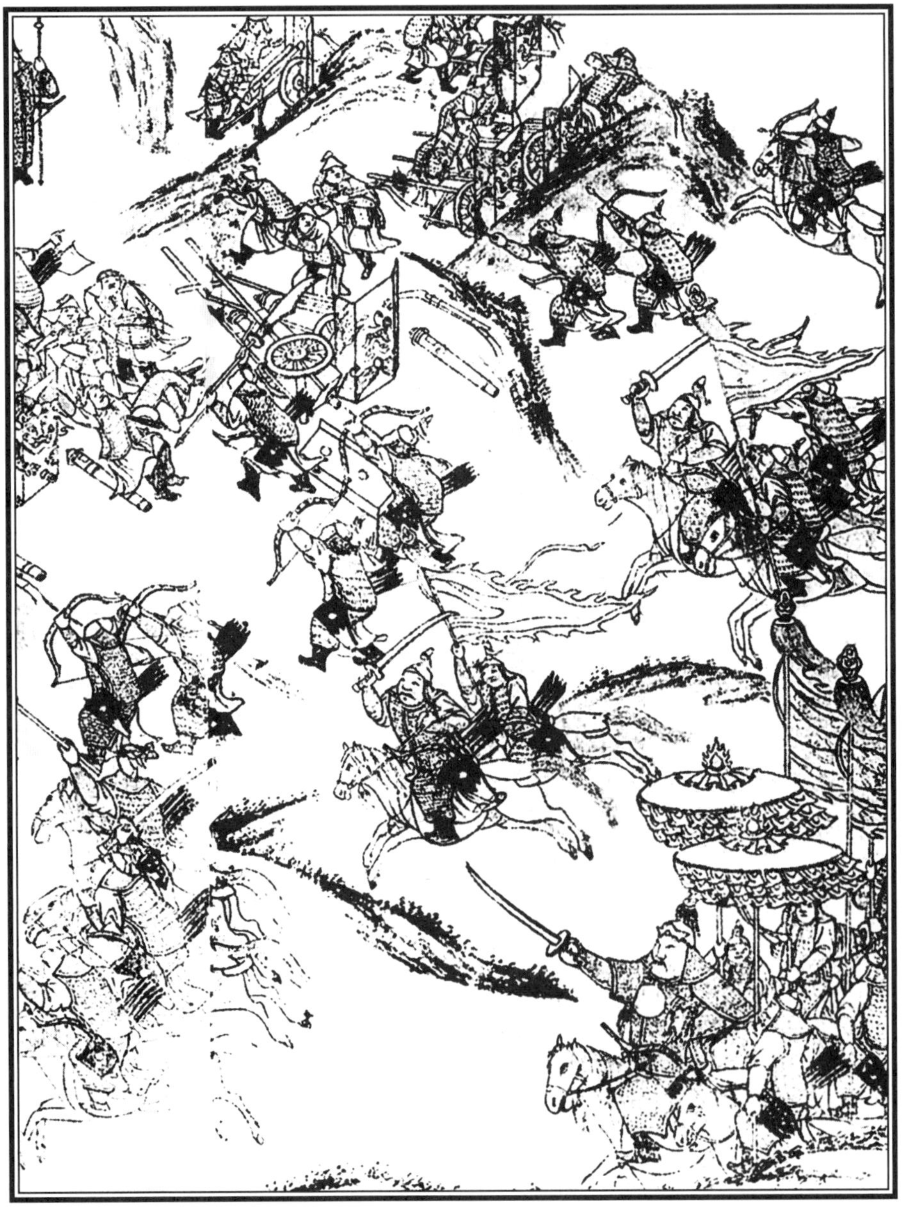

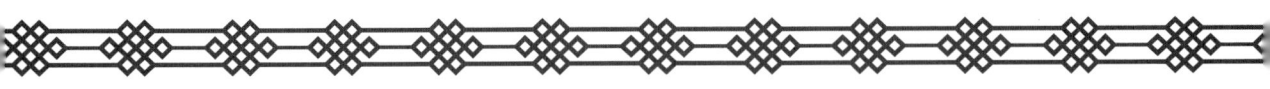

尉繚子
WEI LIAOZI

Translated by Stefan Harvey and Rory Weaver
in association with First Edition Translations Ltd.

天官
THE HEAVENS

1 King Hui of Liang asked Wei Liaozi: "Was it so that the discipline and virtue of the emperor meant that he could win 100 victories?"

Wei Liaozi replied: "Discipline is indeed of use in attacking, as is virtue in defense, but this is not a matter of Heavenly favor, or the coincidence of the right conditions. In fact, when it comes to the Yellow Emperor, his victory is due to naught but human affairs.

2 "Now, if there were a city that could not be taken from east, west, north, or south, then how can it be that no one in the realm can find an auspicious time to take it? The fact is that the city cannot be taken because of the height of its walls, the depth of its moats, the armaments of its soldiers, the preparation of its defenses, the abundance of its grain and the abundance of its supplies, and the unity in purpose of lord and soldier within it. If the walls were to fall, and its moats were shallow and defences weak, then someone would take it. Looked at from this perspective, whether the moment is auspicious according to the Heavens is not as important as human affairs.

3 "Consulting the *Book of the Heavenly Palace*, we say: 'If you line up your army with your back to the river, you will destroy your territory. If you line up your army facing a slope, you will destroy your army.' But when King Wu attacked the tyrant Zhou of Shang, he lined up his army with his back to a rushing river and facing a sheer slope, and with just 22,500 men, he attacked Zhou's boundless hordes and extinguished the Shang Dynasty. How could it be that Zhou lost? Was he not in the favorable position according to the *Book of the Heavenly Palace*?

4 "When the Chu general Gong Zi Xin was at war with the people of Qi, a comet emerged, appearing to favor the state of Qi, and it was thought that the one that received the comet's favor by this omen could not be attacked. However, Gong Zi Xin said: 'How does the comet know who will be victorious? I will certainly topple and defeat those who fight according to comets!' The next day he did battle with Qi and utterly destroyed their army.

5 "Thus the Yellow Emperor said: 'Consulting the omens of spirits and ghosts is no match for examining my own wisdom.' What we attribute to the Heavens is naught but the affairs of humans."

兵談
SPEAKING OF THE MILITARY

1 "When you evaluate the quality of the land and establish a city, construct your walls according to the state of the land, assign manpower according to the size of the walls, and assign grain according to your manpower. If these three things are in balance with one another, then it will be possible

兵談 SPEAKING OF THE MILITARY

to mount a solid defense within the walls and be victorious in battle outside the walls. Victory in battle comes from without, and defense preparations come from within, and the two are employed together just like a pair of matching tallies, for their purpose is one and the same.

2 "In commanding your army, be imperceptible, as if operating from beneath the ground and from above Heaven; exist in a state of non-being, and thus keep your governance secret. Do not use your authority lightly with the great; do not be heavy-handed with the small. Be enlightened in keeping dissent in check; be lenient on minor infractions; find solutions to problems and rectify errors. If this is so, then even vagrants will feel close to the state, and those who fail to cultivate their land will do so.

"When your lands are vast and well maintained, then the state will know prosperity; and when your people are numerous and disciplined, then the state will know order. Those who are prosperous and ordered keep the realm in check through their authority, with neither stirrings from the people nor violence from the army. Thus we call this 'a military victory within the court.' When victory is achieved without mobilizing soldiers, this is the ruler's victory. When victory is achieved by mobilizing troops, this is the general's victory.

3 "The army cannot be mobilized in anger. Proceed if you see a victory, but if there is no victory in sight, then halt. When an enemy is within your borders, mobilize within the day. When an enemy is outside your borders, though the problem may not yet be pressing, mobilize within the month.

Likewise, when an enemy is somewhere within the Four Seas, mobilize within the year lest the danger become more severe.

4 "The general is not checked by constraints of Heaven, nor by Earth, nor by the affairs of man. He is magnanimous and cannot be stirred to anger; his heart is clear and he cannot be stirred to action by riches. The leader with a wild heart is blind to new information and deaf to good advice. He will meet with great difficulties.

5 "Wherever your soldiers go, they must be victorious, whether in narrow and winding roads, in bumpy mountain passes, on mountain slopes, and in valleys and gorges. They must be victorious both when they have encircled an enemy and when they themselves are surrounded. The most serious obstacles are the mountains and the forests, the Yellow River and the Yangtze. In comparison, the cannons and fire of the enemy, or the moment when the enemy hems you in against a wall, or engulfs you like the fog, are minor obstacles. When you order your troops to come together, they must not disperse; when ordered to disperse, they must not remain together. When ordered left, they must not be forced right; and when ordered right, they must not be forced left. If your soldiers are like the many trees of the forest, and your crossbows like the many horns of rams, and each and every man surges forward brave and strong and with all hesitation and doubt having been expunged from them, then they will proceed, mighty and victorious."

制談
SPEAKING OF CONTROL

1   "In warfare, a general's regulations must be foremost in controlling an army. When this is the case, then the soldiers will not be unruly, and only when soldiers are not unruly will the army come into shape. There are none in the realm capable of facing an army in which 100 can fight as one when the battle-drums sound, where 1,000 can fight as one when plunging into battle to break an enemy formation, and where 10,000 can all raise their blades as one to topple an army and kill its general.

2   "In ancient times, footsoldiers were divided into squadrons of 5 and 10, and chariots were arranged into units of 25. When the gongs sounded the attack and the banners directed the army forward, without exception the first over the enemy's battlement would be those whose strength was greatest, and without exception these same soldiers would be the first to perish in battle.

3   "To cost your enemy 1 man but lose 100 of your own in doing so is to benefit your enemy at great cost to yourself. Even the greatest generals of our generation have been unable to avoid this. If the army divides and flees home, or flees after defeat in battle, you will suffer great injury as a result of retreating. Even the greatest generals of our generation have been incapable of avoiding this. Bows and arrows are used to kill men beyond 100 paces. Spears and halberds are what are used to kill men within 50 paces. When the general sounds the drums to advance, but the soldiers and their commanders are immersed in the din of battle, clutching their halberds among snapped arrows and broken spears, and instead retreat and disperse to preserve their own lives—this is defeating yourself from within. Even the greatest generals of our generation have been incapable of avoiding this. If the soldiers lose their squads of 5 and 10 and the chariots lose their units, then even the best troops will forsake the general and flee, and the rank and file soldiers will also flee. Even the greatest generals of our generation have been incapable of avoiding this. If a general can avoid these four situations, then he will scale even the highest walls, traverse even the deepest moats, and break even the strongest enemy formations. If he cannot, then he can no more attain victory than one can traverse the Yangtze having lost one's oars.

4 "People do not despise their lives and die gladly. The reason that the general is able to order soldiers to advance into battle is that his commands and edicts are clear, and his rules and discipline are meticulous. By putting clear rewards in front of his men and decisive punishments behind them, the general gives free rein to his capabilities in battle and will emerge victorious. Thus, when he acts, he will attain great accomplishments.

5 "With a sergeant commanding each 100 men, a lieutenant commanding each 1,000 men, and a general commanding the host of 10,000 men, the few can defeat the many, and the weak vanquish the strong. If you put the words of your humble servant to the test, it will be sufficient to command your armies. If you rule to execute a man and follow through on the sentence, then even a father will dare not shelter his son from punishment, nor will a son dare shelter his father [within the army]. How, then, will mere soldiers dare shelter each other from your punishments?

6   "If a soldier were to attack a man in the marketplace, the masses will surely avoid going there. Your servant says of this: 'Battle is not a matter of individual feats of bravery, but of the deeds of the unexceptional masses.' What do I mean by this? I mean that there is no comparison between the soldier who willingly faces death and the soldier who seeks to preserve his own life. Heed this advice and you will find it sufficient to command your armies such that they will act as a single heroic soldier. None will stand and face them, none will pursue them, and none will compare with them. They will truly be troops worthy of the lords and kings of antiquity.

7   "It is said that the great Huan Gong raised a host of 90,000 men, and none in the realm could face him. It is said that Wu Qi raised a host of 70,000, and none in the realm dared face him. It is said that Wu Zi raised a host of 30,000, and none in the realm dared face him. In present times, there is no host led by any officer in any state that numbers fewer than 200,000 men. The inability to achieve meritorious deeds thus derives from failure to understand the principles by which an army is led, namely keeping dissent in check, being lenient on minor infractions, finding solutions to problems, and rectifying errors that may arise. If you understand these principles of discipline, and you can attain mastery over one man, then this is also true of

ten men. And if you can attain mastery over ten men, then this is also true of men in their hundreds, thousands, and tens of thousands. This is why it is said:

> 'I hone the arms and people at my disposal,
> I nurture the skills of my commanders and the valor of my troops
> Thus when dispatched, my army strikes like an eagle
> Swooping through the winding valleys.'

8 "Now, when the state is attacked, valuable treasure is spent, cherished sons are sent out as hostages, and the boundaries of the state's territory are reduced. If one has attained the aid of other kingdoms in the realm and they claim to send a host of 100,000 men, in reality it will be no more than a few tens of thousands in number. Furthermore, those who have sent soldiers will all have told their generals: 'Do not serve under another general, and do not be first into battle.' In reality, these troops cannot be used to fight.

9 "And imagine that we were to take the measure of our people and find that none among them who were not already assigned to a unit were fit to serve as soldiers. One who would rule as king and exercise control over the masses must surely be able to command them to don military uniforms and take army rations. When it comes to the failure to attain victory in battle or to raise solid defenses, the fault lies not with our people but within us. How, then, if all the states of the realm ride to our aid, like a fine stallion riding to the aid of a lame mule, could we be any match for them, and how could they possibly follow us?

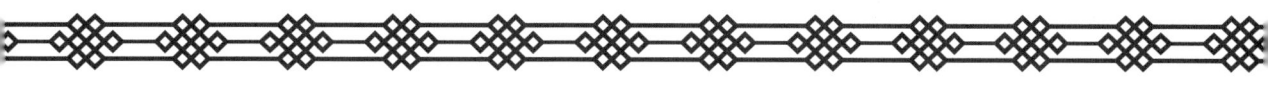

10 "Let us make use of the people and the methods of discipline that are most effective in the realm. Let us cultivate our commands and edicts, and clarify our punishments and rewards. Thus you will command the realm so that no viable land goes uncultivated and no fiefdom goes unconquered, and command your people such that they devote themselves to agriculture and war, and none in the realm will dare to make an enemy of you. This is why it is said: 'Dispatch orders and send out commands, and edify the character of the state.'

11 "If someone says to you that an enemy can be defeated, do not heed their empty words, but instead examine their capabilities in fighting.

12 "If you would covet someone else's land and take their people into your service, you must be able to take in the worthy among them. If you desire to rule but are incapable of this, then you will need to topple armies and kill generals, and though you may be victorious in battle your state will be ever weaker, and though you may expand your territory your state will be ever poorer. This stems from the deficiency of discipline within a state."

戰威
BATTLE AND AUTHORITY

1 "In war, victory is attained through the Way [Tao], through authority, and through strength. When a leader plans stratagems and appraises the enemy, undermining its morale so that its army scatters, and although the army remains intact, it cannot be put to use: this is the victory of the Way [Tao]. When he is meticulous in his regulations and discipline; when he is clear in issuing rewards and punishments; when he hones his armaments and manpower, and through this crafts his people into fine soldiers, thus preventing enemies arising: this is the victory of authority. When he breaks armies and kills generals; storms city walls and launches attacks; assaults the enemy's people and takes their territory; and turns back only once he has attained success: this is the victory of force. These were the means by which kings and dukes of former times became accomplished in the three paths to victory.

2 "Now the means by which a general does battle is the people, and the means by which the people do battle is their morale. When morale is strong, they will fight, and when it is lost, they will flee.

3 "There are five methods by which you defeat your enemy before meeting them in battle and applying punitive measures. First, strategy is discussed in the court; second, the generals receive their orders; third, the army crosses into enemy territory; fourth, it besieges the enemy's city; and fifth, it forms up and goes into battle. These five methods are a

戰威 BATTLE AND AUTHORITY

matter of first examining the enemy, and only then attacking. These are the means by which you defeat an enemy by striking at his weaknesses.

4 "One who is adept at waging war is capable of defeating his enemies and does not suffer defeat himself, so this is a matter of the skills of the general. Commanding is a matter of unifying the hearts of the masses. If the masses are not monitored closely, then orders will change, and if their orders change, then the masses will not trust the orders that you issue.

5 "This is why when it comes to commanding, small errors must not be duplicated, and small doubts must not spread. If there are no doubts concerning the commands of officers, then the masses will not be divided in what they hear, and if there are no doubts concerning the purpose of an action, then the masses will not be divided in their will. There has never been a case of someone being able to find his strength without trusting his heart, and there has never been a case of someone being capable of going to their death in battle without this strength.

6 "For this reason, the state must have the righteous conduct that stems from ritual propriety, honesty, familial love, and affection, and then it is possible for the people to turn hunger into plenty. Likewise, the state must have the customs that stem from filial piety, kindness, honesty, and shamefulness, and then it is possible for the people to turn death into life. In ancient times, the leaders and the people surely valued ritual propriety and honesty over fiefdoms and salaries. They were more compelled by honesty and shamefulness than by the threat of fines and punishments, and found familial love to be a greater motivation than corporal discipline.

7 "Thus, the battle must be rooted in the person of the commander in order to inspire the soldiers, just like the heart commands the four limbs of the body. If their will is not inspired, then the commanders will not die for their honor, and if the commanders will not die for their honor then the masses will not do battle.

8 "Inspiring your soldiers is a matter of placing value on the lives of the people. Whether bestowing ranks and salaries or performing funerary rites, it is essential that the things that the people strive for are made manifest. Understand what people live for, and manifest what the people strive for—namely the security of land and salaries, the comfort of food and drink. In the same village, people toil together; in funerary matters, people help one another; and in battle, soldiers follow one another. These are the things that inspire the people.

9 "If you make the members of each 5-man and 10-man squad brothers, and the members of each 100 friends, then they will be as solid as a wall when holding a position, and they will be as swift as the wind and rain when maneuvering. Your chariots will advance in tandem and your soldiers will not retreat a single step. This is the Way [Tao] that is fundamental to doing battle.

戰威 BATTLE AND AUTHORITY

10 "The land is the means by which a lord nurtures his people. City walls are the means by which the lord defends his land. Battle is the means by which the lord defends his walls. Therefore, those who are tasked with tending the plow do so that the people may not go hungry; those who are tasked with defending the city walls do so that the land not be threatened; and those who are tasked with doing battle do so that the walls are not encircled. These are the three fundamental tasks of the king, and, of these tasks, that of the military is most urgent.

11 "For this reason, the kings of former times first and foremost devoted themselves to military affairs. There are five duties within this sphere: if supplies are not plentiful, then your soldiers will be unable to march; if rewards and salaries are not generous, then your people will not be motivated; if soldiers are not chosen with discrimination, then your army will not be strong; if armaments and manpower are not managed adeptly, then your strength will not be sufficient; if punishments are not appropriate, then the masses will not be in awe of their commander. When you attend to these five tasks, the army remains still, you are able to defend that which you seek to protect, and when you take action, you are capable of accomplishing that which you desire.

12 "When you set out with the aim of attacking an enemy, then when making goals, dwell on the most important; when making formations, desire steadfastness; when destroying the enemy, desire completeness; and when fighting, desire unity.

13 "A state ruled by a king enriches its people. A state ruled by a feudal lord enriches its commanders. A state that hoards its stores enriches the officials. A fallen state enriches the keepers of the granaries. This is the meaning of the saying, 'When rulers become rich at the expense of the people, the state will surely fall.'

14 "Thus it is said: 'Raise up the worthy and appoint the capable, and always use your days to benefit the state. Follow not that which divination declares auspicious, but make your laws clear and your orders meticulous. Depend not on attaining prosperity through sacrifices to the gods, but depend instead on valuing achievement and nurturing diligence.' It is also said: 'The movements of nature are less important than the condition of the land, and the condition of the land is less important than harmony among the people.' The things that the Sages valued were the affairs of people and nothing more.

15 "Now, when it comes to leading a prudent and diligent host, the general must lead by example. Do not spread out a shade in the summer, nor wear extra furs in the winter, and when faced with danger you must step forth into it with your soldiers. Drink only once the army's well has been completed, eat only when the army's food is ready, and sleep only once the army's encampment is fortified. Labor when the army labors, and rest when the army rests. If you do this, then though the host may be long in the field it will not become fatigued."

攻權
METHODS OF ATTACKING

1 "In war, victory is won through calm. In statecraft, victory is won through dedication to a singular cause.

2 "One whose strength is divided is weak. One whose heart harbors doubt will flee. So, if a man's strength is weak, he will not be not bold in maneuvering and will let the enemy slip through his grasp. The general, commanders, officers, and soldiers should move and halt as one. If their hearts harbor doubts of defeat, then when orders are issued, they will not stir, when maneuvers are completed they will not halt, and they will be full of pernicious rumors and empty words. If the general's bearing does not inspire the men and the soldiers do not drill regularly, then when they attack, they will be bloodied. Of this, it is said: 'A soldier that is hastened to the grave is not worthy in battle'.

3 "The general is the heart of the army, and his soldiers are the limbs of the army. If the heart beats strong and true, then the limbs will surely be strong, but if the heart beats hesitantly, then the limbs will surely be defeated. So, if the general does not discipline his heart, then the troops will not act as his limbs, and any victory they win will be a victory of happenstance, and not from mastery of the methods of attacking.

4 "Now, the people cannot be in awe of two things at once. If they are in awe of you, then they will hold the enemy in contempt, and if they are in awe of the enemy, they will hold you in contempt. Of the two, the one who is held in contempt will be defeated, and the one who establishes his authority will be victorious. In every case, the general who is capable of this Way [Tao] will be held in awe by his officials. If the officials are in awe of their general, the people will be in awe of them, and the enemy, in turn, will be in awe of such a people. This is why, to understand the path of victory and defeat, you must first understand the measure of awe and contempt.

5 "If a general does not inspire love, then he cannot make use of men, but if he does not inspire strictness and authority, he cannot mobilize men. If love exists among the ranks and authority is established among the superiors, then as a result of the love the army will be undivided, and as a result of authority the army will not turn on its general. This is why being an adept general is nothing more than a matter of love and authority.

6 "If you do battle, but are unsure of victory, then you cannot speak of doing battle. If you attack, but are unsure of capturing your target, then you cannot speak of attacking. If this were not the case, then though you may issue punishments and rewards, they will not be sufficient for you to be trusted. Trust stems from your past deeds, and the affairs that you are concerned with lie in the future. If you assemble your army, do not disband it without having used it; and if you set out with your army, then do not return home without some achievement. Seek your enemy with the urgency

攻權 METHODS OF ATTACKING

of a father seeking his lost son, and strike at them with the speed of one rescuing a drowning man.

7 "Those who seek to mitigate danger lack the heart for battle. Those who wish to fight only some of the time lack true fighting spirit. Those who are spoiling for battle lack superior skills in war. In all cases, if you fight for the sake of righteousness, then the nobles will rise up for you, but they will also vie for private gain. This will create resentments between them, and you will not be able to resolve this problem. Though resentments may arise, treat them as nobles and lords. Therefore, in times of strife you must treat and receive your subjects equally, and in times of peace you must arm them equally.

8 "There is victory in the court, where strategies are drawn up before the war; there is victory on the field of battle; and there is victory in siegecraft against the enemy's cities. If you fight, making gains whenever you win and bearing losses whenever you submit, and through good fortune are not defeated, this is a false victory that results from the unexpected disarray of your enemy. We say that a false victory lacks completeness, meaning that it does not derive from sound methods in the three arenas of victory. This is why, on the day of an attack, the enlightened lord sounds the drums and gongs in unison, binds together the blades of his soldiers, and is victorious without seeking victory.

9 "In warfare, there are victories attained in spite of the troops abandoning their equipment and forgetting the authority of their general. This is a result of the general's understanding of the methods of war. Where there is complete and detailed planning with regard to armaments and manpower, an army will be well prepared to face the enemy, and its leadership will be supreme. Therefore, when each squad of 5 or 10 men has its leader, each 100 has its captain, each legion has its lieutenant, and each army has its general, your host will be both well prepared and supreme. If an officer perishes in the morning, replace him that same morning. If an officer dies in the evening, replace him that same evening. So first appraise your enemy and carefully assess your leaders. Only after this should you raise your troops.

10 "When gathering your troops, allow ten days to cover an area of 1,000 li, and just one day to cover an area of 100 li, for you must be timely in massing on the enemy's border.[18] When the troops are gathered and the general has arrived, push deep into the enemy's territory, block off their roads, and occupy their cities. Give the order to scale an enemy wall and press them into a dangerous position. Have the men and women at your disposal press in on a fortress and they will take it. If you are encamped outside a city and judge that the roads out have been blocked, then attack immediately. If the enemy's general cannot sincerely believe that he will be victorious, then their commanders and soldiers cannot act in harmony,

---

18. One li is approximately one-third of a mile.

and some among them will not follow the discipline of the army. If this becomes so, then your side will already have defeated them. Thus the entire city will have surrendered before the relieving force arrives.

11 "If you have not destroyed your bridges, repaired your fortresses, fortified strategic locations, and erected shelters on your battlements, then though you may have walls, you have no defense. If the garrison has not entered the city and the troops that patrol your borders have not returned to you, then though you have men under your control, it is tantamount to having no men at all. If you have not gathered livestock, grain, and cash, then though the material to fight a war may be within your possession, it is tantamount to having nothing. So, if a city is empty and its stores exhausted then you will take advantage of its vulnerability and seize it. This is what is meant in the *Rules of Warfare* when they say: 'One who is supreme in commanding his troops will defeat his enemy long before meeting him in battle.'"

守權
METHODS OF DEFENDING

1 "When defensive forces advance without constructing perimeter defenses or retreat without constructing barricades in strategic positions, it shows a lack of skill. Amass heroic commanders, fine troops in sturdy armor, and worthy archers within your city. Collect all of the food in the outskirts and store it in the city. Demolish the outer fortifications before you return to the city walls. Then your own morale will soar and the enemy's morale will be no match for it. Thus when the enemy attacks, you will inflict great harm. Although this is the case, the greatest generals of our generation are incapable of understanding it.

2 "The defenders should not fail in the face of peril. The methods of defending tell us to assign 10 men to defend each 10 feet of wall, not including craftsmen or cooks. If those who leave the city to fight do not defend the walls, and those who defend the walls do not leave the city to fight, then 1 defender will be a match for 10 attackers, 10 defenders for 100 attackers, 100 defenders for 1,000 attackers, and 1,000 defenders for 10,000 attackers. This is why the preparation of the walls and barricades of a city is not a waste of manpower and land, but is truly the essence of defending the city.

3 "If the city walls measure 10,000 feet in length, then assign 10,000 men to defend them. Deepen and widen your moats, build your walls strong and thick, arm your soldiers and people, provide for their provisions and salaries, make your bows and arrows strong and your spears and halberds balanced. This is the method of defense.

守權 METHODS OF DEFENDING

4 "If an attacking force numbers more than 100,000, and if there is an army coming to relieve the city, then you must defend your walls. If there is not an army coming to relieve the city, then it is not the case that you must defend your walls.

5 "If your walls are strong and the prospects of relief are good, then even the foolish men and women in the surrounding area will take refuge behind your walls, and will devote their resources to you and shed their blood upon your walls. The city that can hold out for a long time is one where the defending force exceeds the attacking force, and the relief force exceeds the defending force. If the city walls are strong but without good prospects of relief, then the foolish men and women will weep upon the parapet even as they defend your walls, for this is the nature of people. Even if you open up the granaries to feed and comfort them, you will be unable to stop their grief. You must command your officers, soldiers, and archers to line up at the front of your defense, and keep the old, the weak, and the infirm in the rear.

6 "When a host of 100,000 soldiers is encamped outside your walls, the relieving army must break the siege, and the defending army must come out to meet them. If the defending force sits in the fortress, then there will only be the relief force attacking the rear of the besieging army and their supply lines will not be cut off. The defending army must appear not to believe the relief attempt to be genuine [to confuse the enemy].

7 "If this is the case, then the enemy army will turn, placing their strongest troops to their rear to face the relieving army. The troops on the side of the city walls will thus be their weak and injured, and they will have no way of halting the defending army. This is the strategy of defense."

十二陵
THE TWELVE ATTRIBUTES OF THE GENERAL

1 "Authority lies in not changing course. Wisdom lies in adapting to the circumstances at hand. Strategems are a matter of responding to events. Battle is a matter of morale. Victory when attacking stems from surprising your enemy. Victory when defending stems from the preparation of fortifications. Avoiding errors requires calculation and reckoning. Avoiding difficulties requires prior preparations. Prudence is a matter of taking care over the small. Wisdom is a matter of governing the large. Eliminating threats is a matter of resoluteness and determination. Attaining the favor of the masses is a matter of how you treat the common people.

2 "Regret stems from trusting in what is doubtful. Evil stems from being overly cruel in your punishments. Unfairness comes from placing too much value on your own private gain. Misfortune is a result of unwillingness to hear of your own mistakes. Imprudence is a result of coveting the wealth of others. Ignorance results from receiving the biased opinions of others. Impotence results from reckless actions. Narrowness of thought comes from remaining distant from the talented and worthy. Disaster lies in the love of profit. Harm results from being too close to the common people. Collapse results from failure to prepare defenses. Danger results from a lack of clear orders and commands."

武議
THE UNDERSTANDING OF MARTIAL AFFAIRS

1 "In war, attack no city that is without transgression, and kill no man who is without guilt. If you kill a man's family, avail yourself of a man's wealth, or take the children of a concubine as your servants, then this is mere banditry. Therefore, war is a means of executing those who would cause chaos and constraining those who are not righteous. When a just war is waged, farmers are not pulled from their fields, nor merchants from their markets, nor officials from their seats of government, because the target of a military action is but a single errant lord. This is why the war that avoids bloodshed is the one that attains Heaven's favor.

2 "A great state concerns itself with its agriculture and its military, a medium state concerns itself with preparing armies to defend itself, and a small state concerns itself with feeding its people. With strong agriculture and a strong military, the great state needs no external authority. With strong defense and relief plans, the medium state needs no external assistance. With its people fed, a small state needs no external aid.

3 "If a state lacks the strength to do battle outside its borders or to defend its territory within its borders, the way to solve this is to nurture the marketplaces, for they are the means by which your capacity for battle and for defense are determined. If a great state lacks the support of the large states around it, then it must be able to avail itself of the marketplaces of the small state.

4 "Executions are the means by which one brings clarity to martial affairs. If you will make your armies fearful of you by executing one man, then execute him. If you will please the masses by rewarding one man, then reward him. When you execute a man who is deserving of it, even though he is of great value to you, this chastens the upper ranks of your army. When you extend favor down even to those who tend the horses and cattle, this rewards the lowly in your army. The general's skill in martial affairs is a matter of his ability to chasten the upper ranks and reward the lowly in his army. This is why men and lords think that generals are important.

5 "The general raises his drumsticks and beats the drums to order his troops to set forth into danger and meet the enemy in battle. If his troops face the enemy at the sound of the drum, then he will win great achievements and establish his name, but if they do not, then the general will perish and his state will be lost. The difference between survival and death, between peace and danger, rests in a pair of drumsticks. How could one not think that generals are important?

武議 THE UNDERSTANDING OF MARTIAL AFFAIRS

6 "However, I, your humble servant, do not think that it is such a difficult thing to command men into battle and win a victory by adhering to the principles of martial scholarship. In this way, people say: 'Attacking without the support of warships, and defending without establishing protective barricades' refers to a poorly led army.

"If the people are so poorly fed that their sight and hearing start to fail them, this is because the state lacks marketplaces. The marketplaces must be managed. Officers should only buy for the people those goods that can be bought cheaply and sell those for a high price. A man requires one *dou*[19] of grain, and a horse three *dou* of fodder. [If you have enough food] but your men look starved and your horses emaciated, what is the cause? It is a matter of a lack of management of the products of the marketplaces. So if you attempt to administer the realm but do not manage the marketplaces, then there is no way you are capable of battle.

7 "If we are to raise our troops for a long war, such that lice will grow in the men's armor, then they must be commanded effectively. When a hawk is pursuing a sparrow, sometimes the sparrow perishes by flying into the clutches of a hunter, or into someone's home. This is not because the sparrow desires death, but because there is something more fearful behind it.

---

19. One *dou* is a measurement roughly equivalent to two liters.

8 "When Jiang Ziya was 70 years old, he became a butcher in the Shang capital of Zhaoge, and then fished at a ford on the River Meng. His lord no longer heeded his advice, and the people called him a crazed old man. Then he encountered King Wen of Zhou, raised a host of 30,000 men, and in one battle the fate of the realm was settled. If he had not understood martial affairs, then how did they attain this result? For this reason, it is said: 'With a whip and a fine horse, one can cover great distances. With the convergence of worthy officers, one can arrive at the greater Way [Tao].'

9 "When King Wu attacked the Shang tyrant Zhou, his host crossed the Meng ford, his standard in his left hand and ax in his right, with 300 soldiers ready to die and 30,000 soldiers ready to fight. Zhou's ranks were boundless, with the renowned warriors Fei Lian and Wu Lai brandishing axes and halberds, and his armies stretched for 100 li. King Wu won his victory and executed Zhou without pulling people from the markets to fight, and without excessive bloodshed. He had no auspicious omens, for this was simply a result of cultivating human affairs.

10 "Now, even the best generals of our generation rely on the omens to decide when to attack. They look to sacrifices and oracle bones, and watch for auspicious and inauspicious portents, and changes in the stars and weather. They wish to achieve victory and establish their merit, but I consider this conduct to be disastrous. For the general is not constrained by Heaven, nor by Earth, nor by man. Thus war is an instrument that brings disaster, strife is a perversion of virtue, and the general represents

武議 THE UNDERSTANDING OF MARTIAL AFFAIRS

the death of governance by officials, so use them only when there is no alternative.

11 "Heed no constraints from the Heaven above or Earth below, nor from any lord behind you or enemy before you, for an army that is unified as one is as fierce as the wolves and tigers, as relentless as the wind and rain, and strikes as suddenly as thunder and lightning. It is imposing and august, and all in the realm are fearful of it.

12 "A victorious army is like water. Water is a thing of utmost weakness, but because of the way in which it strikes the mountain slope it makes it collapse. The army is no different. It strikes true with its nature concentrated. Now, if your armies are employed according to the principles of warfare, strong as a rhino and keen as the great sword Mo Ye, then none in the realm will be their match in battle.

13 "When Wu Qi attacked Qin, he made camp on uneven fields and laid down [bamboo] shoots to cover himself to ward off the dew and the frost. Why did he do this? It was because he did not consider himself superior to his men. If you would ask a man to die for you, you cannot seek homage from him, and if you would ask a man to exhaust his strength for you, you cannot demand that he grovel before you. Thus, in ancient times the soldiers did not bow, to show that their lord did not impose hardship upon them. From ancient times down to the present, I have never heard of anyone first put hardship upon a man and then ask him to lay down his life or exhaust his strength.

14 "On the day that a general receives his orders, he forgets his clan. When the army is encamped in the fields, he forgets his family. When he sounds the drum to proceed into battle, he forgets himself. When Wu Qi's troops were advancing into battle all around him, his retinue presented his sword to him. To this, Wu Qi said: 'The task of the general is to devote himself entirely to the banners and drums that direct the army, to clear away doubts when approaching difficulties, and to command the soldiers into combat. Taking responsibility for a single blade is not the task of the general.'

15 "When your armies march and complete one stage, the next day have them complete three stages. Marching more than three stages in one day is like rushing to the source of a river. When you see the enemy in front of you, make use of their advantages. If they fight in white, then whiten the armor of your troops with chalk, and if they fight in red, then redden the armor of your troops with ocher.

16 "Before Wu Qi met Qin in battle, one of his soldiers was overcome by his valor and set out on his own accord, returning with the heads of two enemies. Wu Qi ordered that he be beheaded. Again and again his commanders said to him: 'These are the deeds of a talented soldier, you cannot execute him!' To this, Wu Qi replied: 'He is a talented soldier, but I did not order this.' He then executed the soldier."

將理
PRINCIPLES OF THE GENERAL

1 "Generals are officers of patterns [of the law] and must rule over 10,000 affairs. This must not be the realm of one man alone. When 10,000 affairs arise, since this is not the domain of one man alone, the general is able to govern them all. When 10,000 affairs arise, he can command them all.

2 "The ruler does not arrest a criminal more than five paces away. Although they may fire hooked missiles at him, the ruler will not chase them. This is because the ruler is good at examining the criminal's nature. Without relying on punishment canes, he can still understand the criminal's situation.

3 "If you flog a man's back, brand his ribs, or bind his fingers to question him on his criminality, even an officer of the state would be unable to endure the pain and would falsely accuse himself.

4 "The current generation say: 'Those with 1,000 pieces of gold will not die, while those with 100 pieces will not be punished.' If you try to adhere to my techniques, then even someone as wise as Yao or Shun could not dismiss your charges. Even those with 10,000 pieces of gold could not use a single coin to escape your sanctions.

5 "Now, those awaiting their sentence number no fewer than several tens in the smallest jails, no fewer than several hundreds in the medium jails and no fewer than several thousands in the largest. When 10 men draw 100 [into their affairs], when 100 draw 1,000, and when 1,000 draw 10,000, those they draw together are relatives, brothers, spouses, and old friends who know them well. Thus the farmers are not bound to their fields, traders are not bound to their stores, and officials are not bound to their positions. These criminal acts will drag all the good people drawn together in this way to the bottom.

"The *Art of War* says: 'When an army of 10,000 is dispatched, the daily cost is 1,000 pieces of gold.' Now we have 100,000 good people united in jail, but the ruler cannot remedy the situation. I consider this to be a risk."

原官
THE SOURCES OF OFFICIALDOM

1 "Officials manage affairs and act as the foundation of order. The laws divide the people into the four groups[19] central to dispensing order. The noble, the high-ranking, the rich, and the well-salaried must be named appropriately, since they embody respect and modesty.

2 "Rewarding the good, punishing the bad, and correcting the laws are the tools for organizing and stratifying the people. Sharing out wells and land [equally] and regulating the levies are the measures for taking and giving. Leading artisans [prepare the laws for] the use of equipment and tools that benefit artisans and laborers. Dividing the land and occupying the crucial locations remove oddities and prevent wanton behavior.

3 "Protecting the laws and examining their limits are the duties of subordinates. The ruler highlights the laws and examines their effects. To draw attention to the responsibilities of the bureaucrats and to order things by their level of significance is the duty of the ruler and his ministers. Making rewards clear and strictly handing out punishments are the techniques for stopping malice. Deciding when paths should be opened and closed, and protecting the Way [Tao] is the essence of government.

---

19. The four groups are the officials, farmers, artisans, and merchants.

4 "When messages from below reach superiors, they must be acknowledged with the utmost intelligence. Knowing how much the state possesses allows one to decide how to use what is left over. Knowing the weakness of others is to embody strength. Knowing the movements of others helps to decide when to be peaceful.

5 "Officials are divided between the civil and martial—only the king is capable of both. The vessels for the rituals are reserved for meetings with the Son of Heaven. The technique for holding proper discussions is to prevent traveling debaters and spies from entering the court.

6 "All the feudal lords have their ritual for paying respects to the Son of Heaven. Generation after generation, rulers and ministers follow the orders of the king. When someone recreates the rites [li][20] or alters the convetional, or acts against the king's celebrated virtue, then the king has every right to attack them. When officials have no affairs to govern, when superiors have no rewards to hand out, when people have no lawsuits, when the state has no commerce, this is the epitome of a king's rule! What I have highlighted and said above should be beaten into the king's ears."

---

20. The li were the forms and rituals of proper behavior that were gradually codified into a system similar to the code of chivalry of medieval Europe. The word originally meant a religious sacrifice but came to encompass all forms of human interaction and social behavior.

治本
THE ROOTS OF GOVERNANCE

1 "What is the Way [Tao] of governing people? I say that without the five crops,[21] you have no way to fill people's stomachs. Without silk and hemp, you have no way to cover people's bodies. Therefore, there is grain to fill bellies and garments to clothe them. Husbands weed and plow in the fields, while wives weave at the loom. If the people concentrate on only one affair, then the storerooms will be plentiful. Men must not carve text or make decorative engravings. Women must not embroider or do decorative sewing.

2 "Wooden utensils leak while metal utensils smell unpleasant. The Sage drinks from the earth and eats from the earth, so he uses clay to make utensils, without any waste in the world. These days, the nature of metal and wood is not seen as cold, since people use them to decorate clothes. The nature of horses and cows is to eat grass and drink water, but people give them legumes and grain. This shows governance that has lost its roots and it would be fitting to establish control.

3 "If husbands go out to the southern fields in spring and summer and if in autumn and winter the wives perfect making textiles, then the people

---

21. This refers to the five main grains in ancient China (millet, soybeans, sesame, barley, and rice).

will not face any difficulties. Right now their short, coarse clothes do not conceal their bodies and the grain husk does not fill their stomachs. Clearly governance has lost its roots.

4 "In ancient times, the land was [known as] neither fertile nor barren; the people were [known as] neither hard working nor idle. How is it that people have lost this [understanding] today? Those who plow do not finish all the fields, while those who weave break their machines daily. How could they not be hungry and cold? Overall, where ancient governance was carried out to the end, current governance falls short.

5 "What I call governance is to stop the people from acting selfishly. When the people are not self-centered, the world is like one family. With no selfish plowing or weaving, everyone will shiver in the cold together and suffer from hunger together. This way, someone with ten children would not be even one bowl of rice short, while someone with one child would not have one bowl of rice too many. If this were so, would there be any clamor from excessive drinking undermining the good people?

6 "When people make each other frivolous, from desirous hearts harm emerges and competition arises to take too much. If license lies in just one man, then the people will selfishly gather rice for their own stores and goods for their own uses. If people violate one prohibition and are arrested to face corporeal punishment, then how are you to act as a ruler of men? Be good at governance, impose laws, and ensure the people have no selfish tendencies. This way, your inferiors will not dare be selfish and nobody will do wrong.

7 "Return to the roots [of governance] and follow these principles and go out to meet the Way [Tao]. Then all hearts will be rid of desire and all competition to take too much will be halted. The prisons will be empty and the fields will brim with grain. The people will be at peace and you can take care of distant affairs. Outside your state, there will be no difficulty in the world and inside there will be no violent or chaotic affairs. This is the epitome of governance.

8 "Nobody knows the limits of the deep blue sky! On which ancient emperor or king should you base your methods? Past generations cannot be reached, while future generations cannot be waited for—so search within yourself.

9 "The Son of Heaven has four characteristics: spiritual enlightenment; the glow of brightness; deep conversation; and having no enemies and no enmity. These are the attributes of the Son of Heaven.

10 "The animals in the fields are not for sacrifice, while unfocused studies do not create a refined scholar. Now, people say: 'One hundred li of the sea cannot satisfy one man's thirst, while a three-foot deep spring is enough to end the thirst of the Three Armies.'

"I say: 'Desire comes from a lack of limits, while evil comes from a lack of prohibitions.'

11 "The superiors transform like spirits and are then in accordance with all things. Their subordinates depend on not taking the people away from their appropriate seasonal work, nor damaging the people's goods. Prohibitions must rely on martial measures to succeed, while rewards must have civil measures to succeed."

戰權
AUTHORITY IN BATTLE

1 "The *Art of War* says: 'If 1,000 men give you authority, 10,000 men will allow you to realize your martial affairs. If you employ your men with authority first, the enemy will not have the strength to meet you. If you employ your men with martial affairs first, the enemy will have no dominance with which to meet you.' Therefore, troops value going first to gain victory. If they succeed in doing this, they will have victory. If they do not succeed in this, they will have no victory. When we go, they come and when they come, we go. Out of defeat comes victory and from victory comes defeat. This is the truth behind the principles of battle.

2 "Refined honesty exists in spiritual enlightenment. The authority of battle lies in the extremities of the Way [Tao]. Those who have something should act as if they are without it, while those lacking something should act as if they have it. In this case, how can the enemy trust [what he sees]?

3 "People still listen to what was passed down by the First Kings since they gave responsibility to the just and removed the deceitful. They preserved their compassion and adaptability, though they were never hesitant to decide on punishments. This is why those who understand the Way [Tao] first plan against defeats that arise from not knowing when to stop. Why is it that one must always advance to achieve success? If you think little of advancing and seek out battle, the enemy will plan to stop you and when you advance, the enemy's control will prove victorious. This is why the *Art of War* says: 'If you seek someone, pursue them. If you see someone, attack them. When the enemy's leaders dare not confront you, weaken them and they are bound to lose their authority.'

4 "Those who snatch the initiative away have no vitality. Those who are fearful cannot be protected. Those who fail have no men. These are all troops without the Way [Tao].

"When you commit to advancing and have no doubts, then pursue them. When you snatch the initiative from the enemy and still seem undefeatable, then press on with the attack. If you have a clear vision and remain high up, overcome them with your dominance. These troops are the pinnacle of the Way [Tao].

5 "Those who are not careful with their words can be neglected, while those who are reckless and vicious without reason can be smashed. When an attack is like gushing water or striking thunder, the Three Armies may end up in chaos. You must bring peace to those in crisis; rid them of all damage and make such decisions with wisdom.

6 "Hold debates in court to rise above the enemy. Debate how to give commands to have more integrity than the enemy. Debate crossing their borders to pierce the enemy's defenses. This way the enemy state can be made to obey without having to do battle."

重刑令
ORDERS FOR SEVERE PUNISHMENTS

1 "When the general has 1,000 men or more and flees from battle, drops his defense, or leaves the battleground and abandons his troops, he is to be known as 'a criminal of the state.' Execute him and ruin his family, have his name expunged from all records, expose his family's graves, flaunt his bones in the market place, and force all his children into public service, regardless of gender.

"If the general has 100 men or more and flees from battle, drops his defense, or leaves the battleground and abandons his troops, he is to be known as 'a criminal of the army.' Execute him and ruin his family, force all his children into public service, regardless of gender. If you incite fear of severe punishments among the people, then they will have little fear of the enemies outside.

2 "In this way, the First Kings began by making their laws and measures clear. Only afterward did they render their punishments severe and ensure their domination was heavy. If punishments are severe, there will be fear within the state. If there is fear within the state, the people will think little of the outside [threats]."

伍制令
ORDERS FOR CONTROLLING PLATOONS

1 "When organizing the army, five men make a squadron where each member [of the squadron] is responsible for each other. Ten men make a *shen* where each member [of the *shen*] is responsible for each other. Fifty men make a platoon where each member [of the platoon] is responsible for each other. One hundred men make a company where each member [of the company] is responsible for each other.

2 "If a member of a squadron disobeys orders and violates prohibitions, and another member exposes such misbehavior, the culprit will avoid execution. If another member knows and does not expose such misbehavior, then the whole squadron faces execution.

"If a member of a *shen* disobeys orders and violates prohibitions, and another member exposes such misbehavior, the culprit will avoid execution. If another member knows and does not expose such misbehavior, then the whole *shen* faces execution.

"If a member of a platoon disobeys orders and violates prohibitions, and another member exposes such misbehavior, the culprit will avoid execution. If another member knows and does not expose such misbehavior, then the whole platoon faces execution.

"If a member of a company disobeys orders and violates prohibitions, and another member exposes such misbehavior, the culprit will avoid execution. If another member knows and does not expose such misbehavior, then the whole company faces execution.

3 "Officers from leaders of the *shen* up to the master generals must be responsible for each other, whether superior or inferior [in rank]. If someone disobeys orders and violates prohibitions, and someone exposes such misbehavior, the culprit will avoid punishment. If someone else knows and does not expose such misbehavior, everyone will be considered guilty of the same crime.

4 "When the *shen* and squadrons link together, when superiors and inferiors connect, there is no malice they cannot find, no crime they cannot expose. Fathers cannot show preferential treatment to sons and older brothers cannot show preferential treatment to younger brothers. If this is the case, how can citizens who live in groups and eat together disobey orders and show preferential treatment to each other?"

分塞令
ORDERS FOR BLOCKING AND DIVIDING LAND

1. "Among the military, the left, right, front, and rear armies all have their portion of ground, surrounded by a square of temporary walls, leaving no way of advancing or communicating. The generals have their portion of land; the commanders have their portion of land; the earls have their portion of land. They all set up camp in entrenched areas and make clear their orders for blocking off land, preventing anyone who is not part of their company from entering. If someone from outside the company enters, then the earl will have them executed. If the earl does not execute him, he will be considered to have committed the same crime.

2. "Along the paths that cross through the army camp, establish governing posts every 20 paces. Count your men and measure the terrain so that each post is visible from the next. Ban civilians and keep the paths clear. If someone does not fall under the tally of a general or official, they must not pass through. Those who gather firewood and hay or raise livestock must form squadrons of five. Those who do not form squadrons must not pass through. If an officer has no banner and the troops are not in squadrons, the guards at the gates must execute them. Anyone who goes beyond the demarcations of their territory should be executed, too. Therefore, if there is nobody within the ranks who disobeys orders or violates prohibitions, then outside there will be no malice that cannot be caught."

束伍令
COMMANDS FOR BINDING THE SQUADRONS

1 "The commands for binding squadrons say: 'Five men make a squadron, all under one banner, which they receive from generals and officers. If you lose a squadron but capture another, things even out. If you gain a squadron and nobody is lost, this should be rewarded. If you lose a squadron and do not gain one, men should be executed and their families ruined.

"If you lose a leader and capture another, things even out. If you capture a leader and do not lose one, reward them. If you lose a leader and do not capture one, men must be executed and their families ruined. Nevertheless, if they return to battle and capture the head of a leader, forgive them any faults.

"If you lose a general and capture another, things even out. If you capture a general and do not lose one, reward this. If you lose a general and do not capture one, the culprit should be tried according to the Law of Abandoning One's Position and Fleeing.

2 "The Law for Executions in Battle says: 'The leader of a *shen* has the authority to execute 10 men. The leader of the earls has the authority to execute the leader of a *shen*. The general of 1,000 men has the authority to execute the leader of 100 men. The general of 10,000 men has the authority to execute the general of 1,000 men. The master generals have the authority to execute the general of 10,000 men. There is nobody the general of the entire army does not have the authority to execute."

經卒令
COMMANDS FOR CONTROLLING THE TROOPS

1 "Those who arrange the troops use organizational commands to divide them into three. The left-hand troops have a gray flag and each individual carries gray arrows. The right-hand troops have a white flag and each individual carries white arrows. The central troops have a yellow flag and each individual carries yellow arrows. The troops are drawn up into five sections: the front row has a gray badge, the second row has a red badge, the third row has a yellow badge, the fourth row has a white badge, the fifth row has a black badge.

2 "The next means by which one controls the troops is to execute those who lose their badge. The front five rows place their badges on their heads; the next five rows place their badges on their necks; the next five rows place their badges on their chests; the next five rows place their badges on their stomachs; and the last five rows place their badges on their waists. In this way, the troops are never without their own commanders, while commanders are never without their own troops. If someone notices a commander without his troops or the troops without their commander but does not investigate; or if someone sees chaos but does nothing to stop it, their crime will be considered as serious as the perpetrator's.

3 "When you march to the drums to meet in battle, those marching at the front will combat any difficulty, while those retreating will be a disgrace to the people. Those who advance past the first five rows and march ahead will be rewarded, while those who retreat behind the last five rows will be executed. As a result, the management of advancing and retreating is the [essential] work of commanders. Thus it is said:

"'If you march forward to the drum like a clap of thunder and move like wind and rain, nobody ahead will dare confront you; nobody behind will dare follow you.'

"These words bring everything in line."

勒卒令
COMMANDS FOR RESTRAINING THE TROOPS

1 "Gongs, drums, bells, and banners—there are uses for all four. When the drums are first beaten, advance. When the drums are beaten again, attack. Use the gong to stop the men. Beat the gong again to make them retreat. Bells send out commands. Raise a flag to the left to make the men turn left and raise a flag to the right to make the men turn right. If the troops are unconventional, then the opposite is true.

2 "Beat the drum once and the left will attack. Beat the drum again and the right will attack. If one beat covers each step, this is the beat for a slow pace. If one beat covers ten steps, this is the beat for a quick pace. If the sound never stops, this is the beat for a charge. The *shang* note provides the general's beat. The *jiao* note provides the commander's beat. A small drum provides the earl's beat. If all three beats are the same, then the generals', commanders', and earls' hearts will be as one. If the troops are unconventional, then the opposite is true.

3 "When the drummer loses his rhythm, he is executed. Those who make a racket will be executed. Those who do not pay attention to the gongs, drums, bells, and flags will be executed.

4 "When teaching 100 men how to do battle, once the teaching is complete, unite them with others to make 1,000 men. When teaching 1,000 men is complete, unite them with others to make 10,000 men. When teaching 10,000 men is complete, unite them to make the Three Armies. Then the masses of the Three Armies can separate and unite. When the teachings of the methods of great battles are complete, test the men with examinations.

5 "In a square formation, they are victorious; in a round formation, they are victorious; in an asymmetrical formation, they are victorious; when facing threatening terrain, they are victorious. When the enemy is along the edge of a mountain, they pursue them. When the enemy is deep below, they pursue them. They seek the enemy like they would seek a lost child, following them without any doubts. This is why they are able to defeat the enemy and control their destiny.

6 "Make decisions early, before the enemy [can react]. If you are not the first to settle on a plan and you are beset with indecision, you will be uncertain as to when you should advance and retreat. When doubts are born, you are doomed to fail. Therefore, conventional troops act first, while unconventional troops value acting second. Whether first or second—this is how they control the enemy. Generations of generals have been unaware of this method. After receiving the command to march ahead, they bravely attacked first. There was nobody who was not defeated.

7 "The armies' actions seem full of doubt but they are not. Their directions seem trustworthy but they are not. Their arrival seems early or late but it is neither. These are the three complications of doing battle."

將令
ORDERS FOR THE GENERAL

1. "When the General of the Army is about to receive his mandate, the ruler must first make plans in the temple, then go to the court to give his orders for battle. The ruler himself hands over the labor ax and the battle ax to the general, saying: 'The left, right, and central armies all have their separate roles. If anyone goes beyond their division and seeks promotion, they must die. The army must not be given a second set of orders. Those who try to give alternate orders will be executed. Anyone who hesitates in following orders will be executed as will anyone who forgets their orders.'

2. "The General of the Army may make an announcement, saying: 'When we prepare to leave the gates to go outside the state, we will assemble in the middle of the day. [Within the camp] we will place a table containing schedules. If anyone arrives late, they will be subject to the law.'

3. "When the General of the Army enters the camp, the men must immediately close the gate and clear the paths. Anyone who dares walk along the paths will be executed; anyone who dares talk too loud will be executed; anyone who does not follow orders will also be executed."

踵軍令
ORDERS FOR THE GUIDING ARMY

1 "What is known as 'the guiding army' [the vanguard] keeps a distance of 100 li from the main army. It arranges a meeting time and place, carrying a three-day supply of food. It marches ahead of the main army and lays out a course for joining the battle. When the order for joining the battle is given, the guiding army is mobilized and feasts its troops[22] to give them the sway of power in battle. This is known as 'speeding into battle.'

2 "The advance armies move ahead of the guiding army. When the order for joining battle is given, they move twice the distance [of the guiding army] away from the main army—about 100 li away from the guiding army. When they arrive at the arranged meeting place, carrying a six-day supply of food, they are ready for battle. They divide the troops and place them where they can inflict the most serious damage. If the battle turns to their advantage, they will chase the fleeing enemy. If the enemy bides its time by standing still, they will rush toward them. If the guiding army encounters anyone [from the advance army] who has turned back, they will execute them. Those called 'the troops of all the generals' contain the four unconventional forces and will be victorious.[23]

---

21. Soldiers were fed lavishly before battle to raise their morale.
22. Scholars believe the last sentence of this paragraph is a fragment, belonging to another part of the text, as it bears little relation to the subject discussed above.

3　"Troops can be made up of *shen* and squadrons, who can separate and unite. They are given roles before battle and given crucial passes, connections, and bridges to defend, whereupon they separate and occupy their station. When the order for joining the battle arises, they immediately assemble. The army is mobilized with a daily ration of food and their equipment is always sufficient. They rise when the order to march is given and those who do not comply are executed.

4　"Assign divisions within the Four Borders. Once the advance army and guiding army have set off marching, the people within the Four Borders have no way of leaving. Those who heed the king's military commands, who have been asked to carry the tally, are honored as officials who follow their role. Officers who advance but do not follow their role are executed. When the command for joining the battle is raised, the officers who follow their roles march ahead and must work together to attend to the battle. For this reason, if you want to wage war, you must first have safety at home."

兵教上
FIRST TEACHINGS FOR THE TROOPS

1　"When teaching the troops, the orders should divide men into encampments and have them assume formations. Those who advance or retreat contrary to their orders should be punished for the crime of violating teachings. Those who have marched ahead should teach those in the front lines. Those who have marched at the rear should teach those at the rear. Those who have marched on the left flank should teach the left flank. Those who have marched on the right flank should teach the right flank. When all five men in a squad have been taught, their leader should be rewarded. If they are not [adequately] taught, they should be punished for the crime of violating teachings. If someone drops to the ground and they themselves tell the squadron, and everyone in the squadron reports this together [to the commander], they will avoid any punishment.

2 "When squadrons assemble into formations, if one person does not advance toward the enemy because they fear death, then their teacher will be punished for the crime of violating the law. A *shen* guards all ten of its own men. If one man is lost and the other nine do not face the extreme risk of death against the enemy, then their teacher will be punished for the crime of violating teachings. From the *shen* up to the subordinate generals, if anybody does not heed the law, then their teacher should be punished for the crime of violating teachings.

3 "In general, to illuminate punishments and forfeits, one must ensure incentives and rewards are correct. All must be in accordance with the Law of Teaching Troops.

4 "Generals vary their flags; troops vary their badges. The right-hand army wears its badge on the right shoulder; the left-hand army wears its badge on the left shoulder; the central army wears its badge on the chest. Take note of

兵教上 FIRST TEACHINGS FOR THE TROOPS

their badges, saying: 'A certain armed soldier' and 'a certain officer.' Working from front to rear, for each [platoon of] five rows, you will see the most respected badges are placed on the head and those of lesser esteem are placed below.

5 "When a squadron leader teaches his four men, he uses a panel as a drum, pottery as a gong, and a pole as a flag. If he beats with vigor, the men advance; if he lowers the flag, the men rush ahead; if he hits the gong, the men retreat. When he points the flag left, they should go left, and when he points the flag right, they should go right. When the gong and drum are hit together, then all the men should sit.

6 "When the squadron leader's teachings are complete, they should unite with another squad under a *shen* leader. When the *shen* leader's teachings are complete, they should unite with another squad under a platoon leader. When the platoon leader's teachings are complete, they should unite under a company leader. When a company leader's teachings are complete, they should unite under an army supervisor. When the army supervisor's teachings are complete, they should unite under a subordinate general. When the subordinate general's teachings are complete, they should unite under a major general. When the major general has taught them, they should set up a formation in the fields.

"The major general sets up three large markers every 300 paces. As soon

283

as the formations leave the markers, they first walk 100 paces, then march 100 paces, and finally charge 100 paces. They practice waging war so they can fulfill their duties [as soldiers], after which rewards and sanctions can be applied.

7 "From the supervising official down, all officials have a flag. When you are victorious in battle and capture a flag, observe the rank of every flag that has been captured. This will enlighten the mind as to how to distribute rewards and incentives.

8 "Victory in battle lies in establishing domination. Establishing domination lies in [having] the strength to massacre. The strength to massacre lies in the correct application of sanctions. Correctly applying sanctions determines [the process of handing out] rewards.

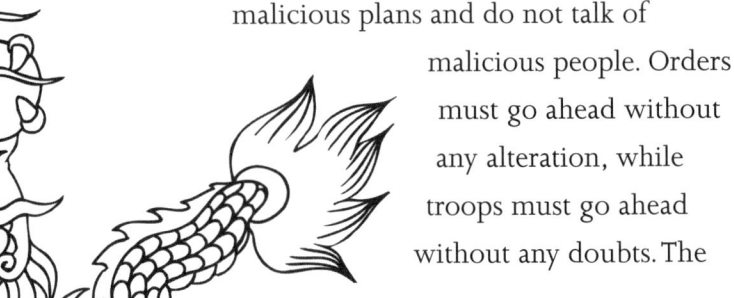

9 "To induce the people to leave the gates of the state and choose between life and death, teach them to have no doubts about death. This gives them purpose. Those who command defenses must be robust. Those who do battle must be willing to persevere. Do not make malicious plans and do not talk of malicious people. Orders must go ahead without any alteration, while troops must go ahead without any doubts. The light troops should be like lightning, shocking the enemy as they advance. Lift up those of merit and distinguish the virtuous as clearly as black and white. Have the people obey orders from above, just as the four limbs on a body react to the mind.

10 "With the main army, separate the enemy's marching men and bring chaos to their formation, smashing their rigidity and forcing it to collapse. This gives them purpose. This is known as teaching the troops. Such teachings allow one to open sealed borders, defend the altars to the gods, eradicate suffering and harm, and realize martial virtue."

兵教下
SECOND TEACHINGS FOR THE TROOPS

1 "I have heard that the ruler of men must be certain in the Way [Tao] of victory. Thus he is able to unite the people and expand [his realm] to make his controls and measures one, whereupon his domination can spread to All under Heaven. There are 12 essential matters:

2 "The first is called 'connecting punishments.' This refers to the shared burden for crimes that protects a squadron.

"The second is called 'prohibitions of terrain.' This refers to banning civilians from walking down restricted paths.

"The third is called 'completing the chariots.' This refers to armored troops and heads of units being dependent on each other, strengthening them through their links.

"The fourth is called 'opening and obstructing.' This refers to dividing up the terrain to highlight the boundaries, so that each man dies in his [correct] position and remains rigid in defense.

"The fifth is called 'dividing limits.' This refers to the left and right imposing prohibitions on each other. This way, the front and rear attend to each other, with a wall of chariots acting as a robust barrier when attacking and defending against the enemy.

"The sixth is called 'distinguishing calls.' This refers to the front rows being committed to advancing. This separates them from the back rows who do not go beyond their stations.

"The seventh is called 'the five badges.' This refers to distinguishing the rows and ranks, so that to begin with the troops are not chaotic.

"The eighth is called 'completing all the parts.' This refers to all the units coming apart one after another, so that each returns to its assigned position.

"The ninth is called 'the gong and drum.' This refers to inciting the meritorious and leading them to virtue.

"The tenth is called 'organizing the chariots.' This refers to ringing the divisions together, placing the spears at the front, and blindfolding the horses.

"The eleventh is called 'officers of death.' This refers to choosing those with talent and wisdom from among the masses of the army to ride on battle chariots. They roam ahead and behind, from side to side, employing unconventional methods to control the enemy.

兵教下 SECOND TEACHINGS FOR THE TROOPS

"The twelfth is called 'troops of strength.' This refers to controlling the flags and securing all the units. If the flags do not sway, nobody moves.

3 "When the teachings of these 12 matters are complete, those who violate orders will not be forgiven. If the troops are weakened, the [teachings] can make them strong. If the master is not esteemed, the [teachings] can make him respected. If the orders are weakened, the [teachings] can reinstate them. If the people leave in floods, the [teachings] can provide enticements for them to return. If there are masses of people, the [teachings] can govern them. If the territory is large, [the teachings] can defend it. This way, even before the chariots leave the city gates and the assembled armor leaves storage, All under Heaven will submit to your domination.

4 "Soldiers must attend to these things: They must forget their homes for the general; they must forget their relatives when they step over the borders; they must forget themselves when they point to the enemy. If they accept the inevitability of death then they will live. To pursue victory with haste is a lowly practice.

5 "One hundred men willing to face the sword can slip through the ranks of the enemy and create chaos among their formations. One thousand men willing to face the sword can capture the enemy and kill their general. Ten thousand men willing to face the sword can march across the world.

6 "King Wu said to Tao Gong Wang: 'Briefly, explain to me all the crucial aspects of employing men.' Wang replied, saying: 'Rewards are like mountains, while sanctions are like gorges. The ruler makes no mistakes and his subordinates smooth out any errors, making men unable to act selfishly. Anyone about to be sanctioned, who asks not to be, ought to die, while anyone about to be rewarded, who asks not to be, ought to die. To attack a state, you must take advantage of its changes. Show it your wealth to observe its poverty. Show it your weakness to observe its sickness. If the rulers are perverse and the inferiors distant [from the rulers' hearts], this is a reason to attack.

7 "When inciting the army, you must inspect the balance of authority between the domestic and the foreign. Plan whether or not to leave for a campaign accordingly. See whether the troops are prepared or lacking and whether they have an excess of food or not enough. Compare the routes for leaving and entering, after which you can raise the troops and attack until chaos ensues. Only then can you cross the borders of the enemy with certainty.

8 "If the territory is large but the cities are small, you must first take their land. If the cities are large but the land is narrow, you must first attack the city walls. If the land is expansive but the people few, then seize their strategic passes. If the land is narrow and the people come in masses, then build great mounds to watch over them. Do not harm their profits and do not upset their seasons. Be open with their government and regulate their occupations. If you save them from ruin, you can apply such methods all over the world.

9 "Today, the Warring States launch great attacks on the virtuous and fight amongst each other. From the smallest squadron to the largest army, there is no unified command. Such a situation makes the common people uneasy and they become arrogant and outlandish. Thus one's plans are harmed and disputes are set off, which officials must investigate. These are the problems that result in defeat. Even after dusk, the roads stretch far ahead, and when troops return, their vitality has been quelled. The troops are aged and the generals are greedy. Those who fight to plunder goods are easily defeated.

10 "When the general is unassertive and the fortifications are low-lying, and the masses unsteady, one can be attacked. If the general is assertive, the fortifications stand tall, and the masses are fearful, one can be surrounded. When encircling a force, make them believe they have a minor advantage [to encourage them to commit their forces] which will gradually render them weaker. If so, the victims will be forced to ration so much that each individual will be unable to eat enough. When the masses fight in the night, they will be greatly alarmed; while if the masses avoid their duties, they will become disheartened. If they wait for men to save them and if during battle they are distressed, they will all lose heart and their vitality will diminish. Diminished vitality defeats armies, while disordered plans defeat states."

兵令上
FIRST ORDERS FOR THE TROOPS

1 "Troops are dangerous tools and competition is contrary to virtue. Affairs must have deep roots. When the king attacks with violence and chaos, its roots are humanity and righteousness. If states are at war, they establish their dominance, resist the enemy, and scheme against one another. They cannot waste their troops.

2 "The troops take martial pursuits as their trunk, while civil pursuits are the seeds. The martial is displayed outside, while the civil is wrapped within. Those who can perceive these two will understand victory and defeat. The civil is used to distinguish the good from the bad, to discern safety from peril. The martial is used to violate and overpower the enemy, to attack and defend with strength.

3 "Focus on one thing and you will win, disperse too widely and you will lose. If formations are kept tight, you will be robust. If the spearhead of the formation is spread out, you can reach your goals. If the troops fear the general more than the enemy, they will win. If they fear the enemy more than the general, they will lose. The comparison of the general with the enemy is used to understand victory and defeat. The enemy and the general are as weights in the balance. If the troops are quiet, they are governable. If the troops are violent and rash, they are chaotic.

兵令上 FIRST ORDERS FOR THE TROOPS

4 "When arranging troops into formation, the army has conventional orders. To line up the squadrons and spread them in numbers is a conventional method. It is appropriate and fitting to line them up one behind the other. Conventional orders are not employed when chasing a fleeing enemy or ambushing a capital city. If rows are not ordered one behind the other, the army will lose. Create chaos first and break them afterward.

5 "Conventional formations face toward the enemy. Some face in, some face out, some formations are standing, some are sitting. Inward-facing formations focus on the center, while outward-facing formations prepare for outside threats. Standing formations are used to advance, while sitting formations are used to defend. Mixed standing and sitting formations cater to both advancing and defending, with the general in the middle. Sitting troops have swords and axes, while standing troops have halberds and crossbows, while the general still occupies the middle.

6 "Those who are good at defending against the enemy first use conventional troops to fight, and unconventional troops afterward. This is the technique for certain victory. Set out the labor and battle axes and display the flags and badges. Those with merit must receive rewards, while those who violate orders must die. Loss and survival, life and death—all depends on the end of a drumstick.

7 "When the arrows are still to be fired and the long blades are yet to connect, those who first make a clamor are known as empty, while those who make a clamor last are known as substantial. Those who make no noise are known as secretive. Emptiness and substance are the embodiment of the troops."

兵令下
SECOND ORDERS FOR THE TROOPS

1 "All of those who leave the main army to prepare advance defenses should establish rows of observation posts every three to five li along the state's border. When you hear that the main army are preparing for battle, begin making plans for defense, and ban everyone from traveling to maintain peace at home.

2 "When domestic troops leave for the garrison, order the commanding general to distribute flags, drums, halberds, and armor. When the troops are dispatched for the borders, anyone who arrives after the commanding general will be subject to the Law for Taking Position Late. All soldiers must serve in a border garrison for one year. Anyone who leaves prior to the new generation of troops arriving will be subject to the Law for Deserting the Army. Any parents, spouses, or children who know of such behavior will be considered guilty of the same crime. If they did not know, pardon them.

3 "If troops arrive at the camp of the head general a day later than their commanding general, their parents, spouses, and children will all share full

兵令下 SECOND ORDERS FOR THE TROOPS

responsibility for this crime. If a soldier escapes home for a single day and his parents, spouse, or children do not arrest, seize, or report him, or if they say nothing, they will share full responsibility for his crime.

4. "If during battle a commander general is lost, or if he gives up on his troops and flees, have them all beheaded. If a commander general at the front gives up on his troops and flees, a commanding general at the rear must behead him and take over his troops, and he must be rewarded. Those without martial merit must be forced to serve in a [border] garrison for three years.

5. "When the Three Armies are in the heat of a great battle, if the head general dies and the officers are unable to kill more than 500 enemy men, have the subordinate officers beheaded. If the troops close to the head general on the left and right were in a central, defensive formation, have them beheaded. The remaining officers and troops should be lowered in rank, even if they have merit in the army. Those who have no merit should serve in a garrison for three years.

6. "If a squadron loses a man in battle, or a man dies and they do not retrieve his body, the whole squadron must be stripped of all its merits. If they retrieve his corpse, everyone should be absolved of the crime.

7. "The strengths and weaknesses of the army lie in its reputation and substance. Reputation currently rests in officialdom, while substance rests in

the family. Officialdom cannot gain you substance, while family life cannot gain you reputation. When the troops are [first] grouped together to make an army, they have an empty reputation and no substance. On the borders, they will not be strong enough to defend against the enemy; while at home, they will not be enough to defend the state. This is how the army cannot give enough and how the general loses his dominance.

8 "When I talk of a soldier escaping back home, the remaining squadron members and officials should be considered guilty, too, and sanctioned for recording the escapee's rations while taking them for themselves. Then the reputation does not match the substance of the army, as the rations of one are recorded as two. If the interior of the state is empty … how can you avoid calamity?

9 "Today, using the law to stop men from escaping back home and preventing desertion from the army are the primary victories of the army. When the *shen* and squadrons connect in the heat of battle, when troops and officials save one another: these are the secondary victories of the army. When the general can establish his dominance, troops can be bound by controls; calls and commands are clear and faithful; and attack and defense are all achieved: these are the tertiary victories of the army.

10 "I hear that in antiquity, those who were good at employing the troops were prepared to kill half of their own officers and troops. Those below them could kill 30 percent, while the lowest could kill 10 percent. Those who could kill half spread their dominance all over the Four Seas. Those who could kill 30 percent extended their strength to all the feudal lords. Those who could kill 10 percent could enforce their orders on the officers and troops. For this reason it is said:

"'When masses of 1,000,000 do heed orders, they are nothing compared to 10,000 men who persevere in battle. Ten thousand men who persevere in battle are nothing compared to 100 men who charge forward.'

11 "When rewards are like the sun and moon; when trust is like the four seasons; when orders are like the labor and battle axes; when laws are like the *ganjiang* sword,[24] I have never heard of troops and officers that do not heed orders."

---

24. A famous sword forged for the King of Wu during the Spring and Autumn period.

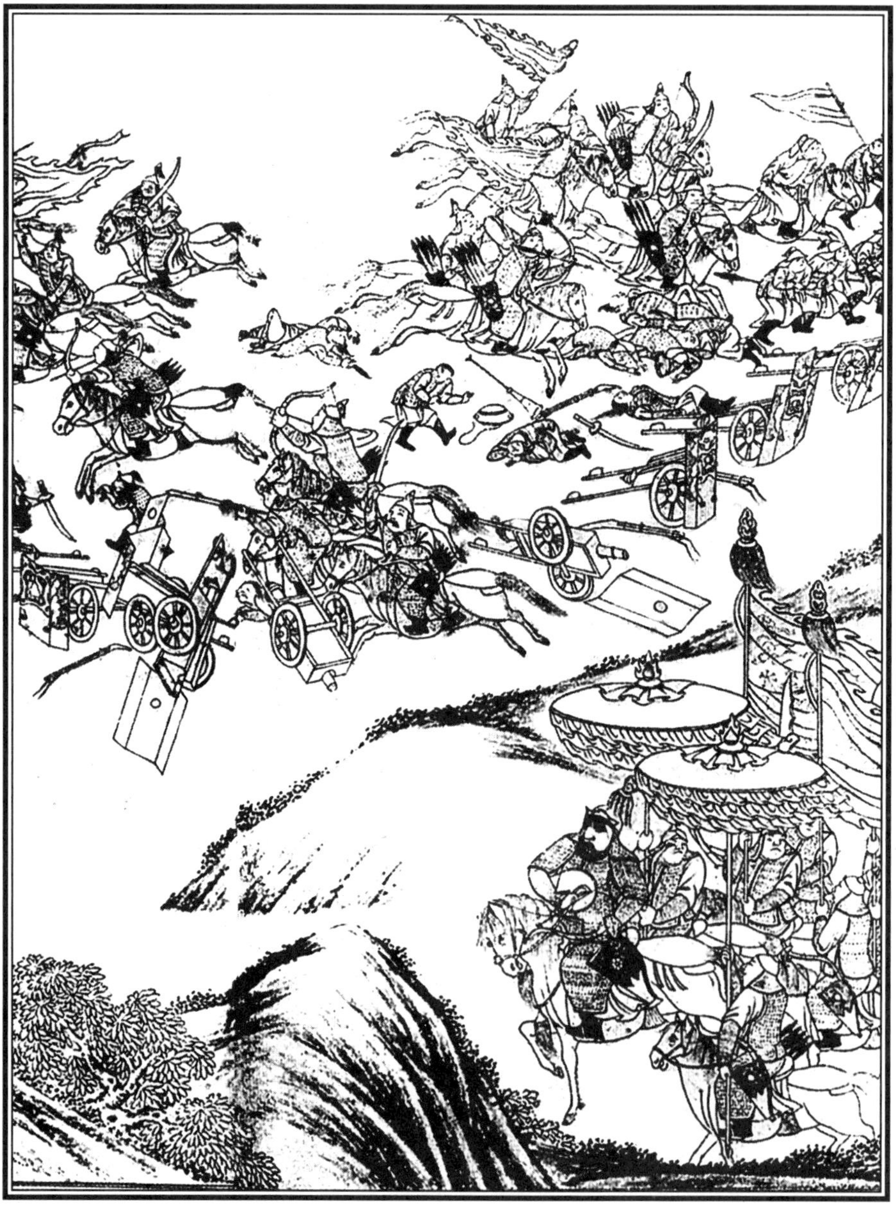

三略
THREE STRATEGIES OF HUANG SHIGONG

Translated by Stefan Harvey
in association with First Edition Translations Ltd.

上略
UPPER STRATEGIES

1. Regarding the methods of the leading general: He engages with and grasps the mind of the hero; rewards and favors the deserving; and communicates his will to the masses. For this reason, if he keeps the same likes as the masses, there is nothing he cannot achieve. If he holds the same dislikes as the masses, there is nothing he cannot overcome. Governing the state and keeping one's family safe are a question of gaining the people's [trust]. Losing the state and destroying the family are questions of losing the people. All life forms wish to achieve their will.

2. According to the *Military Pronouncements*: "The supple can control the rigid, while the weak can control the strong." Suppleness is virtue. Rigidity is villainy. The people will provide aid to the weak while they will resent the strong. Suppleness has its time to be used, rigidity has its time to be implemented, weakness has its time to be deployed, and strength has its time to be increased. Use all four together and control their interactions.

3. When the beginning and the end cannot be seen, then no one can know them. The enlightened spirits of Heaven and Earth change and shift in accordance

with all things. Change your movements and be inconsistent, rotate and transform in response to the enemy. Do not conduct affairs first—allow the enemy to move and then react. Thus one can draw plans that are limitless in what they can control, by propping up and sustaining the authority of Heaven. This brings peace and justice to the eight extremities[25] and contains and gives order to the Nine Barbarians.[26] Those who plan in this way can act as teacher to emperor or king.

4 For this reason, it is said: "There is nobody who does not covet strength but few who can maintain what is subtle." If someone can preserve what is subtle, then he can protect his life. The Sage preserves it in order to respond to all possibilities. If they unfold it, [subtlety] will pervade the Four Seas. If they roll it up, it will not even fill a cup. If they dwell in it, it cannot be used as a home. If they guard it, it cannot be used as city walls. They store it deep in their heart and the enemy states will submit.

5 The *Military Pronouncements* say: "When capable of both suppleness and rigidity, one's state will shine with glory. When capable of both weakness and strength, one's state will be outstanding. When purely supple and purely weak, one's state will certainly be pared away. When purely rigid and purely strong, one's state will certainly perish."

6 Regarding the Way [Tao] of governing the state, you must rely on the

---

25. "The Eight Extremities (八極)" refer to the remotest parts of the world or the "ends of the earth."
26. The Nine Barbarians are the nine outsider tribes listed in the *History of the Later Han* (後漢書).

Worthies and the people. If trust and virtue are like the stomach and the heart and the people are like the four limbs, then one's policies will have no obstacles. If one's objectives are like the limbs and body, as the bones and joints follow each other, then this is the natural Way [Tao] of Heaven and its skill is unbroken.

7 The core of the military and the state lies in observing the hearts of the masses, and carrying out the 100 services [of government].

Those who are threatened must be kept safe. Those who are fearful must be made happy. Those who rebel must be brought back. Those who have grievances must be indulged. Those who have cases lodged against them must be investigated. Those of inferior rank must be valued. Those who are strong must be restrained. Those who are enemies must be attacked. Those who are greedy must be enriched. Those with desires must be employed. Those who are fearful must be hidden away. Those who devise plans must be kept close. Those who make slanderous remarks must be overturned. Those who are scornful must be responded to. Those who turn against you must be got rid of. Those who act favorably must be subdued. Those who are full of themselves must be kept in check. Those who return home to the state must be summoned. Those who submit must be allowed to live. Those who surrender must be released.

If you obtain a strategic position, defend it. If you are in a narrow pass, block it. If you face difficult [terrain], then establish a military post. If you seize a city, divide it up. If you seize a territory, split it apart. If you seize materials, disperse them.

If the enemy moves, spy on them. If the enemy is close, prepare for them. If the enemy is strong, be deferential [to make them arrogant]. If the enemy is in seclusion, leave them. If the enemy crosses boundaries [through insults and taunting], wait for them. If the enemy is violent, calm them. If the enemy is unreasonable, treat them with righteousness. If the enemy is harmonious, then lead them by the hand [to your side].

Act in line with the enemy's movements in order to subdue them. Follow their trends in order to break them. Be wild with your words in order for them to make mistakes. Surround them with your net in order to catch them.

When you gain something, do not keep it. When you occupy somewhere, do not set up long-term defenses. When you seize a city, do not stay too long. When you establish a new ruler, do not take anything away. While it is you who performs the acts, it is your officers who gain from it. Through your actions they know where [their] advantage lies. While they act as the dukes, it is you who act as the Son of Heaven. Render the city able to defend itself and command the officers to position themselves.

上略 UPPER STRATEGIES

8 Previous generations were able to respect their ancestors, but few were able to treat their subordinates appropriately. To respect ancestors is also to show intimacy, while to treat subordinates appropriately is to act like a ruler. Those who treat their subordinates appropriately attend to agriculture and sericulture, not disturbing the [people during the vital] seasons.[27] This means keeping taxes and restraints to a minimum, so that they are not lacking in goods. Keep your labor demands limited, then the state will be rich and families will be happy. Only then select officers to direct and look after [the people].

9 Those known as officers are heroes. For this reason, it is said that if you assemble your heroes, then the enemy state will come to an end. Heroes are the trunks of the state, while the common people are the roots. If you obtain the trunks and gather the roots, then the government will not be resented.

10 The essence of employing the troops lies in esteeming ritual [li] and giving out heavy salaries. If you esteem ritual, then knowledgeable officers will come to your service. If you give out heavy salaries, then the officers will approach death with light hearts. This is why when giving salaries to the worthy, do not covet the goods [that you hand out]. When rewarding success, do not take too much time. This way, the strength of subordinates will come together, while the enemy state is pared away.

---

27. Sericulture was the cultivation of silkworms.

As for the Way [Tao] of employing the troops, if you use respect to hand out titles and keen observation to hand out goods, then officers will come of their own accord. If you connect with them through ritual [li] and encourage them through righteousness, then officers will [be willing to] die for the state.

11 The commanders-in-chief must develop the same tastes as the officers and common troops, and thus confront safety and danger together. Only then can the enemy be punished: This is how troops gain absolute victories and enemies completely succumb to your plans. One example of a good commander comes from former times. The general was presented with a case of good wine. He had it poured into the river and allowed it to flow along its course. From the river he drank the wine along with the officers and the troops. One case of wine cannot be tasted amidst the water of a [whole] river. However, the officers of the Three Armies all fought until death since the wine's flavor had reached them personally.

12 The *Military Pronouncements* say: "When the army's wells have not been completed, the general is not to talk of thirst. When the tents have not been set up, the general is not to talk of exhaustion. When the kitchens have not finished cooking, the general is not to talk of hunger. In winter he is not to wear fur; in summer he is not to wave a fan; in rain he is not to unfold an umbrella; this is called the ritual [li] of the general.

"He faces safety with them, he faces danger with them. In this way the masses can be unified but separated, can be employed but exhausted. He uses his kindness to constantly favor them and uses his plans to constantly unite them.

"For this reason it is said: 'To tirelessly cultivate favor through kindness is to seize ten thousand with one.'"

13 The *Military Pronouncements* say: "What the general uses to achieve domination are his calls and orders. What is used in battle to gain complete victory are the armies and government. For officers to approach death with light hearts they must follow the commands they are given. For this reason, the general does not go back on his commands. Rewards and sanctions must be as sure as Heaven and Earth. Only then can the general control the men. When officers and troops follow orders, only then can they cross the borders into other states."

14 The general is the one who unifies the army and has a grasp on the state of affairs. The masses are those who determine victories and defeat the enemy. For this reason, a chaotic general has no means of controlling and protecting the army, while rebellious masses cannot be made to attack other peoples. If such an army attacks a city, it will not take it. If they surround a city, it will not collapse. If these two are unsuccessful, then the officers' strength will be exhausted. If the officers' strength is exhausted, then the general is left alone with disloyal masses. No defense will be secure and any battle will see them flee—this is what is called an old army.

If an army is old, then the general's domination will have no effect. If the general has no domination, then the officers and troops will take [the threat of] punishment lightly. If they take punishment lightly, then the army will lose its squadrons. If the army loses its squadrons, then the officers and troops will flee. If the officers and troops flee, then the enemy will seize this advantage. If the enemy seizes this advantage, then the army will face certain destruction.

15 The *Military Pronouncements* say: "When a skilled general commands his army, he governs them as he would himself. He extends his favor and employs kindness, which allows the troops to renew their strength daily. In battle they go forth like the wind; when attacking they are like an open river. In this way the masses can be seen from afar but cannot be matched; they can be submitted to but not defeated. If you lead the men yourself, then the troops will be the mightiest under Heaven."

The *Military Pronouncements* say: "The military displays rewards overtly and keeps punishments internal. If rewards and punishments are clear, then the general's domination will take effect. If the correct officials are obtained, then the officers and troops will serve [obediently]. If those with responsibilities are worthy, then the enemy state will be fearful."

上略 UPPER STRATEGIES

16 The Military Pronouncements say: "Wherever the worthy go, they have no enemies before them." For this reason, the officers can be submitted to but cannot be boastful. Generals can be happy but cannot be anxious. Plans can be thorough but cannot be doubted. If officers are boastful, then their subordinates will not follow. If generals are anxious, then their aides and subordinates[28] will not trust each other. If plans are doubted, then the enemy state will rise up. If they use this opportunity to attack, it will result in chaos. The general is the commander of the state. If the general can produce a victory, the state will be safe and assured.

17 The Military Pronouncements say: "The general should be capable of excellence in government, able to be tranquil, to be peaceful, to be regulated; able to accept criticisms, to listen to disputes, to attract capable men; able to know the mores of the state, to map out the mountains and rivers, to expose risks and difficulties, to control the military and the balance of power."

For this reason it is said: "To know benevolence and virtue, to think of sagacity and enlightenment, to pronounce responsibilities and wages, to talk of the hallways of power and court, to manage prosperity and decline—these are what the general must be apt in.

If the general can think of his officers as thirsty, then they will follow his strategies. If the general refuses all criticisms, then the brave and valiant will disperse. If his strategies are not followed, then the officers will

---

28. The literal translation of 內外 *neiwai* would be interior and exterior, which could refer to domestic and foreign affairs, but in a military context may refer to those closer to the general and those further away in terms of rank.

betray his plans. If good and bad are treated equally, then virtuous vassals will become exhausted. If the general takes charge purely by himself, then the subordinates will accept no blame. If he is corrupt himself, then his subordinates will have little success. If he believes any slander, then the masses will lose heart. If he covets goods, then all treachery will go unchecked. If he is obsessed with women, the officers and troops will act wantonly. If the general has just one of these faults, then the masses will not obey. If he has two, then the army will lack order. If he has three, then his subordinates will abandon him. If he has four, then calamity will extend throughout the entire state.

18 The Military Pronouncements say: "The general's plans should be secret; the officers and masses should be unified; attacking the enemy should be done with speed. If the general's plans are secret, then treacherous minds are shut out. If the officers and masses are unified, then the army's hearts are tied together. If the enemy is attacked with speed, then they will not have time to prepare. If the army has all three of these, others cannot seize their plans. If the general's plans are leaked, then the army cannot control the state of affairs [shih].[29] If outsiders spy on internal affairs, then you cannot control the calamity that will befall you. If a taste for wealth enters the camp, then treacherous masses will come together. If the general has all three of these, the army is bound to fail. If the general does not think things through

---

[29]. The *shih* referred to the combination of morale, weaponry, and the natural environment that was required for the successful exercise of military power.

carefully, then the officers will dismiss his plans. If the general is without courage, then the officers and troops will be afraid. If the general moves haphazardly, the army will carry no weight. If the general passes on his anger to others, then the entire army will be fearful."

19 The *Military Pronouncements* say: "Consideration and bravery, these are what the general emphasizes. Mobility and anger, these are what the general employs. These four are the general's observations and warnings."

20 The *Military Pronouncements* say: "When the military is without supplies, the officers will not come. When the military does not hand out rewards, the officers will not go into battle."

21 The *Military Pronouncements* say: "Under fragrant bait there will certainly be dead fish. Under great rewards there will certainly be courageous commanders." For this reason, ritual [li] is what attracts officers, while rewards are what they die for. If you recruit them through what they are attracted to and show them what they will die for, then those you seek will come. Thus if you use ritual [li] and then later retract it, the officers cannot be controlled. If you use rewards and then later retract them, the officers cannot be commanded. If you tirelessly provide ritual [li] and rewards, then the officers will fight to the death.

22 The *Military Pronouncements* say: "A state about to dispatch its army focuses first on dispersing kindness. A state that attacks and captures [another] focuses first on nourishing the people. To defeat many while using few is a question of kindness. To defeat the strong while using the weak is a question of the people. Thus the capable general nourishes his officers as he treats himself. For this reason, if he can command the Three Armies as if they are of the same heart, then his victories can be achieved."

23 The *Military Pronouncements* say: "The crux of employing your troops lies in first examining the enemy's situation. See their granaries and armories, measure their grain and foodstuffs, foretell their strengths and weaknesses, examine their field of activity, carefully watch out for their gaps and cracks." In this way if a state does not have an active military, yet it [is transporting] provisions, its [resources] are depleted.

If the people have an emaciated look, then they are impoverished. If grain is being sent across 1,000 li, the officers will have a hungry appearance. If they have to collect wood and herbs before cooking, then the troops will not spend one night full of food. If one transports food for 1,000 li, that is a year without food; 2,000 li, two years without food; 3,000 li, three years without food. This is called the state being depleted.

If the state is depleted, then the people are impoverished: if the people are impoverished, then superiors and subordinates are not on close terms. When the enemy attacks from outside and people steal from within, this is called "certain collapse (of the state)."

24 The *Military Pronouncements* say: "If the superiors conduct themselves ruthlessly, then the subordinates will soon be disapproving. When taxes are heavy, restraints are numerous, punishments and sanctions have no limit, and when the people harm and commit crimes against one another, this is called 'losing the state.'"

25 The *Military Pronouncements* say: "When officials are covetous on the inside but honest and clean on the outside, dissembling and sycophancy can [improve one's] status. When bureaucrats steal from the public for largess, the distinction between superiors and subordinates becomes unclear. When individuals adorn themselves with an upright appearance so as to gain high office, these are called 'the roots of robbery.'"

26 The *Military Pronouncements* say: "When groups of officials form cliques, each working with those they are close to; when the state hires and promotes the crooked and treacherous, restraining and oppressing the humane and worthy; when the public is left behind and private interests take priority; when those of equal rank ridicule one another, this is called 'the source of chaos.'"

27 The *Military Pronouncements* say: "When a strong clan is treacherous, when people with no rank are respected, when they are dominant but not majestic, these vines intertwine and grow to give the appearance of virtue through their largess. These people seize the balance of power from those of high rank; they encroach upon and humiliate the people below them.

When there is clamor and deceit in the state and vassals shelter from unfaithfulness, these are called 'the roots of chaos.'"

28 The Military Pronouncements say: "When generation after generation carries out evil, they encroach upon and steal county offices. When advancing or retreating they seek only what is convenient for them, and produce crooked and roundabout documents to endanger their rulers, this is called the treachery of the state."

29 The Military Pronouncements say: "When there are many officials but few common people, the respected and the lowly appear the same, while the strong and weak hold contempt for each other. When nobody follows prohibitions or laws, this extends to rulers and the state will take the blame."

30 The Military Pronouncements say: "When the good are regarded as good but do not advance; when the bad are regarded as bad but are not dismissed; when the worthy are hidden and concealed, while the degenerate hold positions of rank, the state will be harmed."

31 The Military Pronouncements say: "When the branches and leaves [the great families] are strong and large; when they form social circles, occupying the positions of authority, so that the base and lowly overstep the nobles; when they gain more and more [power] over time and the ruler dare not get rid of them, the state will fail."

上略 UPPER STRATEGIES

32 The *Military Pronouncements* say: "When sycophantic officials are at the top, the whole army will be quarrelsome. They will rely on their domination to hand out favors and their moves will offend the masses. Without advancement or dismissal on the basis of merit, they will try to ingratiate themselves with those who matter. They focus on serving themselves and brag of their achievements after every action. They slander and defame those brimming with virtue and falsely accuse the good. People may be good or bad, but they are all treated the same by these sycophantic officials. They delay [government] affairs so that commands and orders are not circulated. They fashion a harsh government, changing the governance of old and diverging from tradition. When rulers employ sycophants, they are bound to meet with disaster and calamity."

33 The *Military Pronouncements* say: "When treachery and bravery are given the same labels, this obstructs and conceals the enlightenment of the ruler. When defamation and praise emerge side by side, this limits and conceals the intelligence of the ruler. When everyone is partial to those they favor, the commanding ruler loses loyalty. For this reason, the ruler examines unusual speech so that he may observe the very beginnings [of these issues]. When the ruler hires scholars of virtue, the treacherous yet valiant can then be avoided. When the ruler gives responsibility to experienced hands, the 10,000 affairs will be conducted in an orderly manner. When the ruler hires recluses and hidden scholars, officers will then realize their goals. If plans extend to the timber carriers, then success will continue to be realized. If you do not lose the people's hearts, then virtue will permeate (the state)."

中略
MIDDLE STRATEGIES

1 The Three Great Sovereigns[30] never uttered a word but their transformations flowed through the Four Seas. This is why the world had no way of finding the source of these achievements. The emperors embodied Heaven and followed the example of Earth. Through their words and commands they brought great peace to the world. When the rulers were successful and ministers were deferential, the transformations of the Four Seas proceeded unheeded, while the common people remained unaware, believing the situation to be the natural manner of things. For this reason, they did not rely on ritual [li] and rewards when using their ministers. They enjoyed the beauty of success without harm.

The kings controlled the people by means of the Way [Tao], making their hearts compliant and their will subservient. They established measures so as to prepare for any decline in strength. Everyone within the Four Seas came together and the king's appointments did not go to waste. Although they had prepared armored troops, they did not experience the troubles of warfare. Rulers had no

---

30. The Three Great Sovereigns (三皇 *sanhuang*) are three great gods and/or emperors from distant antiquity. Who exactly they are is a topic of discussion in itself. For example, the *Gu Hanyu Da Cidian* (古漢語大詞典) gives six possible explanations of whom the three individuals might be.

doubts about their ministers, while ministers had no doubts about their rulers. This allowed the state to ensure the safety of the people. Ministers could resign with righteousness and beauty could prevail without harm.

The hegemons controlled the officers through authority, bound them together through trust, and restrained them through rewards. If that trust diminished, officers became estranged and if rewards became insufficient, officers would not carry out their orders.

2 The Military Prowess[31] says: "When the army is dispatched and the troops are made to march, all authority lies with the general. If the court presides over issues of advancing or retreating, then success will be hard to achieve."

3 The Military Prowess says: "Command the wise, the brave, the greedy, and the foolish. The wise take pleasure in establishing their successes. The brave are fond of carrying out their will. The grseedy seek to make quick profits. The foolish do not consider their death. Follow their sentiments and make use of them, since this is the subtle authority of the military."

4 The Military Prowess says: "Do not let argumentative officers discuss the strengths of the enemy, as it may puzzle the masses. Do not let the benevolent have control over goods, since they will dispense large amounts and become attached to subordinates."

---

31. Also translated as *The Army's Strategic Power*. This presumably refers to an older Chinese text that has since been lost.

中略 MIDDLE STRATEGIES

5 The *Military Prowess* says: "Prohibit shamans from praying so that they do not divine the army's good or bad luck on behalf of officials and officers."

6 The *Military Prowess* says: "Do not control the righteous officers only with wealth. The righteous do not die for those who are not benevolent. The wise do not make plans for those who are inward-looking and ignorant."

7 The ruler cannot act without virtue; without virtue, the vassals will betray him. He cannot act without domination; without domination, he will lose authority. The ministers cannot act without virtue; without virtue, they will be unable to serve their rulers. They cannot act without domination; without domination the state will be weak. However, excessive domination is self-defeating.

8 In this way, when the Sage King administers the world, he observes the flourishing and decline [of the seasons], measures [human] gain and loss, and creates institutions for all of them. For this reason, all the feudal lords have two armies, the local earls have three, and the Son of Heaven has six. When the world is in chaos, betrayal and revolt are born. When the king's favor is exhausted, then feudal lords make vows to punish and alliances to attack each other.

9 If your virtue is in a similar state to that of your enemy, so that neither side can have sway over the other, you must win the hearts of the noble and valiant. Once you have also become fond and distasteful of the same things as the masses, then you can attack the enemy using the change in the balance of power [shih]. In this way, without plans and strategies, you will have no means of confirming your suspicions or resolving your doubts. Without deceit or surprise, you will have no means of breaking the treacherous or quelling the bandits. Without devious plans, you will have no means of success.

10 The Sages embody Heaven, while worthy people regulate the Earth. Those who are wise take antiquity to be their teacher. This is the reason the *Three Strategies* have been assembled for a generation in decline. The Upper Strategies establish ritual [li] and rewards, distinguish between the treacherous and the valiant, and mark out successes and failures. The Middle Strategies highlight the inconsistencies between virtue and conduct, investigating changes in the balance of power [shih]. The Lower Strategies explain the Way [Tao] and virtue, examining safety and danger, illuminating what can be attributed to violent or to worthy people.

For this reason, if the ruler has a deep understanding of the Upper Strategies, then he can assume an air of worthiness and capture the enemy. If he has a deep understanding of the Middle Strategies, then he can control his generals and unite the masses. If he has a deep understanding of the Lower Strategies, then he can illuminate the sources of abundance and deficiency, understanding the models for governing a state.

11 When the ministers have a deep understanding of the Middle Strategies, they can be completely successful and protect themselves. When birds high up have been killed, fine bows are put away. When enemy states are exterminated, ministers responsible for planning are lost. When we say they are "lost," this does not mean we mourn their bodies. This refers to [the ruler] seizing their domination and ousting their authority. When they are appointed to court, at the highest rank a vassal may obtain, they make evident their successes. They receive the good states in the central regions, rendering their families wealthy; they bring in charming women and rare curios, rendering their hearts happy.

12 When the masses come together as one they cannot be abruptly taken apart. When authority and domination meet as one, they cannot be abruptly shifted. Making the troops turn back and dismissing the military [at the end of the war] are the difference between survival and loss. This is why weakening a general by appointing him to a new position and seizing his power by granting him a state is known as the strategy of a hegemon. For this reason, a hegemon's actions are made up of persuasion and coercion.

13 Those who preserve the gods of soil and grain and who bring together the noble and valiant are in touch with the practices of the Middle Strategies. This is why, when controlling these practices, the ruler must be secretive about them.

下略
LOWER STRATEGIES

1. If you are able to support those who are endangered under Heaven, then you can seize and manage all peace under Heaven as well. If you can remove all anxieties under Heaven, then you can enjoy all the happiness under Heaven too. If you can save all that face calamity under Heaven, then you can seize all the fortune under Heaven too. In this way, when the kindness of the ruler extends to the people, worthy people will come to him. If his kindness extends to the masses of insects in the world, then Sages will come to him. If worthy people come to him, then his state will be strong. If Sages come to him, then all under the sun will be united [under him]. If he makes demands of worthy people by using virtue, then Sages will use the Way [Tao]. If the worthy leave, then the state will be insignificant. If the Sages leave, then the state will be discordant. Insignificance is a step toward danger, while discord is an omen of death.

2. When governed by worthy people, the people submit through giving their bodies. When governed by Sages, people submit by giving their hearts. When people give their bodies,

one can begin by planning. When people give their hearts, one can end by protecting. People give their bodies through ritual [li] and give their hearts through music.

That which is called music[32] does not refer to the sound of instruments, be they stones, bells, strings, or pipes. The music [joy] of the people refers to their family, their customs, their profession, their capital city, their government and commands, and their Way [Tao] and virtue. The ruler who puts this into practice can make music by moderating these [activities], ensuring they do not lose their harmony. For this reason, the virtuous ruler uses music to bring people joy, while the ruler with no virtue only uses music to bring himself joy. Those who bring other people joy will live long and grow old, while those who bring themselves joy will not last long before dying.

3 Those who give up what is nearby to plan for what is far away will toil to no avail. Those who give up what is far away to plan for what is nearby will be relaxed and achieve results. A relaxed government has many loyal vassals, while a laborious government has many resentful people. For this reason, it is said: "Those who work to expand their territory are reckless, while those who work to expand their virtue are strong." Those who can make use of what they have will be safe, while those who covet what other people have

---

32. This whole passage is a wordplay on the character 樂, which means "music" when read as *yue* and "joy; to take pleasure in" when read as *le*. The metaphor of music has been used as an umbrella term for joy. The reader ought to bear in mind that wherever the words "music" or "joy" occur, the same character is being used in the original Chinese.

下略 LOWER STRATEGIES

will be met with harm. A government that harms and destroys builds up peril for later generations. One that forms and enacts policies beyond its limits, although it may be successful, is bound to fail.

4 To indulge oneself while instructing others is to go against the current, while to correct oneself while transforming others is to follow the current. Those who go against [the current] are inviting chaos, while those who follow [the current] are the key to order.

The Way [Tao], virtue, benevolence, righteousness, and ritual [li]—these five things are all one body. The Way [Tao] is the path people tread along; virtue is what people obtain; benevolence is what people move toward; righteousness is what people agree with; ritual [li] is what people embody. People cannot go without any one of them.

In this way, rising early and sleeping soundly at night are the measures of ritual. To denounce criminality and to take revenge are what determine righteousness. To have a compassionate heart is to show one's humaneness. To make gains for yourself and for other people is the path to virtue. To make all people equal and tranquil, ensuring they do not lose their place, this is the transformation of the Way [Tao].

5 That which comes from the ruler and spreads down to the vassals is termed "commands." That which is distributed on bamboo and silk is termed "orders." That which is respected and carried out is termed "governance." When commands are lost, then orders are not carried out. When orders are not carried out, then governance is not established. When governance is not established, then the Way [Tao] is not communicated. When the Way [Tao] is not communicated, then evil vassals are victorious. When evil vassals are victorious, then the ruler's domination is harmed.

6 If you are to welcome Worthies from a thousand li away, the road is far. If you meet the unworthy, the road is near. This is to say that the enlightened ruler gives up what is near and receives from afar. Thus he can enjoy complete success, value his people, and all his subordinates use their utmost strength.

7 If you cast aside one good individual, then the goodness of the masses will decline. If you value one bad individual, then the masses will be imbued with evil. If the good get assistance and the bad receive punishment, then the state will be safe and the goodness of the masses will be maximized. If the masses are doubtful, the state will be uncertain. When the masses are confused, there is no governance over the people. When doubts are turned to certainty and the people returned from confusion, then the state can be safe. If one order is disobeyed, then 100 orders will be neglected. If one bad act is allowed to slip through, then 100 bad acts will come together. In this way if goodness is used with agreeable people and if badness is imposed on the fierce, then orders will be carried though without resentment.

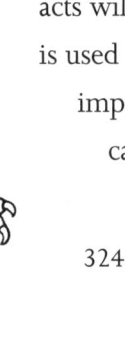

下略 LOWER STRATEGIES

8 Making the resentful govern the resentful is called "betraying Heaven." Making the hateful govern the hateful is a calamity from which one cannot be saved. If you govern the people and make them equal, using purity as a means to reach equality, then they will have their place and all under Heaven will be tranquil.

9 If those who feel enmity toward superiors are respected and if those who covet all things vulgar are rich, even if the ruler is a Sage, he will not be able to impose his control. If those who feel enmity toward superiors are punished and those who covet all things vulgar are imprisoned, then a transformation will take place and all badness among the masses will disappear.

10 Pure and transparent officers cannot be acquired through rank and pay. Temperate and righteous officers cannot be threatened with domination and punishments. For this reason, if the enlightened ruler is to seek the worthy, he must observe what attracts them and reach out to them. To reach out to a pure and honorable officer, the ruler cultivates his ritual [li]. To reach out to temperate and righteous officers, the ruler cultivates his Way [Tao]. If this is done, officers can be reached out to and reputation can be preserved.

11 [Enlightened] Sages and rulers are clear about the sources of abundance and decline, well versed in the roots of success and failure, familiar with the mechanisms of order and chaos [chi], and know the measures used to advance and retreat.

12 Even in difficult times, such people will not take a position in a lost state. Even in poverty, such people will not take salaries from chaotic states in order to eat. They conceal their reputation and hold on to the Way [Tao]; if they move when the time is right, then they will gain the position of an excellent vassal. If virtue unites with the self, then one can establish unique achievements. For this reason, the Way [Tao] of these people is lofty and their name will be spread through later generations.

13 The Sage King does not take pleasure in using his troops. Commands are given to punish the violent and to attack the chaotic. Using righteousness to punish what is not righteous is like having a gushing river and using it to put out a torch, or approaching someone unexpectedly and pushing them down a canyon. Success is certain!

To be carefree and tranquil and not advance [when action is needed] is of great harm to all beings. Weapons are unpromising [instruments]; the Way [Tao] of Heaven detests them. Nevertheless, when it is imperative that the weapons are employed, this is the Way [Tao] of Heaven.

14 People's existence in the Way [Tao] is like a fish's existence in water: If they have water, they live. If they do not, they die. For this reason, the ruler should be in constant fear and dare not lose the Way [Tao].

15 When the elite hold onto office, the state's domination weakens. When issues of life and death lie in the hands of the elite, the state's momentum [shih] will weaken. When the elite bow their heads [to the emperor], then

下略 LOWER STRATEGIES

the state can last a long time. When issues of life or death lie in the hands of the ruler, then the state can be at peace. If the four classes[33] have nothing to use, then the state will have nothing to store. If the four classes have plenty to use, then the state will be secure and contented.

16 When worthy vassals are on the inside, malicious vassals will remain on the outside. When malicious vassals are on the inside, worthy vassals will perish. When the inside and outside are in discord, calamity and chaos will pass down through generations.

17 When great vassals doubt the ruler, then masses of treacherous people will group together. When vassals usurp the respect due to the ruler, superiors and subordinates will be confused. When the ruler assumes the place of the vassals, superiors and subordinates will lose their order.

18 To harm the worthy is to let damage extend through three generations. To conceal the worthy is to bring damage to oneself. To envy the worthy is to leave one's reputation incomplete. To promote the worthy is to have fortune flow down to your sons and grandsons. For this reason, the ruler should be quick to promote the worthy and create for himself an excellent reputation.

---

33. The Four Classes, or Four Occupations, in descending order, were the gentry scholars (士 shi), the peasant farmers (農 nong), craftsmen and artisans (工 gong), and merchants (商 shang).

19 If you help one person while 100 are harmed, the people will leave the city. If you help one person while 10,000 are harmed, the people of the state will then consider dispersing. If you do away with one person while helping 100, the people will admire kindness. If you do away with one person while helping 10,000, the government will not then be in chaos.

宋高宗像

唐太宗李衛公問對
QUESTIONS AND REPLIES BETWEEN EMPEROR TAIZONG OF TANG AND GENERAL LI JING

Translated by Stefan Harvey
in association with First Edition Translations Ltd.

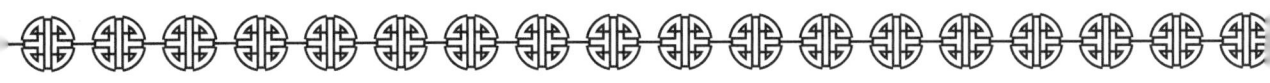

卷上
FIRST SCROLL

Taizong said: "Koguryo has invaded Silla several times.[34] I sent a mission to give them instructions, but they did not heed them. If I am to send a punitive expedition, how should we go about it?"

Li Jing said: "We have found out that Gai Suwen is overconfident regarding his knowledge of the military. He claims the Central Kingdom is unable to carry out punitive expeditions. This is why he goes against your commands. May I request 30,000 troops to take him with force?"

Taizong said: "Our troops would be few and the land (Koguryo) is far away. What method would you use to approach him?"

Li Jing said: "I would use conventional[35] troops."

Taizong said: "When you suppressed the Turks,[36] you used unconventional troops. Now you speak of conventional troops—why is this?"

Li Jing said: "Zhu Geliang[37] captured Meng seven times and never used a different way. He used conventional troops and that was all."

---

34. Koguryo and Silla were states on the Korean peninsula during the Three Kingdoms of Korea (1st century CE—7th century CE).
35. Conventional and unconventional are translated from 正 zheng and 奇 qi respectively. They were first coined in Sunzi's Art Of War as contrasting types of troops and military tactics.
36. "Turks" refers to the Turkic Khanate, which was the main power in the Mongolian Plateau during the Tang. The Khanate established a strong empire covering huge areas of Central Asia.
37. Zhuge Liang was recognized as the most accomplished strategist during the Three Kingdoms era. He was later popularized in the historical novel Romance of the Three Kingdoms (三國演義).

唐太宗李衛公問對 QUESTIONS AND REPLIES BETWEEN EMPEROR TAIZONG OF TANG AND GENERAL LI JING

Taizong said: "When Ma Long plotted against Liangzhou, he too used the 'Eightfold Maze'[38] and built special chariots. If the ground was expansive, he set up camps of deer-horn chariots. If the paths were narrow, he would build wooden huts upon the chariots. This way, men could both do battle and advance. Is it not believable that the people of antiquity prized conventional troops?"

Li Jing said: "When I went on a punitive expedition against the Turks, we traveled thousands of li to the west. Had we not used conventional troops, how would we have gone so far? Special chariots and deer-horn chariots are the crux of the military.[39] On the one hand, they allow us to control how we exhaust our strength. On the other, they provide defense at the front. They also constrain our ranks and squadrons. All three of these functions are carried out in turn. These are the methods Ma Long learned from antiquity."

Taizong said: "When I defeated Song Laosheng, as the ranks collided, our righteous troops retreated a little. I myself led our armored cavalry to speed down from the south to cut off the enemy with a surprise attack. After Laosheng's troops were isolated, they were heavily defeated and I was able to capture him. Were these conventional methods? Or unconventional methods?"

Li Jing said: "By the will of Heaven, your majesty is a Sage of martial affairs, wholly capable [of understanding] even without studying. I have observed and studied the methods of war since the Yellow Emperor and have established that first one must be conventional, then afterward unconventional. First one must be benevolent and

---

38. A plan drawn out by Zhuge Liang depicting his formation for deploying troops.
39. Deer-horn chariots were named for the btlades attached to the front that prevented the enemy from approaching.

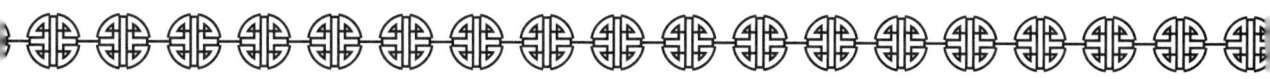

righteous, then afterward flexible and deceitful. At the battle of Huo Yi, that which the troops initiated through righteousness was conventional. When Jian Cheng fell off his horse and the right-hand army retreated a little, this was unconventional."

Taizong said: "That time when they retreated a little almost destroyed our great affairs. How can you call it unconventional?"

Li Jing said: "Generally, when troops advance, it is considered conventional, while retreating is considered unconventional. What's more, if the right-hand army had not retreated, how would we have made Laosheng come forward? *The Art of War* says: 'Tempt them with advantages. Seize them with chaos.' Laosheng knew nothing of the military; he relied on courage and advanced with haste. He did not consider the possibility of being cut off at the rear, or being captured by your majesty. This is called making unconventionality through conventionality."

Taizong said: "When Huo Qubing's actions by chance coincided with [the strategies] of Sunzi and Wuzi, was this truly the case? When our right-hand army retreated, Gaozu[40] went white in the face. Then when I seized [the opportunity] and attacked, it was in fact to my advantage, unintentionally following [the strategies of] Sunzi and Wuzi. My minister [Li Jing] certainly knows the words of such great men."

Taizong said: "In general, when troops retreat, can it always be referred to as unconventional?"

Li Jing said: "It cannot. When the troops retreat and their flags are in disarray and uneven; when large and small beats of the drums do not correspond with each other; when orders are called out in a clamor and have no unity: this is truly a failed retreat, not unconventional military methods.

---

40. Taizong's father.

"If the flags are even and the drums responsive; if calls and orders work as one; when the men are numerous and organized: even if they retreat, they will not fail. This is certainly the use of unconventional methods. The *Art of War* says: 'Do not pursue those who pretend to flee.' It also says: 'When capable, present yourself as incapable.' These are all called unconventional methods."

Taizong said: "During the battle for Huo's capital, the right-hand army retreated a little. Was this due to Heaven? When Laosheng was captured, was this due to men?"

Li Jing said: "If conventional methods had not changed to unconventional and unconventional methods had not changed to conventional, then how would you have been able to win? In this way, those who are good at employing troops use both unconventional and conventional methods with their men, nothing more! As he changes his men, he lends them a spiritual quality, which is attributed to Heaven."

Taizong lowered his head [in acknowledgement].

Taizong said: "Can unconventionality and conventionality be distinguished at all times or are they forged temporarily [during battle]?"

Li Jing said: "Lord Cao's *Hsin shu* [*New Book*] states: 'If for every one man the enemy has, you have two, then have one use conventional techniques and another unconventional techniques. If for every one man the enemy has, you have five, then have three use conventional techniques and two use unconventional techniques,' which states the main strategy. As Sunzi said: 'The state of a battle [*shih*][41] cannot go beyond unconventionality and conventionality, while the changes in unconventionality and conventionality cannot be completely depleted. Unconventionality and conventionality give birth to each other

---

41. The *shih* referred to the combination of morale, weaponry, and the natural environment that were required for the successful exercise of military power.

in a limitless cycle—who could exhaust them?' This is the core of the issue. How could they be distinguishable beforehand?

"If the officer and troops are not accustomed to my methods and the deputies are not familiar with my orders, then we must carry out two techniques. When giving instructions for battle, every soldier must recognize the flags and drums, must disperse and unite in turn. For this reason, [Sunzi] said: 'To disperse and to unite are changes.'

"These are the techniques for giving instructions in battle. When the instructions and inspections are completed and the masses know my methods, only then can they be driven like a flock of sheep, following the direction in which the general points. Who then can make a distinction between unconventional and conventional? What Sunzi calls 'forming other people but being formless oneself' is the epitome of using unconventional and conventional methods. Therefore, to see them as distinguishable beforehand is for [the purpose of] instruction and investigation. When determining changes [at the time of battle] between conventional and unconventional, the changes cannot be overcome or exhausted."

Taizong said: "How deep! How profound! Lord Cao must have known this! But what the *New Book* teaches is aimed only at his generals and no one else. [It does not contain] the fundamental unconventional and conventional methods."

Taizong said: "Lord Cao said: 'Conventional troops attack from the flank.' What do you, minister, say to this?"

Li Jing said: "I remember Lord Cao noted of Sunzi: 'To go out first to do battle is to act conventionally and to go out afterward is to act unconventionally.' This differs from [his discussion about] capturing the enemy by attacking

唐太宗李衛公問對 QUESTIONS AND REPLIES BETWEEN EMPEROR TAIZONG OF TANG AND GENERAL LI JING

from the flank. If I may, I refer to the engagement of the great masses as conventional; and when the general himself advances as unconventional. Where are the constraints when one attacks first or after, or from the side?"

Taizong said: "My own conventionality makes the enemy regard my actions as unconventional; my unconventionality makes the enemy regard my actions as conventional. Is this what is called 'displaying a form?' To be conventional through unconventionality, to be unconventional through conventionality, and to change and transform in enigmatic ways, is this what is called 'having no form?'"

Li Jing bowed twice and said: "Your majesty is a spiritual Sage. You return to [the wisdom of] the ancients, reaching further than I will ever be able to."

Taizong said: "As for those who carry out change through division and unity, where exists their unconventionality and conventionality?"

Li Jing said: "Those who are good at employing troops are not conventional or unconventional. They make the enemy unable to fathom [their actions]. In this way not only the conventional can lead to victory but the unconventional can also lead to victory. The officers of the Three Armies merely know the victory and nothing more—none knows what is actually done to bring it about. Without being able to understand change, how could the generals attain victory? Only Sunzi was able to understand where division and unity come from. Since the time of Wu Qi, nobody has been able to reach such an understanding."

Taizong: "What was Wu Qi's technique like?"

Li Jing said: "Please allow me to briefly outline

it. Marquis Wu of Wei asked Wu Qi about [the strategy to use] when two armies are facing each other. Wu Qi said: 'Make the bravest of the lower ranks attack at the front. When blades begin to clash, have them flee and do not punish them for doing so. Observe the enemy in case they advance into [the trap that had been laid]. If the enemy sit and stand as one, not pursuing those who had fled, then the enemy has sound strategies. If all their troops chased those who flee, some marching, some halting, going in all directions, then the enemy's men have no talent. Attack them without any doubts.' If I may say so, Wu Qi's strategy was generally of this sort—not what Sunzi would call a conventional engagement."

Taizong said: "My minister, your uncle Han Qinhu once said you talk about Sunzi and Wuzi with him. Did you also talk about conventionality and unconventionality?"

Li Jing said: "How could Qinhu know about the epitome of unconventionality and conventionality? He only took the unconventional as unconventional and the conventional as conventional. He never knew about the interchangeability of the unconventional and the conventional—that never-ending cycle."

Taizong said: "In antiquity, people approached enemy formations and sent out unconventional [troops] to attack where people would not expect. Was this the method of interchangeability?"

Li Jing said: "When previous generations struggled in battle, most used little technique to defeat those with no technique. That is to say, those with a hint of excellence defeated those with no excellence at all. How can [these examples] be enough to discuss the methods of war? Just like Xie Xuan's crushing of Fu Jian. It was not to do with Xie Xuan's excellence but rather Fu Jian's lack of excellence."

Taizong ordered the ministers in attendance to seek out the biography of Xie Xuan. After examining it, he said: "Ultimately, was the way Xie Xuan managed affairs not good at all?"

Li Jing said: "I observed that in the records of Fu Jian it says: 'All of Qin's armies had collapsed in defeat, only Mu Rongchui's unit remained. Fu Jian led over 1,000 cavalry to join him. Chui's son Bao urged him to kill Jian but to no avail.'

"From this, we can see that when Qin's troops were in chaos, only Mu Rongchui remained intact. That is to say, Fu Jian was betrayed by Chui. Is it not particularly difficult to defeat the enemy when somebody is so inclined toward treachery? This is why I can say for certain that Fu Jian was one of those without any technique."

Taizong said: "Sunzi says: 'Many plans defeat few plans.' Although there are those who know that few plans still defeat those with no plans. This is so in all cases."

Taizong said: "As for the Yellow Emperor's methods in war, they have been passed down generations through the *Writings on Seizing the Unconventional*, also known as *Writings on Seizing Opportunity*.[42] What might you say about this text?"

Li Jing said: "The pronunciation of 'irregular' is the same as 'opportunity.' This is why someone passed the text down with the title *Opportunity*, though their meaning is the same. If we examine the actual words [of the text], it says: 'Four are conventional, four are unconventional. Everything remaining is for seizing opportunity.' Here, the [character] 'unconventional' means the remainder. Because of this, it is pronounced [the same as] 'opportunity.' May I dare say that the troops are not without opportunity, so how is it that we talk of seizing such things? If we are talking about unconventionality as the remainder, then this is right.

"Conventional troops receive orders from the ruler, while unconventional troops receive orders from the general. *The Art of War* says: 'If one teaches the people through typical moral conduct, then the people will obey.' This is an order received from the ruler. Sunzi also says:

---

42. Also known as *The Classic of Grasping the Unorthodox* and *The Classic of Grasping Subtle Change*.

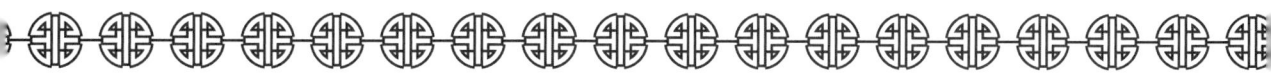

'The [use of the] troops cannot be predicted, since the ruler makes some commands that are not accepted.' This comes from the general. If generals use conventional [tactics] and no unconventional ones, then they are defensive. If they use unconventional [tactics] and no conventional ones, then they are aggressive. If they have both, then they can assist the state. In this way, seizing opportunity and seizing unconventionality are not two fundamentally different methods. Those who study military methods are proficient in both."

Taizong said: "[The *Writings on Seizing Opportunity* says:] 'There are nine formations, with the mass at the heart, which the general commands. The "Four Sides" and "Eight Directions" are all regulated in relation to these formations. Within [the main] formation other formations exist. Within platoons, other platoons exist. Have the front act as the rear and the rear act as the front. When advancing, do not rush ahead. When retreating, do not hurry away. There are four heads and eight tails. Wherever contact is made, this acts as the head [of the army]. If the enemy attacks the center, two heads will come to the rescue. The numbers start at five and end at eight.' What do you have to say about this?"

Li Jing said: "Zhuge Liang laid stones horizontally and vertically to make eight rows. The methods for a square formation rely on this plan. When I used to teach the examination of texts, I of course put this formation first. The *Writings on Seizing Opportunity* passed down by previous generations grasps the rough idea of such formations."

Taizong said: "Heaven, Earth, the wind, clouds, dragons, tigers, birds, and snakes—what do these eight formations mean?"

Li Jing said: "Those who transmitted them made a mistake. The people of antiquity kept such methods secret.

唐太宗李衛公問對 QUESTIONS AND REPLIES BETWEEN EMPEROR TAIZONG OF TANG AND GENERAL LI JING

In this way they slyly established these eight names. The [eight] formations were originally one and then divided into eight. 'Heaven' and 'Earth' originated in banners. 'Wind' and 'clouds' originated in pennant names. 'Dragons,' 'tigers,' 'birds,' and 'snakes' originated in the distinctions of squadrons and platoons. Later generations transmitted them with errors. If they were slyly established, these images of animals, why stop at eight?"

Taizong said: "The numbers begin with five and end with eight, so if they were not established as images, they must be the treasured products of antiquity. Could my minister try to explain them?"

Li Jing said: "I see that the Yellow Emperor began by establishing the methods of 'the well and the household,' with which he controlled his troops. Therefore the 'well' was divided into four paths, on which eight families dwelled. Its shape looked like the character for a well [井], so nine squares were formed by it. Five were used for formations; four were open spaces. This is known as 'beginning with five.' The middle square was left empty for the general to dwell in. The four sides around it connected the various sections of the army. This is known as 'ending with eight.'

"To control the enemy through change and transformation, appear as 'numerous and varied; attack as if chaotic but in fact have an ordered method; be turbulent and surging; take the formation of a circle but do not disperse your momentum [shih].' This is known as 'dispersing and becoming eight, returning, and becoming one again.'"

Taizong said: "How profound! Such was the Yellow Emperor's control of his troops! Although later generations had the knowledge of Heaven and the strategies of spirits, none was able to surpass his ability to do battle. Who best continued his reputation?"

Li Jing said: "When the Zhou dynasty first emerged, Taigong essentially copied his methods. He started at the Qi capital by setting up wells and fields with banks surrounding them, [constructing] 300 chariots, and 300 brave warriors, which he used to establish control of the army. They taught the methods of battle: '[Make] six steps, seven steps; [make] six attacks, seven attacks.' When the soldiers set camp in the herding fields, Taigong had only 100 officers, though he still managed to realize his military success. With 45,000 men, he overcame King Zhou's[43] masses of 700,000.

"In the Zhou dynasty, *The Methods of the Sima* was based upon Taigong. When Taigong passed away, the people [of Qi] inherited his methods. When Lord Huan was hegemon of the world, he made Guan Zhong responsible for managing [the military], who again adopted Taigong's methods. The army was known to be strictly controlled and all the feudal lords were obedient."

Taizong said: "The classical scholars mostly say that Guan Zhong governed as the hegemon's minister and nothing more. They did not know that his methods in war were rooted in the king's authority. Zhuge Liang compared his talent in assisting the king to that of Guan and Yue. Because of this, we know that Guan Zhong also assisted the king. However, when the Zhou was in decline, the king could not employ him. This is why he mobilized the troops of Qi."

Li Jing bowed twice and said: "Your highness is a spiritual Sage, knowing the nature of man so well! Even if I, your old minister, were to die, your highness would have no shame going before the Worthies of antiquity. May I speak about Guan Zhong's methods of controlling Qi?

---

43. Different to the Zhou dynasty mentioned before.

唐太宗李衛公問對 QUESTIONS AND REPLIES BETWEEN EMPEROR TAIZONG OF TANG AND GENERAL LI JING

"He divided the state of Qi into three, so as to create three armies. Five families made a basic unit, so five men made a squadron. Ten units made a hamlet, so 50 men made a platoon. Four hamlets made a village, so 200 men made a company. Ten villages made a town, so 2,000 men made a battalion. Five towns made an army, so 10,000 men made the military. Guan derived his meaning from *The Methods of the Sima*, which says: 'One army is five battalions. One battalion is five companies.' In fact, all his work uses the methods passed down by Taigong."

Taizong said: "As for *The Methods of the Sima*, people say that it was written by Rangju. Is this the case or not?"

Li Jing said: "The biography of Rangju in the *Shiji* has it that during the time of Duke Jing of Qi, Rangju was adept in employing the troops, defeating the soldiers of Yan and Jin. Out of respect, Duke Jing made him Minister of War (*Sima*). From then on he was known as Sima Rangju. His sons and grandsons took the surname Sima too. During the rule of King Wei of Qi, people pursued and discussed the ancient methods of the Minister of War. They also recorded the studies of Rangju. This became *The Book of Sima Rangju*, divided into ten chapters. Furthermore, the knowledge the military specialists have passed down to the current generation is divided into four: 'balance of power and plans', 'form and circumstance,' 'Yin and Yang,' 'skill and craft'—all of which come from *The Methods of the Sima*."

Taizong said: "During the Han, Zhang Liang, and Han Xin [dynasties], they [the rulers] curated the writings on military methods. There were 182 thinkers, but after removing the unworthy and selecting the most important, they were left with 35. Now we seem to have lost what they passed on—why is this?"

Li Jing said: "Zhang Liang studied Taigong's *Six Secret Teachings* and *Three Strategies*. Han Xin studied Rangju and Sunzi. Their main principles do not exceed the Three Gates. There were Four Kinds and that is all."

Taizong said: "What do you mean by the Three Gates?"

Li Jing said: "If I am to refer to the 81 chapters of Taigong's *Plans*, that which is known as the secret strategies cannot be exhausted through words. The 71 chapters of Taigong's *Sayings* cannot be exhausted through battle. The 85 chapters of Taigong's *Warfare* cannot be exhausted through materials. These are the Three Gates."

Taizong said: "What is meant by the Four Kinds?"

Li Jing said: "It is what Ren Hong of the Han discussed. In general, the trends of the military thinkers followed this pattern: 'the balance of power and plans' were one kind, the 'form and circumstance' another, while 'Yin and Yang' and 'skill and craft' were the last two. These are the Four Kinds."

Taizong said: "*The Methods of the Sima* began with the spring and winter hunts—why is this?"

Li Jing said: "To follow the seasons; to show their importance to the spirits; and to highlight the importance of their affairs. These hunts were the most important political affairs, according to the *Zhou Rituals*. King Cheng held the spring hunt on the south side of mount Qi. Kang held court at Feng Palace, while Mu held a gathering at Mount Tu. These are the affairs of the Son of Heaven.

"When the Zhou dynasty was in decline, Huan of Qi gathered the troops at Zhao Ling, while Wen of Jin formed alliances at Jian Tu. These were cases where all the feudal lords carried out the Son of Heaven's affairs. They in fact used the Nine Methods to overpower the unscrupulous. They used the hunt to hold court, and gave instructions during the hunt to train the troops. *The Methods of the Sima* also says that if there are no affairs to attend to, the troops must not be rashly mobilized. However, they must not forget their martial preparations between the farming seasons. In this way, the spring and winter hunt were prioritized. Is this not profound?"

Taizong said: "In the *Spring and Autumn Annals*, the Ruler of Chu's *Methods for Double Fleets of Chariots* says: 'The 100 officials should act according to [the nature of] things. The military and government should be prepared without [needing] instructions.' Does this fit in with the commands of Zhou?"

Li Jing said: "According to Zuo Shi,[44] the Ruler of Chu's fleets [*kuang*] consisted of 30 chariots.[45] Each chariot had a company [of infantry], who would have as many men as chariots.[46] As the army advanced, those to the right of shafts [of chariots] used the shafts to position themselves. Therefore, they stayed close to the shafts during battle. These were the commands of Zhou.

"When I say 100 men, I mean a company [*zu*]; by 50 men I mean a platoon [*liang*]. This is to say, 150 men accompany each chariot. This is far more than Zhou. For every chariot of Zhou, there were 72 foot soldiers and three armored officers. There were 25 foot soldiers under each officer, meaning that there were 75 in total. Zhou is a hilly and marshy state, with few chariots and many people. If the troops were to be divided into three platoons, then they would be arranged the same as Zhou."

Taizong said: "During the Spring and Autumn period, when Xun Wu attacked the Di

---

44. The historian to whom *Spring and Autumn Annals* is attributed. He is often called Zuo Zhuan.
45. A *kuang* (廣) is typically made up of 15 chariots, hence the "double fleets."
46. This phrase is unclear. *Zu* could refer to one commander but could also refer to a company of men. Equally, *pian* and *liang* could refer to 25 chariots and men respectively.

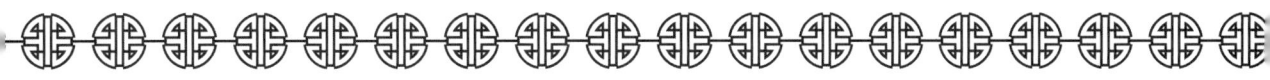

tribe, he abandoned his chariots to arrange his troops in file. Was this conventional or unconventional?"

Li Jing said: "Xun Wu employed his strategy for chariots. Even though he abandoned his chariots, such methods were still among them. One platoon flanked left, one flanked right, and another resisted at the front. Dividing into three platoons is one method for fighting with chariots. Be it 1,000 or 10,000 chariots, the method would be the same. If I might refer to Lord Cao's *New Book*, which says: 'Attacking chariots have 75 men with them. The platoon resisting at the front, and the two platoons flanking left and right. The defending chariot has 10 men to cook, 5 to protect the equipment, 5 to attend to the stables, and 5 to gather wood and draw water—25 in total. One attacking and one defending chariot together have 100 men. If you mobilize 100,000 men, then use 2,000 chariots—1,000 light and 1,000 heavy.' This is a summary of Sun Wu's old methods.

"Having also looked at the period from the Han to the Wei, I noticed that [army regulations stated] five chariots make a platoon, with one representative. Ten chariots make a regiment, with one commander. If you were to have 1,000 chariots, you would have a general and an official. With more chariots, the organization would follow this pattern. If I compare this with our current methods, then our front line is the cavalry. Our attacking troops are made up of the infantry and cavalry, half and half. Our stationed platoons go out together as chariots and men.

"When I went to punish the Turks, we braved several thousand li of terrain. Not once did I dare to alter such methods of organization, since the methods and regulations of old are highly trustworthy."

Taizong granted Ling Zhou an imperial visit. Once he had arrived, Taizong called Li Jing and asked him to be seated, saying: "I commanded Dao Zong, A Shi Na Shi Er, and others on a punitive expedition against Xue Yantuo. Various departments from the Tie

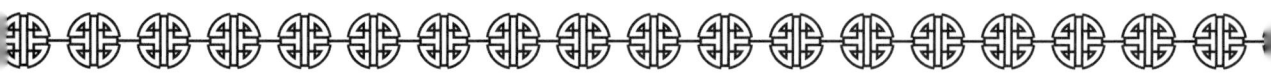

唐太宗李衛公問對 QUESTIONS AND REPLIES BETWEEN EMPEROR TAIZONG OF TANG AND GENERAL LI JING

Lie people pleaded that a Han administration be established and I accepted all of their requests. Yantuo fled west, but I feared there would be more trouble later. This is why I sent Li Ji to further punish him. Currently, everyone in the North is at peace. Still, the various barbarians are interspersed among the Han. What long-term path should one take to make the two live in total peace?"

Li Jing said: "Your highness decreed the installment of 66 observation posts from the Turkic tribe all the way to the Uighurs, so as to connect all the scouts. This [policy] fully implements these measures, though if I may give my foolish opinion, I would say that the Han garrisons should be left to their own methods, as should the barbarian tribes. Since each group's teachings and customs are different, there is no need to mix them into one. If we come across a foe, then we can secretly order the generals to change the military symbols and outfit at the last moment, allowing them attack through unconventional means."

Taizong said: "What kind of way is this?"

Li Jing said: "This technique is called 'deceit through many methods.' If the barbarians present themselves as Han and the Han present themselves as barbarians, the other will not be able to tell whether they are Han or barbarian. In such a case, nobody will be able to surmise our plans for attack and defense. Those who are good at employing troops must above all be impossible to read, so the enemy will be baffled by where the troops are going."

Taizong said: "This is certainly in line with my thoughts. Minister, you may go and secretly teach our generals on the borders that only through these distinctions between barbarian and Han can we distinguish unconventional and conventional methods."

Li Jing bowed twice and said: "Your sagely considerations are threads from Heaven—you sense one thing and understand ten! How could I even articulate it all?"

Taizong said: "Zhuge Liang said: 'Well-ordered troops, even with an incapable general, cannot be defeated. Disorderly troops, even with a capable general, cannot be victorious.' I suspect his words do not reach the levels of finer discussions."

Li Jing said: "This was what the Marquis of Wu said for [the] motivation [of the troops]. Allow me to refer to Sunzi: 'If the Way [Tao] of instruction is unclear, the officials and troops will have no constant routine. The formation of troops will be all over the place—that is to say, they will be chaotic.' One can never properly record all the instances since antiquity in which a chaotic army invited the enemy to victory. As for 'those whose way of instruction is unclear,' Sunzi says their teachings and readings are not those of ancient methods. When the officials and troops have no constant routine, he says that the generals and ministers who hold authority and responsibility will not do so for long. When a chaotic army invites the enemy to victory, he says it is due to one's own collapse and failure—it is not a case of the enemy winning.

"This is why the Marquis of Wu said: 'If the troops are well organized, even an average general will not face defeat. If the troops are chaotic themselves, even a worthy general is at risk.' Is there anything to doubt in this?"

Taizong said: "One cannot overlook the methods of teachings and readings."

Li Jing said: "If instructions accord with the Way [Tao], then the officers are happy to be employed. If instructions do not follow the [correct] methods, even if one examines them by day and upbraids them by night, there will be no benefit. The reason I labored through the ancient ways of organization, compiling them all, was to achieve a well-ordered army ourselves."

唐太宗李衛公問對 QUESTIONS AND REPLIES BETWEEN EMPEROR TAIZONG OF TANG AND GENERAL LI JING

Taizong said: "Please can my minister select the ancient methods of formations and compile them on my behalf."

Taizong said: "Barbarian troops only use their most vigorous horses to charge forward. Is this unconventional warfare? The Han soldiers only use their strongest crossbows to corner the enemy. Is this conventional warfare?"

Li Jing said: "Allow me to refer to Sunzi: 'Those who are good at employing troops seek [victory] by capitalizing on [the strategic] circumstances [*shih*], not by placing a high value on men. Therefore, they are able to select men while benefiting from circumstances.' To 'select men' is to do battle by playing to the strengths of both the barbarians and the Han. The barbarians are adept with horses, and so the cavalry benefit from attacking quickly. The Han are adept with crossbows, and so bows are beneficial in slow warfare. Each group benefits from its own circumstance, though this is not to distinguish between unconventional and conventional warfare. Before, I mentioned how the barbarians and Han must change their signs and uniforms—this is the method by which unconventionality and conventionality give way to one another. Horses also have conventional features, as crossbows have unconventional features. Is there anything that is constant?"

Taizong said: "Can my minister discuss such techniques in more detail?"

Li Jing said: "First take your form, then make the enemy yield to it. Such is the technique."

Taizong said: "I see! Sunzi said: 'The epitome of troops taking form culminates in them having no form.' He also said: 'Follow your form, and you will achieve victory without the masses even realizing how [you brought it about].' This is what he is saying!"

Li Jing bowed twice and said: "How profound! Your majesty considers things with such sagacity. Your thoughts are already halfway there!"

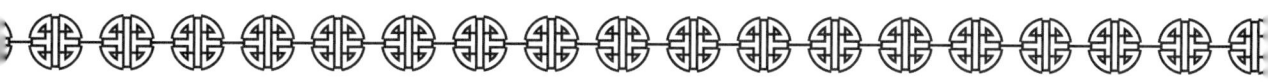

Taizong said: "Recently the Khitan and the Xi have all become subordinates. I have placed the two commanders-in-chief of Song Mo and Rao Le to unite and protect Anbei. I would like to employ Xue Wanche—what do you think?"

Li Jing said: "Wanche is not as good as A'shina She'er or Zhishisi Li and Jibihe Li. They are all barbarian ministers who understand warfare. I once discussed with them the mountains and rivers that lead to Song Mo and Rao Le, about how the nature of barbarians goes against the flow, as well as the tens of tribes far out in the west. These ministers are clear and trustworthy. I taught them the methods of formation and there was not one at which they did not nod their head in recognition of what I meant. I hope your majesty will entrust them with responsibility, free of suspicion. If you choose Wanche, he may be brave but he has no plans. He will struggle to hold responsibilities alone."

Taizong said: "The barbarian men have all served my minister well. The ancients said: 'Using the Man and Di to attack the Man and Di is the central kingdom's strategic advantage.' My minister certainly understands this."

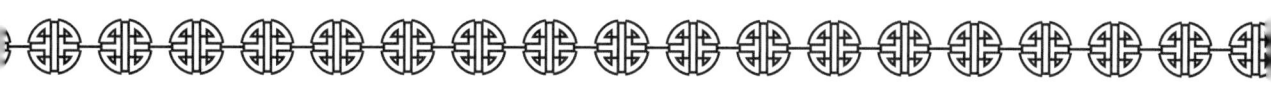

卷中
MIDDLE SCROLL

Taizong said: "I have observed the various books on military strategy and none is better than Sunzi. In all 13 of Sunzi's chapters, none surpasses [the chapter on] the 'empty' and the 'substantial.' When employing troops, if one recognizes the empty and the substantial, there is no instance in which one will not be victorious. All the current generals can only say 'reject the substantial and attack the empty.' When they approach the enemy, few can recognize the empty and the substantial. That is to say, they cannot draw the enemy to them, which is why they are drawn to the enemy. What is to be done? My minister ought to explain to all the generals what is important."

Li Jing said: "First teach them the technique of alternating between unconventional and conventional warfare. Afterward one can explain to them the form of the empty and the substantial. Since many of the generals do not know how to turn unconventionality into conventionality and vice versa, how are they to recognize when the empty is the substantial and the substantial is the empty?"

Taizong said: "Sunzi said: 'Make plans and know how to calculate gain and loss. Take action and know the reasons for moving and staying silent. Arrange your formation and understand where one might die and one might live. Corner the enemy and discern where there is space and where there is not.' If I follow this, will the unconventional and conventional lie with me, while the empty and substantial will lie with the enemy?"

Li Jing said: "The unconventional and conventional are the [means to reveal] the empty and the substantial in the enemy. If the enemy has substance, then one must use

唐太宗李衛公問對 QUESTIONS AND REPLIES BETWEEN EMPEROR TAIZONG OF TANG AND GENERAL LI JING

conventional methods. If the enemy is empty, then one must act unconventionally. If a general cannot distinguish the unconventional from the conventional then, although he knows of the enemy's emptiness and substance, how can he draw them out? I respect your edict, but one must teach the generals to use the unconventional and conventional, after which they themselves will know of the empty and the substantial."

Taizong said: "When using the unconventional to act conventionally, if the enemy senses the unconventional, I will use the conventional to attack. When using the conventional to act unconventionally, if the enemy senses the conventional, I will use the unconventional to attack. I will render the enemy's situational advantage constantly empty and render my own substantial. If you lecture the generals on these methods, they should easily understand."

Li Jing said: "One thousand texts and 10,000 phrases simply cannot surpass the phrase 'draw the man and do not be drawn toward him.' I will certainly use this to teach the generals."

Taizong said: "I have placed Yao Chi as commander-in-chief to serve the Anxi governor. Where and how shall we position the barbarian and Han troops?"

Li Jing said: "When Heaven first gave life to people, there was no distinction to be made between barbarian and Han. However, now their [barbarian] land is distant and desolate and they are forced to hunt with bows in order to survive. From this, they become accustomed to battle and struggle. If I were to nurture them with kindness and trust, to clothe and feed them adequately, then we would all be Han. As your highness has established this governor, I request that you gather all your Han garrison soldiers and station them in the central lands. This will help economize on grain and provisions—what military experts term 'the method of ordering strength.' However, select Han officials familiar with the nature of barbarians and establish defenses all over. These [techniques] are enough to run the area for a long time. If we come across an emergency, then we can use the [Han] troops to deal with it."

Taizong said: "This 'controlling strength' of which Sunzi speaks—what is it?"

Li Jing said: "'With the near, await those far away. With the idle, await the fatigued. With the sated, await the hungry.' This is the strategy he generally means. Those who are skillful at employing troops take these three points and turn them into six: Wait for them to come with lures; wait for the intensity in silence; wait for the light with the heavy; wait for the relaxed with the disciplined; wait for chaos with order; wait for the attack with defense. If you go against these, victory will be beyond your reach. If you have no technique for ordering your men, how can you face the enemy troops?"

Taizong said: "As for those who study Sunzi today, they merely recite hollow words. Few are competent enough to understand his meaning further. The method for ordering strength should be expounded among all the generals."

Taizong said: "Our old generals and aged troops are withered and exhausted. All our armies are newly deployed and cannot manage their formations against the enemy. How should we teach them the essentials?"

Li Jing said: "I tend to teach the officers through three steps. I must first assemble the squadrons of five. Once the 'Method of Assembling Squadrons' is complete, I show them how to arrange [the troops] into armies and battalions. This is one step. To organize the armies and battalions, I turn one into ten, ten into 100. This is another step. Then I instruct them on picking subordinate generals. The subordinate generals then bring together the platoons among all the battalions, assemble them into formation, and instruct them in your plan. This is the third step.

唐太宗李衛公問對 QUESTIONS AND REPLIES BETWEEN EMPEROR TAIZONG OF TANG AND GENERAL LI JING

"When the head general teaches these three steps, he should make detailed examinations, ascertaining their orders and measures. He divides them into unconventional and conventional, gains allegiance from the masses, and implements punishments. Should your majesty observe all of this from above, there will be nothing you cannot implement."

Taizong said: "Several thinkers have discussed the method of assembling squadrons. Whose thoughts are the most essential?"

Li Jing said: "Allow me to refer to the *Spring and Autumn Annals*. Zuo Shi says: 'First a fleet of chariots, and after a squadron of five.' *The Methods of the Sima* also says: 'Five men make a squadron.' The *Wei Liaozi* has a section titled 'Commands for binding warriors [into squadrons].' Han organization had records of the number of enemies killed and mutual agreements that each squadron would help another. Later generations used paper to write their records and agreements, whereupon they lost control.

"I have deliberated over their methods. They changed from 5 to 25 men and then from 25 to 75 men. Then they had 72 foot soldiers controlled by 3 armored officials. When they abandoned their chariots and rode their horses, then they had 8 horses to 25 men. Therefore, they kept control through 5 soldiers acting as 5. In discussing the military methods of all the thinkers, all that is essential is the method of assembling squadrons itself.

"A small arrangement would have 5 men, while a large arrangement would have 25. Altogether there would be 75 men and if you were to multiply this by 5, you would get 375 men. Three hundred men would act conventionally, while 60 would act unconventionally.[48] In this case, there could be two conventional divisions of 150 along

---

47. The remaining 15 men would be the armored officers.

with two unconventional divisions of 30—to cover the left and the right. This is what Rangju means by 'five men make a squadron, while ten squadrons make a platoon.' To the present time, it remains essential to follow this."

Taizong said: "I discussed warfare with Li Ji. He is mostly in agreement with you, but Ji has not researched the origins [of such ideas]. From what technique did you create the Six Flowers Formation?"

Li Jing said: "My creation has its roots in Zhuge Liang's method of Eight Formations. A large formation surrounds a smaller formation as a large camp surrounds a smaller camp. The corners all lock together, while the bends and breakages are interlocked. The ancients controlled their men like this, so I have planned my formations in accordance with it. This is why the outside drawing is a square, while the inner ring is a circle, which becomes the Six Flowers Formation, as commonly termed."

Taizong said: "A circle inside and square outside—what do you mean by this?"

Li Jing said: "The square produces the conventional, while the circle produces the unconventional. The square is used to regulate the troops' steps, while the circle composes the organization of their flags. Using this method, the number of steps is decided by the Earth, while the composition of the flags corresponds with Heaven. When the pace is decided and the composition is unified, then [the army's] transformations will not bring chaos. The Eight Formations become the Six Flowers—this is the old method of Zhuge Liang."

Taizong said: "I draw the square to see the steps and set out the circle to see the troop arrangements. The steps teach the methods for the feet, while the troop arrangements teach the methods for the hands, benefiting [the training of] both hands and feet. Have I grasped the general meaning?"

Li Jing said: "Wu Qi said: 'Even when cut off, do not become separated. Even when retreating, do not disperse.' This is the method of marching. Instructing the officers is like setting up a chessboard. If there are no outlines to mark the pathways, how does one use the chess pieces? Sunzi said: 'The terrain produces measurements; measurements produce estimates [of forces]; estimates [of forces] allow the determination of the numbers [of men]; the numbers [of men] allow the estimates of [an army's] weight; while comparing [an army's] weight produces victory. The victorious troops are like a boulder compared to a grain, while defeated troops are like a grain compared to a boulder.'[49] This all arises from measuring and estimating the square and the circle."

Taizong said: "How profound Sunzi's words are! If one does not measure the distance of terrain or the width of a formation, how can one control arrangements within the army?"

Li Jing said: "The average general is rarely able to understand the army's arrangements. 'Those who are adept in warfare strategically benefit from their circumstance and make concise arrangements. The way they benefit from circumstance is like a fully drawn bow; their arrangements are like the release of the arrow.' I have cultivated this technique: position [infantry] platoons 10 paces apart and place cavalry platoons 20 paces from the infantry at the front. Between each platoon, place one battle platoon. To advance 50 paces is to make one measure.

"When the horn sounds, all the platoons will disperse and go to their positions: they must be no further than 10 paces apart. When the horn sounds for the fourth time,

---

49. The Chinese here refers to two measures of weight—Yi (鎰) and Zhu (銖). One yi is at least 400 times the weight of a zhu.

they will grab their spears and squat down. Whereupon the drum will beat—three calls to three strikes. They advance 30 to 50 steps to control the changes among the enemy. The chariots come out from the rear, also advancing 50 paces when the time is right. The conventional are in front and the unconventional are behind. Observe the enemy. When the drums beat again, act unconventionally in front and conventionally in the rear. Beckon the enemy to come and wait for an opportunity to break through a gap. This is generally how the Six Flowers method works."

Taizong said: "Lord Cao's *New Book* says: 'When establishing your formation opposite the enemy, you must first establish the arrangement [of the pennants], drawing the troops into formation by going into the arrangement. When one part is attacked, if the other parts do not go to save them, they will be beheaded.'"

Li Jing said: "To face the enemy and then establish the arrangement is incorrect. This is only a method used when instructing how to battle. Among the ancient people who were good at employing troops, they taught the conventional but not the unconventional. They chased the masses as if driving a herd of sheep. The masses advanced and retreated with them, unaware of where they were going. Lord Cao was boisterous and took pleasure in victory. Of all the current generals who praise the *New Book*, none dare criticize its shortfalls. Furthermore, if you establish an arrangement before the enemy, is it not already too late? I secretly observed the music and dance you created for 'Smashing Formations.' Four pennants go out from ahead; eight flags intertwined stitch together at the back, while the left and right break off in rotation, pursuing the gongs and drums, each according to their instructions. This is the diagram for Eight Formations, a system of four heads and eight tails. Society only sees the abundant nature of music and dance—how could they know that the army is composed in such a way?"

Taizong said: "In antiquity, when Emperor Gao of Han established All under Heaven, he composed a song with the lyrics: 'How can I find fierce officers to defend all four corners?' In short, military methods can be taught through thought but not passed on in speech. For my dance and music, I made the 'Smashing Formations,' but only you, my minister, already understand the layout. Later generations will know that I did not carelessly create it."

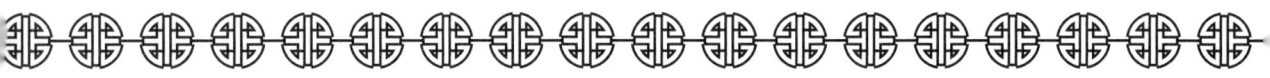

Taizong said: "Are the five flags in an array of colors conventional? If they separate and unify through change, what is the correct number of platoons?"

Li Jing said: "I have examined and employed the ancient methods. Generally, when three platoons unite, their flags lean on each other but do not cross; when five platoons unite, two flags cross; when ten platoons unite, five flags cross. When the horn blows, the five crossed flags separate, the unit disperses and acts as ten platoons again; when the two crossed flags separate, the unit disperses and acts as five again. When separating two flags that lean on each other but are not crossed, the platoons disperse and act as three again. When the troops disperse, to unite is unconventional. When they unite, to disperse them is unconventional. Give orders three times and arrange them five times. Disperse them three times and unite them three times. Have them return to conventionality, after which the Four Heads and Eight Tails can be taught to them. This is what is appropriate for the methods of the platoon."

Taizong gave his praise.

Taizong said: "Lord Cao had 'battling cavalry, trapping cavalry, and roaming cavalry.' What arrangement can the current army of horses be compared with?"

Li Jing said: "Allow me to refer to the *New Book*, which says: 'The battling horses lie at the front, the trapping horses lie in the center, and the roaming horses lie at the rear. If this is the case, then each has an established role and title, so they were divided into three kinds. In general, the cavalry battalions of 8 were equivalent to 24 foot soldiers. Twenty-four cavalrymen were equivalent to 72 foot soldiers. These were the ancient methods of organization. The foot soldiers were usually taught to use the conventional, while the cavalry battalions were usually taught to use the unconventional.'

"According to Lord Cao, the front, back, and center are divided into three covering forces. He did not discuss the two wings however, so he only mentioned the end of the spectrum. Later generations have not understood the meaning of the three covering forces, so they [believe] the battling horses must go ahead of the trapping horses. How does one then employ the roaming horses? I am well versed in employing such methods. If you rotate the formation back, then the roaming horses will take the front, the battling horses the back, and the trapping horses will divide when responding to change. This is what Lord Cao refers to."

Taizong laughed and said: "How many people have been duped by Lord Cao?"

Taizong said: "Chariots, infantry, and horses—these three are all one method. Does their use lie with man?"

Li Jing said: "I refer to the Fish and Deer Formation in the *Spring and Autumn Annals*. First comes a battalion of chariots, then a squadron behind. In this case, the chariots and infantry are without cavalry, which we call resisting from the left and right. The writings speak of resisting and defending—that is all! They did not use unconventional means to win. When Xun Wu of Jin attacked the Di, he abandoned his chariots and had his men go on foot. In this case, numerous cavalry would have been useful. His only concern was victory, so he used unconventional means, not only resisting and defending.

"If I am to summarize their techniques,

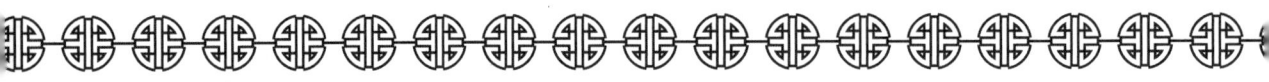

唐太宗李衛公問對 QUESTIONS AND REPLIES BETWEEN EMPEROR TAIZONG OF TANG AND GENERAL LI JING

then generally one horseman counts for three men. Chariots and infantrymen are likewise matched. When they are mixed, they use a single method and its employment lies with the men. How can the enemy know where my chariots will ultimately appear? Where my cavalry will ultimately come from? What my foot soldiers will ultimately follow? 'Will we lie in the depths of Earth or move in the heights of Heaven?' Your knowledge is spirit-like, your majesty! How could I adequately understand such a thing?"

Taizong said: "Taigong's book says: 'On a terrain of 600 or 60 steps square, arrange the 12 celestial bodies.' What is this technique?"

Li Jing said: "If you mark out an area of 1,200 paces in a square, each part will cover a square of 20 paces. Place a man every five paces horizontally and every four paces vertically, making 2,500 men divided over five areas with four empty grounds remaining; this is called forming a formation within a formation. When King Wu attacked Zhou, each Tiger Warrior controlled 1,000 men. Each formation had 6,000 men. Altogether there was a mass of 30,000 men. This was Taigong's method for marking out the terrain."

Taizong said: "How does my minister mark out the terrain for the Six Flowers Formation?"

Li Jing said: "After great examination: An area of 1,200 paces means six formations are established. Each occupies an area with a border of four hundred paces, divided into two wings of east and west. An empty ground of 1,200 steps is reserved for instruction of battle practices. I once taught 30,000 men, divided into formations of 5,000. One set up camp, while five practiced the square, round, curved, straight, and pointed formations. Each formation practiced all five variants, giving a total of 25 changes before all were used up."

Taizong said: "What is the Five Moves Formation?"

Li Jing said: "The names were originally established in relation to the colors of the five shapes. In fact, they are square, round, curved, straight, and pointed due to the shapes of the terrain. If the army does not generally cultivate and practice these five formations, how can they face the enemy? When it comes to warfare, deception is the Way [Tao]. Therefore they named them the Five Moves. They were described to explain how technique and number produce and overcome the patterns of each other. In fact, the form of warfare is like that of water—the terrain controls the course of flow. This is the implication of it all."

Taizong said: "Li Ji spoke with merit, of 'male and female, square and round methods for troops in ambush.' Did they have such methods in antiquity?"

Li Jing said: "The methods of male and female have been passed down through folklore. In fact, the two simply mean Yin and Yang. Allow me to refer to Fan Li: 'If you go afterward, then use Yin. If you go first, then use Yang. Exhaust the enemy's ties with Yang and allow your ties with Yin to flourish, then seize the enemy.' This is the military scholar's trick for Yin and Yang.

"Fan Li also said: 'Establish the right as female and increase from the left to be male. Use this to flow with the Way [Tao] at dawn and dusk.' In this way, left and right, dawn and dusk, differ from time to time. The changes lie in the unconventional and conventional. The left and right are the people's Yin and Yang. Dawn and dusk are Heaven's Yin and Yang. The unconventional and conventional are the interchangeability of Yin and Yang in man and Heaven. If one grabs these and does not change, then Yin and Yang are wasted. How does one preserve nothing more than the form of the male and female? Therefore, when you take form, display unconventionality to the enemy, not conventionality. When

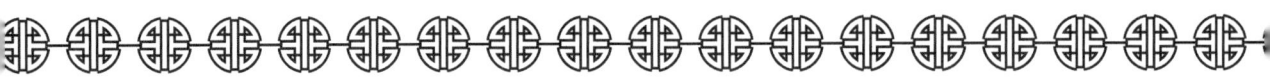

唐太宗李衛公問對 QUESTIONS AND REPLIES BETWEEN EMPEROR TAIZONG OF TANG AND GENERAL LI JING

you are victorious, use conventionality to attack the enemy, not unconventionality. This is called the interchangeability of the unconventional and conventional. When attacking in ambush, do not stop at waiting in mountains, valleys, grass, and trees, for hiding them away is only a means of carrying out an ambush. Their conventionality is like a mountain, their unconventionality like thunder. Although the enemy is [standing] opposite, one cannot infer the location of their unconventionality and conventionality. At this point, what form does one take?"

Taizong said: "The Four Beasts Formation has the notes *shang*, *yu*, *zheng*, and *jiao* to represent them. What is the way of this?"

Li Jing said: "The Way [Tao] of deception."

Taizong said: "Can they be abandoned?"

Li Jing said: "By preserving them, one can abandon them. If they are abandoned and not employed, then deceit will reach extremes."

Taizong said: "What are you talking about?"

Li Jing said: "Imagine we are using the Four Beasts Formation, assigning them titles according to Heaven, Earth, Wind, and Thunder. Then we matched them with gold and *shang*; water and *yu*; fire and *zheng*; and wood and *jiao*. These have been the ways of deceit of all military scholars since antiquity. Preserve them and the deceit cannot continue. Abandon them and what can one do to control the covetous and stupid?"

After a long time Taizong said: "My minister should keep this secret and not allow it to be leaked outside."

Taizong said: "Severe punishments and stern measures make people fear me and not the enemy. This confuses me. In ancient times, Guang Wu used a single army to match Wang Mang's masses of millions. He did not inflict punishments and laws on his people, so where did [his] victory come from?"

卷中 MIDDLE SCROLL

Li Jing said: "Whether an army is victorious or defeated depends on thousands of particulars. You cannot just pick one issue. When Zhen Sheng and Wu Guang crushed the Qin troops, how were they victorious? Were Guang's punishments and measures more extreme than the Qin? When Guang Wu rose up, it was generally because he acknowledged the people's disdain for Wang Mang. Moreover, Wang Xun and Wang Yi did not understand military methods and merely boasted of the size of their armies, so they brought failure upon themselves. Allow me to refer to Sunzi: 'If you punish the troops before they feel a sense of closeness, they will not obey. If troops already feel a sense of closeness but punishments are not carried out, then the troops cannot be employed.' These words mean that in each case a general must first have love to bind his officers, after which he can enact strict punishments. If a general has not fostered their love, few can control or benefit an army with severe measures alone."

Taizong said: "The *Shang Shu* says: 'When domination surpasses the ruler's love, this is guaranteed to help [one's affairs]. When the king's love surpasses domination, he will certainly have no success.' What does this mean?"

Li Jing said: "Establish love first and domination later—you cannot act contrary to this. If domination takes priority, and love is left behind, you will have no advantage in conducting affairs. The *Shang Shu* is cautious at the end, but this is not how plans should be made at the beginning. This is why Sunzi's *The Art of War* will not change for ten thousand generations."

Taizong said: "When you suppressed Xiao Xian, all the generals wanted to take over the subversive officials' homes to reward their officers and troops. You alone did not comply since the Han did not execute Kuai Tong and so the Han and Jiang rivers flowed home smoothly. This makes me think of the ancient saying: 'The civil can draw the masses near, while the martial can dominate the enemy.' Does this not refer to you, minister?"

唐太宗李衛公問對 QUESTIONS AND REPLIES BETWEEN EMPEROR TAIZONG OF TANG AND GENERAL LI JING

Li Jing said: "When Guang Wu of the Han suppressed the Red Eyebrows, he entered and observed the bandit camp. The bandits said: 'King Xiao offers his sincere heart unto others.' This was mainly due to his having first recognized their nature as fundamentally not evil. Did he not consider the future?

"When I punished the Turks with masses of the Barbarians and Han working together, though we went 1,000 li from the fortress, not once did I kill a Yang Gan or behead a Zhuang Jia. Rather, I extended my sincerity and encouraged the common good—nothing more. What your majesty has heard would place me in a rank of undeserving esteem. As for my dealing with the civil and the martial, which would I dare act upon?"

Taizong said: "In ancient times when Tang Qian was an ambassador to the Turks, you took the chance to attack and defeated them. People say you were willing to risk [the life of] Qian as a go-between."

Li Jing bowed twice and said: "Qian and I shouldered the responsibility for affairs equally. I expected that Qian's words would not succeed in making the enemy yield peacefully. This is why I gathered the troops and attacked. I overlooked minor righteousness so as to get rid of a major evil. Although people say Qian was an expendable go-between, [the thought of his death] never crossed my mind.

"Allow me to refer to Sunzi on employing spies, which he says is a lowly strategy. I once compiled a discussion regarding this and at the end said: 'Water may carry a boat but it can also overturn it. Some employ spies to have success; others rely on spies and veer toward failure.' If one braids his hair and serves the ruler with a just demeanor in court; if one is loyal and sincerely trustworthy, although he is a good spy, how can he be used [to create discord]? [The use of] Tang Qian is a matter of minor righteousness. What has your majesty to doubt?"

Taizong said: "How sincere! 'If there is no humanity or righteousness, one cannot manage spies.' How can a less majestic person carry this out? Since Lord Zhou, with his great righteousness, destroyed all his relatives, why not one more subject? There are clearly no doubts to be had!"

Taizong said: "The army values acting as the host, not the guest. It values speed, not longevity. Why is this?"

Li Jing said: "The military is only employed when nothing else can be done, so how can it act as a guest or use longevity? Sunzi says: 'When supplies are transported afar, the common people suffer from poverty.' This is the downfall of acting as a guest. He also said: 'People should not be conscripted twice, while grain should not be carried [transported away] three times.' This is the experience that comes from not being able to use longevity. If I compare and measure the trends of hosts and guests, then [I see that] techniques exist for changing guests into hosts and changing hosts into guests."

Taizong said: "What do you mean by this?"

Li Jing said: "Accumulating supplies from the enemy is to change guests into hosts. 'Making the full hungry and making the idle work' is to turn a host into a guest. This is why the military is not restrained by the roles of host or guest, delay or speed. Troops must only insist on keeping the laws as appropriate."

Taizong said: "Did the ancients use all these [methods]?"

Li Jing said: "In ancient times when Yue attacked Wu, they used two armies, one on the left and one on the right. They sounded the horns, beat the drum, and advanced. Wu divided up its troops for defense. Yue used the central army to lie low and wade through the river. No drum was beaten and they launched a surprise attack on the Wu troops. This was the experience of changing a guest into a host."

"When Shi Le and Ji Dan battled, Dan's troops came from afar. Le sent out Kong Chang as the spearhead to retaliate against Dan's troops. Kong Chang retreated and Dan came to pursue him. Le used troops in ambush to attack them, whereupon Dan's army was greatly defeated. This was the experience of changing toil into idleness. There were many ancient cases like this."

Taizong said: "The iron vines and obstructions for enemy troops were put together by Taigong, were they not?"

Li Jing said: "They were, although they were for resisting the enemy and nothing more. The troops valued devoted men and did not want to resist them. Taigong's Six Secret Teachings talks of the tools for defending, not what is employed when attacking."

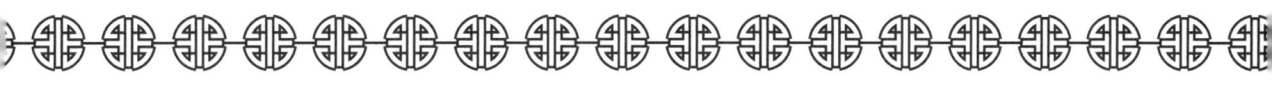

卷下
LOWER SCROLL

Taizong said: "Taigong said: 'When infantry battle against armies of chariots and cavalry, they must rely on hillocks, mounds, steep rocks, and strategic obstructions.' Sunzi also said: 'When the terrain appears as gaps in Heaven, hillocks, mounds, and fortified cities, troops should not be stationed there.' What about this [contradiction]?"

Li Jing said: "Employing the masses [successfully] relies on their minds being as one. Their minds being as one relies on forbidding omens and clearing all doubts. If the commanding general doubts or dreads anything, then the group will be shaken. If the group is shaken, then the enemy will seize this weakness and attack. For this reason, when settling a camp or occupying land, it should accommodate human activities and nothing more. Mountain streams, deep drops, pitfalls, crevices, and places that create natural traps—all such terrains are unsuitable for human affairs. For this reason, military thinkers avoid drawing troops toward these areas, preventing the enemy from capitalizing on such faults. Hillocks, mounds, and old fortified cities are neither cut off nor risky places. To gain them works to one's advantage, so why turn away and abandon them? What Taigong said is the core of military methods."

Taizong said: "I thought that among the tools of violence, none were more powerful than the troops themselves. If mobilizing the troops will benefit human affairs, how can one doubt [mobilizing the troops], merely to avoid taboos? From now on, if any generals have misgivings due to Yin and Yang and therefore fail to deal with affairs appropriately, my minister should exhort and admonish them."

Li Jing bowed twice in acknowledgement and said: "I note that the *Wei Liaozi* says: 'The emperor uses virtue to protect the good but uses punishments to condemn the bad. This is called punishment and virtue. It does not refer to astrology or [the following of] appropriate seasons or days.' Since this is the case, people can be made to follow this [punishment and virtue] but cannot be allowed to know of it. Ordinary generals in later ages drowned in [mystical] strategies, which led to many defeats. One cannot but admonish them. I will promptly spread your majesty's sagely guidance among all the generals."

Taizong said: "When the army divides or assembles into one great mass, it is crucial that in each case its actions are appropriate. Who excelled at this according to the records of previous generations?"

Li Jing said: "Fu Jian led a mass of one million and lost at the Fei river. This is what happens when troops are able to unite but are incapable of dividing. Wu Han went on a punitive expedition against Lord Sun Shu and divided his forces with his deputy general Liu Shang. They went 20 li apart, whereupon Shu came to attack Wu Han. Liu Shang went out to join the offensive and greatly defeated Shu. This is what happens when troops divide but are also able to unite. Taigong said: 'When troops are unable to divide, they are a "tied up army." When they are unable to group, they are an "isolated force."'"

Taizong said: "This is the case. Fu Jian first got Wang Meng. He certainly knew about managing troops and consequently seized the Central Plains.[50] When he availed himself of Wang Meng's troops, Jian was ultimately defeated. Is this what is called a 'tied up army?' When Guang Wu gave Wu Han responsibility, the army was not controlled from afar. In this way Han ultimately subdued the state of Shu. Does this not fall into the category of an 'isolated force'? The historical records of gains and losses can be used as a reference for 10,000 generations."

Taizong said: "Having observed 1,000 chapters and 10,000 sentences, none go further than the single sentence, 'Use an array of methods to force an error.'"

After quite a while, Li Jing said: "Your words are truly sage. Generally, when employing troops, if the enemy does not make an error, how can our troops exploit them? Compare it to chess, where the two enemies begin evenly but one false move and nobody can be saved. Therefore, from antiquity until now victory and failure have been forged by a single error and nothing more. Imagine when many mistakes are made!"

Taizong said: "Are the two affairs of attack and defense in fact one method? Sunzi says: 'When one is good in attack, the enemy does not know what to defend; as for those who are good in defense, the enemy does not know what to attack.' He never spoke of the enemy coming to attack one's own army or of one's army attacking the enemy. Assuming we defended ourselves and the enemy did so too, if our defending and attacking [strength] were identical, what technique is best to use?"

Li Jing said: "Previous generations had several cases like this, with mutual attack and mutual defense. Everyone said: 'To defend is not enough but to attack is too much.' That is to say, insufficiency is weak, while a surplus brings strength. Overall, they did not understand the methods for attack and defense.

---

49. The middle and lower regions of the Yellow river, including Henan, western Shandong, southern Shanxi, and Hebei.

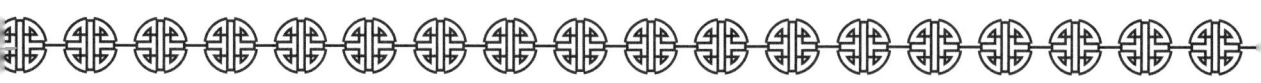

"Allow me to refer to Sunzi, who says: 'Those who cannot win go on the defensive, while those who can win go on the offensive.' This implies that if one was unable to defeat the enemy, one then defended oneself. When one waits until the enemy can be defeated, then one attacks. There is no talk of strength or weakness. When later generations did not understand the meaning of this, they defended when they ought to attack, and vice versa. The two phases are distinct—this is why they cannot be one method."

Taizong said: "Really? Ideas of surplus and insufficiency made later generations confused about strength and weakness. In particular, what they did not know about the methods of defense was that the essence lies in displaying an insufficiency to the enemy. When attacking, the essence lies in displaying a surplus to the enemy. If you display an insufficiency to the enemy, they are bound to come and attack. In this case, the enemy does not know what to attack. If you display a surplus to the enemy, they are bound to defend themselves. In this case, the enemy does not know what to defend. Attack and defense may be one decision—but the enemy and oneself are two separate affairs. If one succeeds in such an affair, the enemy fails. If the enemy succeeds, then one fails. Gain, loss, success, and failure are all divided among the enemy's and one's own affairs. As for attack and defense, they are one and nothing more! Those who understand that they are one will win 100 battles. For this reason, it is said: 'Know the enemy and know oneself. Then you will not suffer in 100 battles.' Is this talking about understanding such unity?"

Li Jing bowed twice and said: "How profound are the methods of the Sage! Attack is the mechanism for defense, while defense is the strategy for attack. Both lead to victory, nothing more! If one does not understand defense when attacking, or does not understand attack when defending, and not only makes them into two affairs but also assigns them to two separate offices, then, although one may quote the words of Sunzi or Wuzi, if he has not thought about the subtleties surrounding the identical nature of attack and defense, how can he know what is true?"

Taizong said: "*The Methods of the Sima* says: 'Even if a state is large, it is bound to decline if it takes pleasure in battle. Even if the world is at peace, those who forget how to battle are bound to be at risk.' Is this also a method for unifying attack and defense?"

Li Jing said: "If a man has a state and a family, how could he not discuss attack and defense? Attacking does not end with attacking the city walls or launching an offensive on a camp and nothing more. One must attack the techniques at the heart of the enemy. Defending does not stop at completing one's walls or strengthening one's camp and nothing more. One must also defend one's vitality [chi] and await the enemy. To speak of warfare in great terms is to conduct the Way [Tao] of the ruler; to speak of it in specific terms is to conduct the Way [Tao] of the general. Those who attack the heart are said to understand the enemy; those who defend their vitality are said to understand themselves."

Taizong said: "How true! Usually, when I was on the verge of battle, I first evaluated the enemy's mind by comparing it with my own to see who was more vigilant. Only after this could I understand the enemy and [learn] whether I could gain an advantage over them. I compared the enemy's vitality with my own to see whose was more controlled. I could then know myself. This is to know the enemy and to know oneself—an essential maxim for military thinkers. Although the generals and ministers of today may not know the enemy, if they are able to know themselves, how could they lose the advantage?"

Li Jing said: "When Sunzi said: 'First make yourself undefeatable,' he referred to those who understood themselves. Those who 'waited until the enemy was defeatable' were those who understood the enemy. He also said 'the capacity to be undefeatable lies in the self, the capacity to be defeatable lies in the enemy.' I do not dare lose thought of this warning for one second."

唐太宗李衛公問對 QUESTIONS AND REPLIES BETWEEN EMPEROR TAIZONG OF TANG AND GENERAL LI JING

Taizong said: "Sunzi spoke of the methods by which the vitality of the Three Armies could be seized: 'At dawn their vitality is vigorous; during the day their vitality is sluggish; at dusk their vitality is exhausted. Those who are good at employing troops avoid an army when their vitality is vigorous and attack when it is sluggish or exhausted.' How is this?"

Li Jing said: "For those who have life and blood within them, when they go to do battle at the beat of the drum, even if they die without any reservation, it is their vitality which made them so. For this reason, when using the methods for employing troops, one must first scrutinize one's officers and masses and then stimulate their victorious vitality. Only then can they meet the enemy with an offensive.

"Wu Qi's *Four Mechanisms* places the mechanism of vitality at the top, suggesting that there is no other Way [Tao]. If one can make all men fight individually, then nobody will be able to surmount their vigorous force. That which is called the vigorous vitality of dawn is not limited to an instant in time. Sunzi merely used the beginning and end of the day as metaphors. Generally, if after three beats of the drum, the enemy's vitality is neither ailing nor depleted, how can one render it sluggish and depleted? Most of those who study the texts tend to recite empty rhetoric and are [easily] duped by the enemy. If they knew the principles for seizing their vitality, then the troops could be entrusted to their responsibility."

Taizong said: "My minister once spoke of Li Ji's ability in military methods. Can his methods be employed long-term or not? If this is the case, but I am not around to control and guide him, then [I fear] he cannot be employed. How will my heir guide him in later days?"

Li Jing said: "If I were to plan for your majesty, nothing would be better than dismissing Ji and then have your heir employ him again. Ji would certainly be confused by such kindness and seek to repay it. Is there any harm in this logic?"

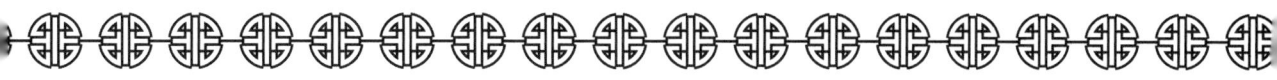

Taizong said: "Good idea! I have no doubts regarding this."

Taizong said: "If Li Ji and Zhangsun Wuji one day took hold of the state's government together, what would you think?"

Li Jing said: "Li Ji is loyal and righteous. I imagine he can maintain his responsibilities. Zhangsun Wuji heeded your commands, resulting in great success. Since he is a relation with a place deep in your heart, you appointed him as deputy minister. While on the outside he is deferential to officers, on the inside he is actually jealous of the Worthies. This is why Yuchi Jingde highlighted his shortcomings before his face and retired thereafter. Hou Junji resented him for forgetting his former friends and rebelled because of this. This all occurred because of Wuji. As your majesty has asked me about this, I dare not avoid talking about it."

Taizong said: "Do not let this be leaked. I will think carefully about how to deal with this."

Taizong said: "Emperor Gaozu of the Han was able to command his generals, although afterward Han Xin and Peng Yue were executed and Xiao He was thrown in jail. Why was this?"

Li Jing said: "I observe that Liu and Xiang were both rulers unable to command their generals. When the Qin fell, Zhang Liang initially wanted revenge for his state of Han. Chen Ping and Han Xin were both bitter about Chu not employing them. For this reason, they took advantage of Han's strategic power [*shih*] for themselves. As a result, Xiao, Cao, Fan, and Guan made every effort to flee their doom. Because of this, Gaozu gained All under Heaven. If he had installed ministers from descendants of the six states to be reestablished and each individual gained their old state, then although he had a talent for commanding generals, whom could the Han have employed? I mentioned that the Han gained All under Heaven by Zhang Liang's plan of borrowing [Gaozu's] chopsticks and

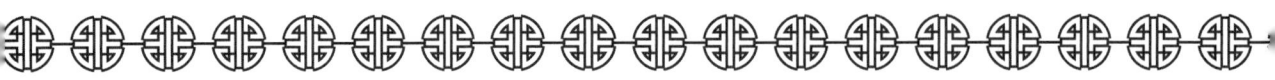

唐太宗李衛公問對 QUESTIONS AND REPLIES BETWEEN EMPEROR TAIZONG OF TANG AND GENERAL LI JING

Xiao He's successes in water transport and management. By saying this, Han and Peng being executed and Fan Zeng not being employed are equally important. This is why I refer to Liu and Xiang as rulers unable to command their generals."

Taizong said: "Emperor Guang Wu, who restored the dynasty, was able to protect his ministers and realize their achievements. He did not entrust them with civil affairs. Is this better than commanding the generals?"

Li Jing said: "Although Guang Wu applied the methods of previous systems and easily gained success, Wang Mang's balance of power was not inferior to Xiang Yu's system. Kou Xun and Deng Yu were unable to surpass Xiao He and Zhang Zao, who alone were able to extend their sincerest hearts, employ a well-rounded government, and protect and realize the achievements of ministers. They were far more worthy than Gaozu! If we were using this to talk about the Way [Tao] of commanding generals, I would say that Guang Wu has attained it."

Taizong said: "In ancient times when troops were sent out and generals were given commands, the ruler would abstain from meat for three days and then hand over to the general a battle ax, saying: 'The general of the army will control this from now until Heaven.' The ruler would then push the hub of the general's [chariot] wheel and say: 'Advancing and retreating should only be done at their proper time. When you are on the march, the army will only listen to the general of the army's commands and not heed the commands of the ruler.' I would say that such rituals have long been forgotten. I would now like to set up a ceremony with my minister for dispatching the general—how about this?"

Li Jing said: "If I may say so, the Sages created this ceremony as well as the vegetarian regime at the ancestral temple. It was so that the spirits lent them the ability to dominate. Handing over the labor ax and the battle ax, then pushing the hub of the wheel were the ruler's way of entrusting the general with authority. Today, when your majesty dispatches the troops, he must discuss things with the lords and ministers and visit the ancestral temple. Only then may he dispatch the general. If all this is done, then you will be inviting the spirits to come forth. Every time you entrust the general with responsibility, you must make him capable of obeying his duties. If you do so, then you can lend him great authority. What is this compared to a vegetarian regime and pushing the wheel hub? It is totally in line with ancient ritual, with the same meaning. There is no need to convene and decide on something new."

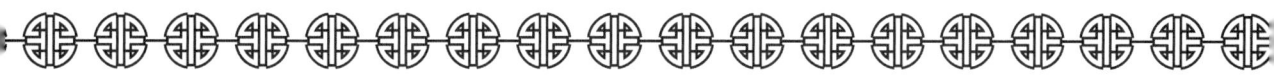

The ruler said: "How good!" and then ordered his nearby officials to note down these two affairs to be used as methods for later generations.

Taizong said: "Can one disregard the numerous strategies of Yin and Yang?"

Li Jing said: "No. The troops are the Way [Tao] of deceit. If we trust them to use the strategies of Yin and Yang, then they can control the greedy and influence the foolish. These strategies cannot be disregarded."

Taizong said: "My minister once said: 'The management of astrology and proper seasons and days are not the methods of enlightened generals. Dim generals are confined by them.' So it seems apt to disregard them!"

Li Jing said: "In ancient times, King Zhou died on the *jiazi*, the first day of a 60-year cycle. King Wu however ascended on the same day. According to astrology and proper seasons and days, the *jiazi* day is the first. The later Shang was chaotic, while the Zhou was well ordered. Rising and falling have their differences. Emperor Wu of the Song raised his troops on the 'Day for Approaching Death.' The army officials deemed this impossible, so the emperor said: 'If I go forth, he [the enemy] will perish,' whereupon he overcame him. From talking about this, it is clear that one can disregard certain things. Despite this, when Tian Dan was surrounded by Yan, Dan commanded one man to imitate a spirit. Dan

唐太宗李衛公問對 QUESTIONS AND REPLIES BETWEEN EMPEROR TAIZONG OF TANG AND GENERAL LI JING

bowed to him and offered sacrifices. The spirit said: 'Yan can be broken,' upon which Dan went out to attack Yan with fire oxen and greatly defeated him. This is the Way [Tao] of deceit of military strategists. [The use of] astrology and proper seasons and days should be like this."

Taizong said: "Tian Dan entrusted [their fate to] the mysterious nature of the spirit and destroyed Yan. Taigong burned the yarrow and the tortoise shell, but exterminated Zhou. In what way do these two affairs oppose each other?"

Li Jing said: "Their mechanisms are the same. One rebelled and seized the enemy, while the other went with the enemy and carried out his plans. In antiquity when Taigong was assisting King Wu, they reached the herding fields where they encountered a thunderstorm. The flags and drums were snapped and destroyed. San Yisheng wished to make a divination for good luck before he marched on. Due to doubts and fears among the army, he had to rely on divination to ask the spirits. Taigong deemed festering grass and withered bones not worth consulting. Furthermore, if a vassal attacks his ruler, how can this happen more than once?

"Having observed that San Yisheng displayed his mechanisms at the beginning while Taigong completed his at the end, although rebellion and compliance have their differences, their patterns are ultimately the same. When I previously said not to disregard these strategies, my overall aim was to preserve their vitality [chi] while it was still young. Their success lay in human affairs and nothing more!"

Taizong said: "Currently there are only three real generals—Li Ji, Dao Zong, and Xue Wanche. Besides Dao Zong, who is a relative of mine, who can handle such great employment?"

Li Jing said: "Your majesty once said that in employing troops, Li Ji and Dao Zong saw neither great victories nor great losses. However, if Wanche did not see a great victory, he was bound to experience a great defeat. In my foolishness I have pondered your words. Those who do not seek great victories but also do not suffer great defeats are troops who are well bound and controlled. Whether they seek victory or defeat, if they have good fortune then they will be victorious. This is why Sun Wu said: 'Those who are good in battle stand on ground where they will not be defeated. They also never lose sight of the opportunity to defeat the enemy.' To be disciplined and controlled lies in the self."

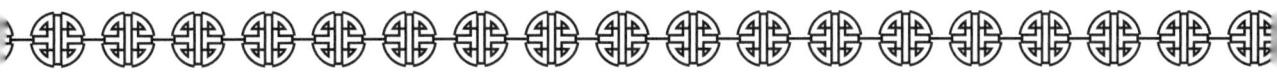

Taizong said: "As two formations approach each other, if one does not wish to fight, how can this be achieved?"

Li Jing said: "In ancient times the troops of Jin attacked Qin. They did battle then retreated. *The Methods of the Sima* says: 'Do not chase a fleeing enemy far or follow those withdrawing for too long.' I describe withdrawing as being constrained by the reins. If our troops are already disciplined and controlled, while the enemy also arranges its platoons in an ordered fashion, how could anyone dare to take battle lightly? In this way, when some go out and do battle, while others retreat but are not pursued, each side is defending against victory and defeat. Sunzi said: 'Do not attack well-ordered formations and do not pursue upright flags.' If two formations have an equal balance of power, when one body goes slightly off course and the other capitalizes on this, then they will be greatly defeated. The patterns of warfare make this so. For this reason, there are times when the troops do not need to do battle and times when they must. Refraining from battle lies with the self, while the compulsion to do battle lies with the enemy."

Taizong said: "Refraining from battle lies with the self—what is meant by this?"

Li Jing said: "Sunzi said: 'If one does not wish to do battle, mark the ground and defend your territory. The enemy cannot do battle with you when one capitalizes on their movements.' If the enemy has sufficient men, then the period between engagement and retreat cannot be mapped out. For this reason, I said refraining from battle lies with the self and the compulsion to do battle lies in the enemy. Sunzi said: 'Those who are skillful at moving the enemy take form in such a way that the enemy can only submit. They offer something that the enemy must seize. They use their advantage to move the enemy and await them with their main body of men.' When the enemy has insufficient men, they will certainly advance and do battle. I would capitalize on this and smash them. This is why I said that the compulsion to do battle lies with the enemy."

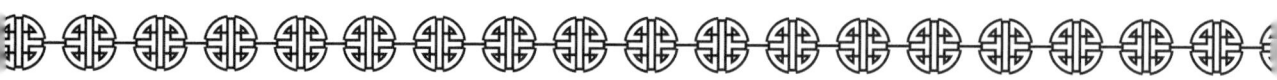

Taizong said: "How profound! Disciplined and controlled troops—they prosper when they realize their methods, but fall when they lose their methods. Could my minister collate and recount all the figures in history that were good at disciplining and controlling troops? Draw up some clear diagrams and then I will select the most apt and subtle ones to beat into the minds of later generations."

Li Jing said: "The two formation diagrams of the Yellow Emperor and Taigong that I previously submitted, as well as *The Methods of the Sima* and Zhuge Liang's methods of the unconventional and conventional, are already clear and detailed. Famous generals throughout history have employed one or two of these and a number of them have been successful. However, few official historians have managed to understand military matters and so were unable to record true events. Still, dare I disregard your order? I should collate and recount something for you to hear."

Taizong said: "What is the most profound element of military methods?"

Li Jing said: "I once divided things into three to make students gradually understand what they ought to. The first I call the Way [Tao]. The second I call Heaven and Earth. The third I call the Methods of the General. The Way [Tao] is the most subtle and most profound. It is what the *I Ching* calls: 'intelligence and astute knowledge, spiritual and martial without killing.' To talk of Heaven is Yin and Yang, while to talk of Earth is risk and ease. Those who are skillful at employing troops can use Yin to seize Yang and use risk to attack ease. It is what Mengzi calls 'the timings of Heaven and the advantages of the Earth.' To talk of the general's methods is to give men responsibilities and to benefit from weapons. It is what the Three Strategies calls 'the prosperity of those who gain good officers' and how the *Guanzi* says: 'Weapons must be strong and sharp.'"

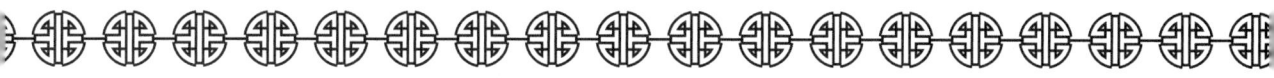

Taizong said: "This is true! I have remarked that troops who force men to give in without fighting are superior. Those who win 100 battles are mediocre. Those who build deep trenches and high ramparts are inferior. If we use this as a measurement for comparison, Sunzi's works have all three of these."

Li Jing said: "We can also make distinctions by observing people's writings and by recounting their affairs. For instance, when Zhang Liang, Fan Li, and Sunzi rid themselves of nature and pulled themselves to lofty heights, no one knew where they were going. If they did not understand the Way [Tao], how could they have done this? Yue Yi, Guan Zhong, and Zhuge Liang fought to certain victory and defended to certain security. Had they not examined the seasons of Heaven or the advantages of Earth, how would they have done this? After this there was Wang Meng's protection of Qin and Xie An's defense of Jin. If they had not given generals responsibility and selected great talents, nor amended and completed their defense, how could they have done this? For this reason, becoming accustomed to military studies should come up from below to the middle to the top. In this way, understanding gradually becomes profound. If not, then beating out empty words and learning recitations like disciples will not be enough to seize [opportunities]."

Taizong said: "Daoists ignore three generations of families who serve as generals. While military studies should not be passed on rashly, that is not to say that they should not be passed on at all. My minister must be prudent over such matters."

Li Jing bowed twice, then went out, whereupon he passed all his books onto Li Ji.

INDEX

Art of War, The
    army on the march 167–73
    attacking strategy 143–7
    background to 11
    battle preparation 147–50
    battle tactics 150–9, 164–6
    dividing forces 150–3
    fire in warfare 189–91
    military maneuvers 159–64
    planning for war 137–40
    spies 192–5
    terrain 173–88
attacking strategy
    in *Six Secret Teachings* 55–6, 92
    in *The Art of War* 143–7
    in *The Questions and Replies Between Tang Taizong and Li Weigong* 371–4
    in *Wei Liaozi* 247–51
battle preparation
    in *Six Secret Teachings* 72–4
    in *The Art of War* 147–50
    in *Wei Liaozi* 233–6, 273
battle tactics
    in *The Art of War* 150–9, 164–6
    in *The Questions and Replies Between Tang Taizong and Li Weigong* 333–51, 354–68, 369–81
    in *Wei Liaozi* 255–60
    in *Wu Zi* 221–5
benevolent rule
    in *Methods of the Sima* 107–11
    in *Six Secret Teachings* 42–3
border preparations
    in *Six Secret Teachings* 71–2
breaking out
    in *Six Secret Teachings* 68–70
cavalry warfare
    in *Six Secret Teachings* 99–101
    in *The Questions and Replies Between Tang Taizong and Li Weigong* 360–2
chariots
    in *Methods of Sima* 114
    in *Six Secret Teachings* 96–9
defensive strategy
    in *Six Secret Teachings* 27–9
    in *The Questions and Replies Between Tang Taizong and Li Weigong* 371–4
    in *Wei Liaozi* 251–4
deployments in battle
    in *Methods of Sima* 130–2
    in *Six Secret Teachings* 67

discipline
    in *Methods of the Sima* 124–30
    in *The Questions and Replies Between Tang Taizong and Li Weigong* 364–7
    in *Three Strategies of Huang Shigong* 299–310
    in *Wei Liaozi* 237–46, 268–72, 274–8, 280–95
    in *Wu Zi* 212–17
dividing forces
    in *Six Secret Teachings* 88–9, 91
    in *The Art of War* 150–3
    in *The Questions and Replies Between Tang Taizong and Li Weigong* 369–71
doubts, military
    in *Six Secret Teachings* 43–4
emergency commands
    in *Six Secret Teachings* 53–4
empty fortifications
    in *Six Secret Teachings* 78–9
equipment
    in *Six Secret Teachings* 61–7
fire in warfare
    in *Six Secret Teachings* 77–8
    in *The Art of War* 189–91
flags
    in *Methods of Sima* 114
    in *The Questions and Replies Between Tang Taizong and Li Weigong* 360
forest warfare
    in *Six Secret Teachings* 81
generals
    in *Six Secret Teachings* 47–53
    in *The Questions and Replies Between Tang Taizong and Li Weigong* 375–6
    in *Three Strategies of Huang Shigong* 299
    in *Wei Liaozi* 254–5, 261–3, 279
    in *Wu Zi* 217–20
Han Dynasty 7, 9
    and *Methods of Sima* 11
    and *Three Strategies of Huang Shigong* 11
infantry warfare
    in *Six Secret Teachings* 102–3
insignia
    in *Methods of the Sima* 114
irregular forces
    in *The Questions and Replies Between Tang Taizong and Li Weigong* 353–4
Jiang Ziya 10
Jin Dynasty 10
leading into battle
    in *Six Secret Teachings* 70–1
Li Jing 12

INDEX

Liao Dynasty 10
Liu Tao see Six Secret Teachings
march, army on the
    in *The Art of War* 167–73
marsh warfare
    in *Six Secret Teachings* 86–7
Methods of Sima
    background to 11
    benevolent rule 107–11
    chariots 114
    deployments in battle 130–2
    discipline 124–30
    insignia 114
    military maneuvers 118–24
    rewards and punishments 113–14, 116–17
    righteousness of ruler 111–17
    state and military 112, 115–16
    wise rulership1 110–17
military maneuvers
    in *Methods of the Sima* 118–24
    in *Six Secret Teachings* 33–5
    in *The Art of War* 159–64
mixture of forces
    in *Six Secret Teachings* 94–6
motivating armies
    in *Six Secret Teachings* 52–3
    in *Wu Zi* 226–8
mountain warfare
    in *Six Secret Teachings* 85–6
music
    in *Six Secret Teachings* 58–9
non-military equipment
    in *Six Secret Techniques* 61–2
non-military methods
    in *Six Secret Teachings* 40–2
observation of enemy
    in *Six Secret Teachings* 60–1
    in *Wu Zi* 207–12
planning for war
    in *The Art of War* 137–40
Qin Empire 7, 9
Questions and Replies Between Tang Taizong and Li Weigong, The
    attacking strategy 371–4
    background to 12
    battle tactics 333–51, 354–68, 369–81
    cavalry warfare 360–2
    defensive strategy 371–4

discipline 364–7
dividing forces 369–71
flags 360
generals 375–6
    irregular forces 353–4
    terrain 362–4
rapid assault
    in *Six Secret Teachings* 82–3
rewards and punishments
    in *Methods of Sima* 113–14, 116–17
    in *Six Secret Teachings* 33
    in *The Questions and Replies Between Tang Taizong and Li Weigong* 364–7
    in *Wei Liaozi* 270–2
    in *Wu Zi* 226–7
righteousness of ruler
    in *Methods of the Sima* 111–17
sage principles
    in *Six Secret Teachings* 39–40
Shang Dynasty 11
Shenzong of the Song, Emperor 9
sieges
    in *Six Secret Teachings* 76–7
Six Secret Teachings
    attacking strategy 55–6, 92
    background to 10–11
    battle preparation 72–4
    benevolent rule 42–3
    border preparations 71–2
    breaking out 68–70
    cavalry warfare 99–101
    chariots 96–9
    defence of country 27–9
    deployments in battle 67
    dividing forces 88–9
    emergency commands 53–4
    empty fortifications 78–9
    equipment 61–7
    fire in warfare 77–8
    forest warfare 81
    generals 47–53
    infantry warfare 102–3
    King Wen meets teacher 19–21
    leading into battle 70–1
    marsh warfare 86–7
    military doubts 43–4
    military maneuvers 33–5
    mixture of forces 94–6

INDEX

motivating armies 52–3
mountain warfare 85–6
music 58–9
non-military equipment 61–2
non-military methods 40–2
observation of enemy 60–1
rapid assault 82–3
rewards and punishments 33
sage principles 39–40
sieges 76–7
soldier selection 93
state instability 21–3
strong enemies 83–5, 87–8
subordinates of rulers 24–5, 29–32, 45–7
supply routes 75
training 94
unconventional strategies 56–8
wise rulership 23–4, 25–7, 37–8
soldier selection
    in *Six Secret Teachings* 93
Song Dynasty 9, 10
spies
    in *The Art of War* 192–5
state instability
    in *Six Secret Teachings* 21–3
state and military
    in *The Methods of the Sima* 112, 115–16
    in *Three Strategies of Huang Shigong* 311–14
strong enemies
    in *Six Secret Teachings* 83–5, 87–8
subordinates of rulers
    in *Six Secret Teachings* 24–5, 29–32, 45–7
    in *Wei Liaozi* 263–5
Sunzi 11
supply routes, protecting
    in *Six Secret Teachings* 75
Taizong, Emperor 12
Tang Dynasty 10
    and *The Questions and Replies Between Tang Taizong and Li Weigong* 12
terrain
    in *The Art of War* 173–88
    in *The Questions and Replies Between Tang Taizong and Li Weigong* 362–4
Three Strategies of Huang Shigong
    background to 11–12
    disciple 299–310
    generals 299–310
    state and military 311–14

wise rulership 315–19, 321–8
training
    in *Six Secret Teachings* 94
unconventional strategies
    in *Six Secret Teachings* 56–8
Warring States 7–8
    and *Art of War* 11
    and *Six Secret Teachings* (Liu Tao) 10
    and *Methods of Sima* 11
    and *Wei Liaozi* 11
    and *Wuzi* 11
Wei Liaozi
    attacking strategy 247–51
    background to 11
    battle preparations 233–6, 273
    battle tactics 255–60
    defensive strategy 251–4
    discipline 237–46, 268–72, 274–8, 280–95
    generals 254–5, 261–3, 279
    rewards and punishments 270–2
    subordinates of rulers 263–5
wise rulership 265–8
wise rulership
    in *Methods of Sima* 111–17
    in *Six Secret Teachings* 23–4, 25–7, 37–8
    in *Three Strategies of Huang Shigong* 315–19, 321–8
    in *Wei Liaozi* 265–8
    in *Wuzi* 201–6
Wu Zi
    background to 11
    battle tactics 221–5
    discipline 212–17
    generals 217–20
    motivating armies 226–8
    observation of enemy 207–12
    rewards and punishments 226–7
wise rulership 201–6
Yao, Emperor 22–3
Zhang Liang 11
Zhou Dynasty 10

384

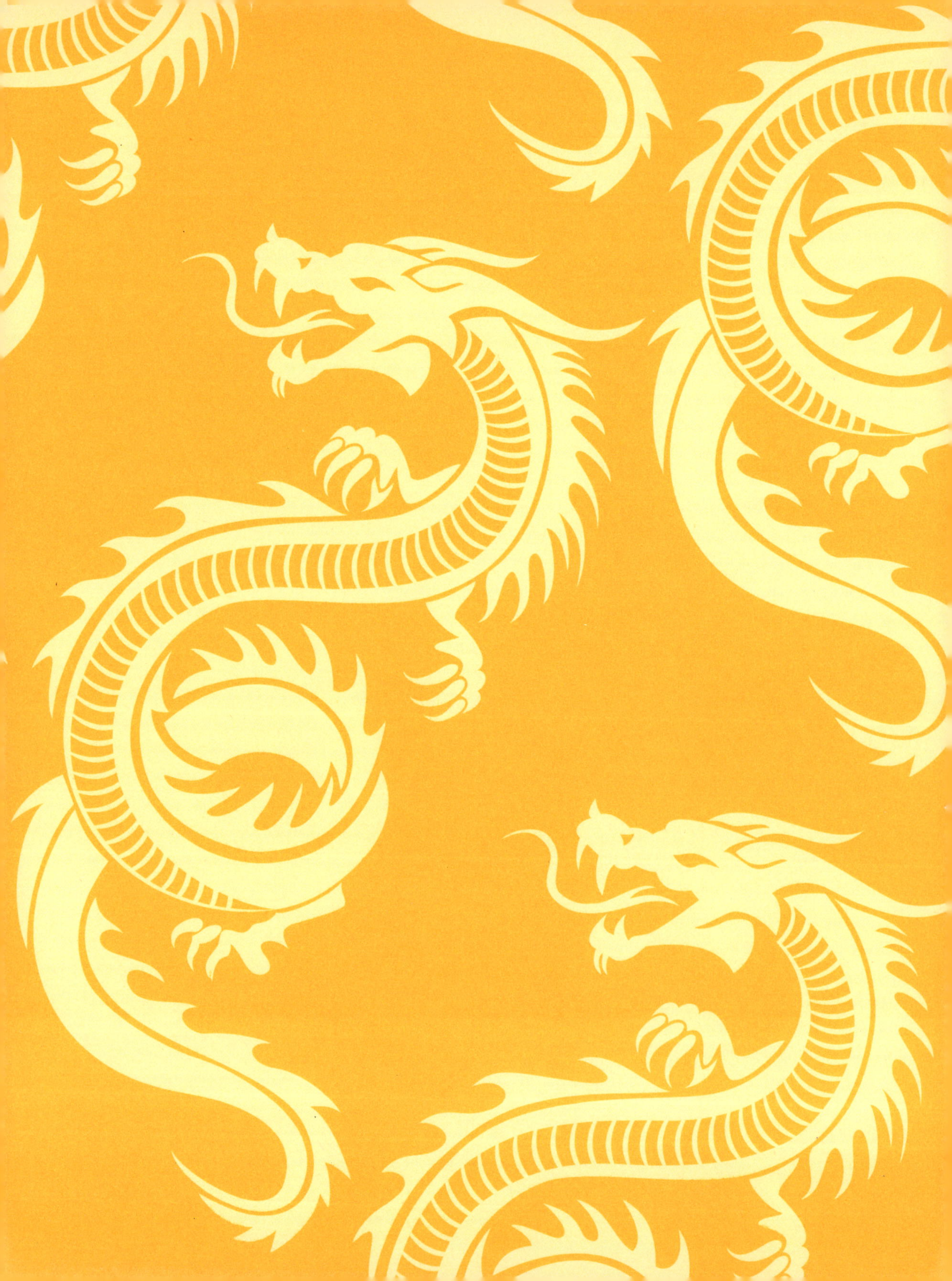